88

JK 2319 .C4 G87 cop.1
Guterbock, Thomas M.
Machine politics in transition

Machine Politics in Transition

Studies of Urban Society
Morris Janowitz, Gerald D. Suttles, and Richard Taub, *series editors*

Other books in this series

Elijah Anderson, *A Place on the Corner*

Michael Crozier, *The World of the Office Worker*

Carole Goodwin, *The Oak Park Strategy*

Albert Hunter, *Symbolic Communities*

William Kornblum, *Blue Collar Community*

Robert McKenzie and Allan Silver, *Angels in Marble*

David Popenoe, *The Suburban Environment*

Gerald D. Suttles, *The Social Construction of Communities*

Gerald D. Suttles, *The Social Order of the Slum*

Mayer N. Zald, *Organizational Change*

Thomas M. Guterbock

Machine Politics in Transition

Party and Community in Chicago

The University of Chicago Press
Chicago and London

THOMAS M. GUTERBOCK is assistant professor of sociology at the University of Virginia.

The University of Chicago Press, Chicago 60637
The University of Chicago Press, Ltd., London

Printed in the United States of America
84 83 82 81 80 5 4 3 2 1

Credits
P. 1: Photo by Jack Lenahan, courtesy of the *Chicago Sun-Times*
P. 13: Photo courtesy of the *Chicago Sun-Times*
P. 71: Photo courtesy of the *Chicago Sun-Times*
P. 147: Photo courtesy of the *Chicago Sun-Times*
P. 239: Photo by Bob Kotalik, courtesy of the *Chicago Sun-Times*

Library of Congress Cataloging in Publication Data

Guterbock, Thomas M
Machine politics in transition.

(Studies of urban society)
Bibliography: p.
Includes index.
1. Democratic Party. Illinois. 2. Party affiliation—Illinois—Chicago. 3. Chicago—Politics and government—1950– I. Title.
JK2319.C4G87 329'.0211 79–16131
ISBN 0–226–31114–7

For Carole, who lived it too

Contents

Appendixes

Tables

Foreword

Thomas Guterbock has written a careful and penetrating community study of Chicago ward politics. Each community case study in the tradition of the Chicago school of sociology raises the question: How representative is the particular case analysis? Of this one, the same question can also be raised. The regular Democratic organization under Richard J. Daley was the last of the big-city machines, a special case hardly typical of inner-city politics in the United States.

To the practitioners of the intensive community case study, including Thomas Guterbock, the answer is self-evident. Representativeness in a narrow sense is not the real issue. Each case study deals with unique human experiences. This is what is meant by the "humanistic" element in sociological research. But it is the task of the sociologist to analyze the uniformities in his case study and thereby to test general conceptions and propositions which make up the debates and controversies among social researchers. This objective, or rather this aspiration, runs through the tradition of Chicago community studies. Thus, for example, in 1926, when Harvey Zorbaugh published *The Gold Coast and the Slum,* the classic study of Chicago's Near North Side, he was not dealing with a typical community. But it was a community in which the theories of urban interaction and institutions could be extensively scrutinized. Likewise, the ward Guterbock selected supplies a highly appropriate locale for exploring in depth both the conventional wisdom and the social science models of the big-city machine. Precisely because it is the last "machine," it supplies a relevant example.

It is very wrong to believe that the pursuit of intensive community research, including the task of selecting one's research site, is a calculated decision based only on research criteria. Methodological issues weigh heavily. The pursuit of the research typified by this book rests on elements of chance and of underlying personal impulse and sheer fascination. Guterbock was schooled in the practicalities and frustrations of independent politics in Chicago, having worked in various capacities for the Independent Voters of Illinois. He was drawn by the urge to understand the opposition. How does "the machine" maintain the loyalty of its active members? How does it actually produce "the vote"? Of course, an excellent opportunity for direct access arose, and that strongly influenced the actual selection of the research setting. But strong personal sentiments were required to carry through this undertaking. It must be remembered that he spent three years living in the ward collecting a mass of data. In the end, his personal motives and experiences, I believe, strengthened his persistent search for objectivity.

Guterbock goes directly to the heart of the matter: Is machine politics at the ward level best described by an exchange model? Are personal favors and particular personal services exchanged for political support and votes?

The result is a rich and rewarding case study which updates rather than challenges our understanding of "machine politics" in its later phases. The exchange model was described by Harold Gosnell in *Machine Politics: Chicago Model,* published in 1937, and was encountered in a variety of other studies. But that model does not encompass the realities of the 1970s. Instead Guterbock draws a strong distinction between the loyal workers in the party hierarchy and the electorate in the ward. Patronage dominates the organization and motivates participation, especially at the lower ranks. It produces the essential compliance and commitment.

Material incentives from patronage are augmented by venal and illegal practices which are in effect defended by elements in the party. These elements of the party in the city make possible favors for insiders and permit various forms of corruption and near corruption. The scope of such activities has been documented repeatedly by journalists' reports and by a series of court cases.

The party ward organizations believe that the favors and personal services they render generate citizen loyalty and support at elections. They therefore work hard not only to "service" the requests of clients but also to search out opportunities to assist local residents. But Guterbock concludes that there is little effective linkage between favors and personal service on the one hand and the patterns of voting support for organization candidates on the other. This conclusion is not based on an assertion that the favors and personal services that the local organization renders have atrophied or even declined. There is no doubt that they have changed over time and Guterbock enumerates these changes. But these continue to be of relevance and significance in the daily life of the citizenry.

Nor does Guterbock argue that Harold Gosnell was in error about the consequences of these services in the earlier period that he studied. To the contrary, in the 1970s the recipients no longer see these services as requiring political reciprocity. The electorate has come to believe that these services are now citizen rights. They are not only entitled to receive these services, but it is their civic duty to demand them in order to improve the neighborhood and the local community. An important element in Guterbock's findings is that this outlook, which one would associate with the middle-class or suburban electorate, has penetrated deep into the lower strata.

Instead of a specific exchange model, Guterbock emphasizes the general sense of attachment to the Democratic Party as the basis of support for the local organization in elections. Sentiments of attachment to the local community are also important in this regard. Defection from the regular ticket reflects the weakening of Democratic partisanship, the importance of particular single issues, or the popularity of specific candidates in local, state, and national elections.

Guterbock seeks to explain the continued emphasis of the party on favors and personal services. He does not believe that efforts to maintain a flow of favors and services are the result of tradition or miscalculation. Nevertheless, his data do suggest that if the party were to reduce such efforts it would incur additional criticism from opposition groups. Moreover, he argues that these efforts assist the Democratic ward organization indirectly. They permit access by the local political leaders, although not so much by precinct captains, to important voluntary associations where the Democratic party affiliations and sentiments can be reinforced. Guterbock is struck by the energy with which local political leaders participate—almost as nonpartisan figures—in the extensive life of local voluntary associations and groups.

The data were collected and the analysis completed before the events of the winter of 1979, which led to the election of Ms. Jane Byrne. The adaptation of the regular Democratic organization to social and economic change will depend on her political skill in building new coalitions. But the 1979 election serves to underline Guterbock's argument that favors and personal services do not ensure machine political support.

This is not only an important contribution to our understanding of the transformation of urban politics in the United States; it is also a most effective continuation and enrichment of the tradition of community-based research, for it combines participant observation with extensive statistical methodologies. From its very beginning, the Chicago school of sociology saw no inherent opposition between fieldwork and statistical analysis. But the task of using these approaches concurrently is difficult and requires considerable self-discipline. The richness of the field reports captures the institutional life of the ward organization. To test his argument, however, Guterbock needed as well a careful statistical analysis of the organization records and a meaningful sample survey of the citizenry. The study would not have been possible without all three approaches.

I continue to be impressed with the willingness of individual representatives of each new generation of sociologists to put forth the extensive effort and time required to produce such case studies in depth. It does not take more than a handful to keep such traditions alive. Professional commitments no doubt motivate these young scholars, but their work represents their personal attraction to an academic tradition that has become effectively diffused throughout the discipline. It is a tradition that epitomizes the continued relevance of individual scholarship in a period in which the growth of group research must of necessity be the dominant trend.

Morris Janowitz

Near South Side
University of Chicago

Preface

This book is about politics as it is practiced at the grass roots level in one ward of the city of Chicago. The ward's politics are typical for Chicago in that elections and decision making are dominated by the local unit of the Regular Democratic Organization, the political machine that has controlled the city's government since 1932. Inevitably, a case study of Chicago's local politics is a study of machine politics. This book, then, seeks to establish how a political machine secures popular support in a contemporary urban setting.

Recent events in Chicago have focused renewed attention on the mechanisms by which political machines have sustained themselves. The victory of Jane Byrne over the Regular Democratic incumbent Mayor Michael Bilandic in 1979 left most political analysts dumbfounded, for it gave the lie to the conventional wisdom about how the machine works. The fact that Byrne received a majority of the primary election vote put to rest the notion that Chicago's electorate was controlled by party bosses. Yet if the evolutionary forces of economic and social progress had at last made Chicago ready for reform, how was it that the new mayor reached such rapid rapprochement with the old-line party leadership and that the city council remained solidly in machine control?

These puzzling circumstances were part of an undreamt-of future when I began the research reported in this book. In the spring of 1972, when I began participant observation in the ward I studied, the late Richard J. Daley was in his fifth term as mayor, and his political organization appeared invincible. My project seemed at first to be straightforward. It was my intention to document the process by which the machine harnessed the political loyalty of economically or politically deprived individuals. In accordance with what I had heard and read, I thought the process to be one of social "exchange" in which favors were traded for votes. In pursuit of data to test this thesis, I lived in the ward for three years, participated in the activities of the Regular Democratic Organization there, and conducted interviews with a sample of ward residents.

The quantitative and qualitative data that I gathered proved to be contrary to my expectations and to the accepted models of how the political machine operates. The data were fully compatible, however, with the remarkable events that followed in 1979. For I found that the services distributed by party workers have no direct effect on the political loyalties of the voters who receive them. The support the Regular Democrats receive at the polls and in community gatherings is based on traditional loyalties and on the local attachments of many ward residents. The motivations of voters who support the party are similar to the motivations of partisan voters in other localities and cannot be equated with the motivations of members of the actual party organization, the recipients of patronage. The party and its community are organized around conflicting moralities, and party agents and full-time party politicians must create linkages across this moral gap. The political life of the ward I studied is thus imbued with ambivalence, concealment, and paradox. That the same qualities prevail in the citywide political system became evident when the Bilandic administration met its end amid the relentless snows of 1979.

This book has four principal parts. Part 1 contains a theoretical introduction and a description of the setting and method of the research. The chapters in part 2 present an inside look at the Regular Democratic Organization. I do not attempt to present a strict insider's view of the organization, but rather to describe the activities of its members and to give a plausible account of their motives based on their deeds and words.[1] I begin with an account of the ways in which the club secures compliance from its members despite the divergence of its activities from the moral expectations of the larger community. I then describe the club's service activities and try to demonstrate that, despite rhetoric to the contrary, party members perform favors in the hope of winning votes in return.

Part 3 examines the success of the club's service activities in winning support from ward residents. Much of this part is based on the statistical results of a sample survey. Here the extent of party service activities is measured and changes in these activities over the last fifty years are explored. The characteristics of the voters who make use of party services are then analyzed, and the effect of party services on the party loyalty of voters who use them is examined in some detail.

Part 4 returns to more qualitative data that shed light on the relationship of the party to ward residents. Here I describe the typical activities of full-time politicians in ward politics and the strategy by which they maintain a positive public image. In the light of the findings reported in part 3, I reevaluate the importance of the party's service activities. The concluding chapter reviews the argument of the book and considers some of its broader implications.

I came to this study from an advantageous background of political marginality. I was raised in the Hyde Park neighborhood on Chicago's South Side, an area that has supported liberal Independent politics for nearly as long as the Democrat machine has held sway in the rest of the city. I was enlisted into precinct work on behalf of the Independent Voters of Illinois before I was a teenager and continued to help out in election campaigns intermittently through 1971, when I proudly and somewhat naively captained a precinct for Richard Friedman's dismally unsuccessful attempt to unseat Mayor Daley. The liberal Democrats with whom I worked in these campaigns liked to depict the machine as evil incarnate—somewhere just this side of Hitler's

SS in its efficiency, power, and cruelty. But I never could muster such zealousness. It never seemed to me that the Daley administration was doing as bad a job of managing the city's affairs as the Independents insisted; nor did our Independent political representatives seem to be notably efficacious. Even more troubling to me was the strength of electoral support at the command of the machine candidates whom we fought so hard to beat. If they were as bad as our Independent organizers insisted, then why did so many people vote for them? The explanation offered by most Hyde Parkers I knew was a simple one: the supporters of the machine were coerced. For example, I was told to have pity on a woman in our neighborhood who worked at the County Hospital. Our Independent precinct captain explained to me that the woman would have liked to sign nominating petitions for our Independent candidates, but could not for fear of losing her job. Yet the woman stayed on her job—indeed she prospered—and as I grew older I gradually came to realize that she was in fact quite securely and sincerely committed to the machine. I became increasingly impatient with the superciliousness of the Independent ideology. Thus, I began intensive study of the machine neither as its enemy nor its friend, yet with a compelling urge to probe its secrets. As I came to know the Regular Democrats better, I learned that the ambivalence that I had experienced was not merely a reflection of my own disaffiliation from local politics, but was rooted in the contradictory nature of the machine itself.

A great many people—more than I can thank here by name—were of help to me in completing this work. I completed the fieldwork and much of the analysis while a graduate student at the University of Chicago, where I received financial support from a Mellon Foundation Urban Studies Fellowship, a Ford Foundation Urban Research Grant, and a University of Chicago William Rainey Harper Fellowship. The Center for Social Organization Studies at the Department of Sociology provided official backing for the sample survey which I conducted and, more importantly, provided an atmosphere of congenial criticism in its series of student-faculty seminars. Martin Frankel assisted me in designing the sampling procedures. My friends David Gordon and Paul Anderson were always ready to hear me talk of my work and gave me countless insights into it. Many of my teachers at Chicago took a special interest in this research, not only Barry Schwartz and Edward Laumann, who served on my dissertation committee and gave freely of their time and expertise, but also Charles Bidwell, Terry Clark, Leo Goodman, and Richard Taub, each of whom offered invaluable guidance and encouragement. I would particularly like to acknowledge my intellectual debt to courses taught by Victor Lidz and Gerald Suttles. The works of two predecessors in Chicago fieldwork, William Kornblum and Albert Hunter, have served as models for me. But my greatest debt is to my *Doktorvater* Morris Janowitz. My references to his work in the text do not begin to do justice to his share in this study; he guided it from the outset with profound insight.

Since leaving Chicago I have benefited from the colleagueship and clerical support provided by the departments of sociology at Memphis State University and the University of Virginia. For competent typing of various drafts, I thank Sherry Crone, Cleva Burner, Joycelyn Smith, and Gail Wooten-Votaw. Joseph Galaskiewicz, Mark Granovetter, Hagen Koo, and Kenneth Wald provided helpful comments at an earlier stage of this research; Theodore Caplow, Murray Milner, Gresham Sykes, and an anonymous reviewer provided useful feedback on a prior draft of this book. Lester Kurtz helped me to obtain recent Chicago election statistics, and Roberta Allen conducted a diligent and creative search for illustrations. A small grant from the University of Virginia helped defray the costs of final preparation of the manuscript.

Finally, I have three debts of a different kind to acknowledge. First, I thank my parents, who have served me both as a model of the academic calling and a source of support in my efforts to follow it. Second, I thank my wife, to whom this book is dedicated. She shared with me the joys and frustrations of fieldwork and helped me to observe, to understand, and to write. Lastly, although

I cannot thank them by name, I am deeply grateful for the cooperation of my friends and informants in the Regular Democratic Organization and in the community where we lived. It has been my goal to set down a just account of their situation, and I hope they will judge it a fair one.

Part 1 Introduction

One The Problem of Machine Support

Machine is a venerable word, evocative of both quaint and sinister images.[1] In political discourse the term is usually pejorative, but social scientists use it as a descriptive term for a specific type of political party: one which has a tight, hierarchical organization, includes party agents at the grass roots level, and systematically distributes patronage among its members.[2] Initially the concept appears simple enough, but those who encounter the machine, either in the political arena or as an object of scholarly inquiry, continue to find its manifest attributes contradictory and its essential nature mysterious.[3]

Wherever and whenever party organizations of this type have existed, they have been controversial—assailed by some as evil and defended by others as beneficent. People differ in their evaluations of the machine partly because they judge it from the standpoint of different values, but also because they disagree over certain facts. The purpose of this book is to contribute to this evaluative debate by advancing understanding of how political machines operate today. Toward that end, the first step is to delineate the central empirical issues in the debate.

The Problem of the Machine

By definition, the machine seeks to gain office in a competitive democracy but is organized primarily around the material interests of its members. Therefore it is dependent on voluntary support from a broad public, but at the same time must, to a substantial extent, operate in direct conflict with institutionalized values of that public.[4] The fact that machines have been able to achieve and maintain power despite this fundamental contradiction is what makes them scandalous, admirable, or merely fascinating, depending on the viewpoint of the observer. The contradiction is a problem for the machine itself, which must find the means to surmount it, and for social scientists, who would discover what those means are.[5]

The contradiction between the machine's venal nature and the ideals of democracy is a threat to the party's survival only if the people whose support the party requires (1) believe in the ideals of democracy, (2) act according to those beliefs, and (3) perceive the machine as being venal. It is possible for the machine to survive if the combination of commitment to democratic ideals and perception of the machine's nature as self-serving is confined to groups on whose support the machine does not depend—such as unsuccessful reformers.

On whom does the machine depend for its success? A successful patronage party must be able to distribute money, jobs, and other material incentives to its members. It acquires control of some power resources, such as patronage jobs, by successfully influencing election outcomes. It also depends on money contributions from business organizations. It need not control all voters or all businesses, but to keep itself in existence the machine must receive support from significant sectors of each of these groups. Support from business usually is no problem. Businesses, like the machine itself, operate on the profit motive, and tend to cooperate with an organization that will protect their interests. Control of regulatory and law enforcement agencies by the successful machine even makes it possible for businesses to receive illegal benefit with little risk of penalty. Thus, even businessmen who hold democratic values may contribute because the benefits of doing so are substantial. The more difficult issue, the one to which this book is primarily addressed, is how the machine secures electoral support.

Models of Machine Support

The internal organization of the "classic" machines and the service activities of grass roots party agents have been documented in a series of primarily qualitative studies that spans the last half century.[6] These studies assert that the machine controls votes by using distinctive vote-getting methods. It is generally supposed that the service activities—favors—performed by ward and precinct politicians for individuals and organized groups are crucial in generating and maintaining voter support. Democratic ideals dictate that the voter's electoral choice should be based on informed consideration of which candidates will best serve the interest of the entire political community, but the machine is thought to gain support from voters who act in violation of these ideals. These machine supporters base their votes on more immediate incentives that are distributed through the service activities of the party.

Beyond this assertion there is little agreement among either popular or scholarly accounts of machine politics. There has not been any polarization of scholarly camps around opposed systematic theories; rather a variety of competing ideas have gained wide acceptance and seem to be passed on from textbook to textbook, with little attempt to resolve the internal inconsistencies in the received wisdom.[7] Some of the points of ambiguity are crucial to evaluating the machine: does the "boss" win support by coercing people or by satisfying their wants? Is the machine a channel for effective political participation by the lower classes, or does it subvert their interests? Other points of ambiguity center around the quality of life in urban subareas which support political machines, and the nature of the relationship between voters and grass roots party agents ("precinct captains"). Alternative answers to two fundamental questions seem to be at the core of these ambiguities: What kind of incentives does the machine offer its supporters?[8] Do machine supporters respond to these incentives because they do not hold democratic values, or because their circumstances compel them to act contrary to those ideals? The answers to these questions are logically interdependent, and it is therefore possible to abstract from the rich descriptive literature on the machine two competing traditional models of machine support.

The Material Exchange Model

The older of the two traditional views was subscribed to by movements for political reform at the turn of the century and is still held today by many of the amateur politicians who oppose existing political machines. According to this view, machine support has its roots in the long-term decline of community autonomy and cohesion which Roland Warren has called "the Great Change."[9] The societal transformation to increased scale of social organization, and in particular the dislocations involved in urbanization, produce large numbers of city dwellers who are without linkage to sources of authority and without roots in a network of primary relationships.[10] They are thus unable to identify their own self-interest and to participate responsibly in democratic processes.[11] They are amenable to manipulation by the mass media and by the predatory agents of the political machine. Harvey Zorbaugh offers this argument in his classic study of community life in Chicago's Near North Side:[12]

> The growth of the city, with its mobility and anonymity, its organization along lines of interest rather than sentiment, its specialization, its breaking down of local life, greatly changed the nature of political life . . . . Party organizations were indifferent to social questions. Politics narrowed down to the struggle for office and the booty of office. It was the day of the "spoils system" of the "ring" and the "machine."

In the material exchange model, the communities which support the machine are anonymous, atomistic slums characterized by social disorganization.[13] The absence of shared standards and effective sanctions in such settings means that even though some residents may hold democratic ideals, they have little incentive to act in accordance with their values. In this environment the party agents are able through their service activities to generate a network of obligations which people repay by voting as they are told. The relationship of the voter to the precinct captain is face-to-face but essentially utilitarian and "segmental" (i.e., narrow in its functional scope). The relationship is built around the exchange of specific material incentives for votes. Because of his lack of resources the voter values the bucket of coal or other small favor he receives, and because of his lack of community ties he has no support for any attempts he might make to arrive at his own electoral choice. The machine supporter is materially motivated and responds to material incentives.[14] Thus dominated, he permits the machine, in the words of Lord Bryce, to "set up a tyranny under the forms of democracy."[15]

The Affectual Exchange Model

Where the material exchange model depicts the political machine as coldly predatory, an alternative theoretical tradition depicts it as warmly personal—if no less exploitative. This second tradition, which I call the affectual exchange model, has its origin in Harold Gosnell's even-handed examination of the Chicago machine and Robert Merton's analysis of machine functions; it is most clearly expressed in the work of Edward Banfield and James Q. Wilson.[16] According to this view, support for the machine has its roots in the incomplete social integration and cultural assimilation of urban immigrants. Rural and preindustrial forms of community—and the political orientations that accompany them—persist in the industrial city. Instead of assuming that immigrants are isolates in an anomic setting, the affectual exchange model presumes them to be urban villagers embedded in a closed community with a backward political morality.[17]

The people who support the machine are assumed to be linked to others in their neighborhoods by primordial ties of ethnicity and kinship and by bonds of intimate friendship. The precinct captain is able to mobilize support for the patronage party because he has gained a place in this localized network of intimacy. As Banfield and Wilson phrase it,[18] "the voter is the one contributor to the machine's system of activity who is usually given non-material inducements, especially 'friendship.'" By the use of quotation marks these authors imply that the friendship of the precinct captain is inauthentic, but apparently they do suppose the voter to be genuinely friendly. The voter regards the bucket of coal or other favor as a token of esteem and evidence of the party worker's good character. In support of this view, Banfield and Wilson quote from a description of the machine published in 1902 by pioneer social worker Jane Addams:[19] "On the whole, the gifts are taken quite simply as an evidence of genuine loving kindness. The alderman is really elected because he is a good friend and neighbor." In this view, then, the relationship of the voter to the precinct captain is face-to-face, personal, affective, and functionally diffuse. The specific incentives that the party's agents offer in exchange for votes are "solidary"[20] rather than material and the distribution of favors is but a mechanism by which personal attachments can be developed and maintained.

Why are the electoral choices of these ethnic villagers so strongly influenced by personal attachments, even to the detriment of what we would judge to be their objective interests? Here Banfield and Wilson introduce an explanation that is essentially cultural.[21] Ethnic villagers vote for machine politicians not because they lack moral standards or a local structure to support their values, but because they judge their leaders by standards different from those invoked by more cosmopolitan, middle-class citizens.[22] They act within a "private-regarding ethos" that values the welfare of those personally linked to them above the welfare of the city as a whole.[23] It is a combination of cultural predisposition and community structure which leads supporters of the machine to vote on the basis of emotional ties.

The Commitment Model

Each of the traditional models stresses that machine support is constituted differently from support for normatively organized (i.e., nonpatronage) parties. Despite the disagreement over the nature of the inducements, the two exchange[24] models have in common the notions that the inducements are specific (that is, they "can be offered to one person while being withheld from others"[25]) and are made available on a regular basis in face-to-face encounters in the precincts. The findings I will report in the chapters that follow contradict these basic notions. Since the exchange models do not fit these findings, an alternative model is needed which does not assume the motivations of machine supporters to be fundamentally different from the motivations of other voters.

Like the affectual exchange model just described, the alternative model posits a contrast between the motivation of party agents and the motivation of the multitude of voters who support the party. The support of the former is generated by material inducements (primarily patronage jobs) distributed through the party's patronage apparatus. The well-staffed precinct organization is an important mobilizing force which activates the party's supporters at each election, giving a strong advantage to the party's slate of candidates. But the voters mobilized by the organization support the machine primarily out of normative commitment to the patronage party and its candidates.

This commitment does not necessarily have anything to do with the voter's relationship to the local party agent. This relationship varies, but in most cases it is a transitory, segmental, and impersonal one in which opinions, and little else, are exchanged. Voters may believe that the party represents the interests of a social class, an ethnic group, or a locality with which they identify. They may believe the party can provide more effective leadership than the competing parties can. The distribution of services *is* relevant to the success of ward politicians, for voters judge local leaders in part according to their performance as advocates of community improvement and monitors of city services. But these beliefs and judgments are formed on the basis of what the voter hears from acquaintances, community leaders, the press, the pulpit, and the political candidates themselves. His or her vote is not controlled by direct linkage to party agents; it is won by the party's continuous efforts at legitimating itself. While the machine's supporters are certainly not models of informed and rational voting, they are not any less committed to democratic ideals than other mass constituencies. They give their support to a materially motivated party not because they lack political morality or knowingly act in violation of the norms of democratic citizenship, but simply because they do not perceive the party as being self-interested.

This *commitment model* is based on a revised view of the urban subcommunity in which machine supporters reside. The material exchange model saw supporters as isolated in a mass society; the affective exchange model saw them as captives in a closed network of primary ties. The tension between these approaches corresponds to the classic debate over whether urbanization causes "community" to disappear. That debate has for the most part been abandoned as sociologists have developed new concepts of community and documented the sustained viability of these redefined entities. Urban communities and subcommunities are now seen as socially constructed collectivities that serve the psychic needs and perceived interests of certain urban residents. Hence, community sentiments vary among people and change over the life-cycles of individuals and neighborhoods, but are a systemic and consequential component of urban social organization.[26] Support for the patronage party is linked to the existence of these voluntary and functionally specific local ties. Machine support does not flow automatically from community attachment; rather, patronage politicians consciously pursue a public strategy that articulates with the notions locally-attached residents have about what is best for their communities. The service activities of the party are just one of a variety of means the party employs to appeal to widely shared localistic values.

The task of this book, then, is to advance our understanding of how machines generate electoral support. As I have noted, a number of previous researchers have reported in rich detail the procedures used in "old-style" precinct work and the shared understandings among party activists about how voters are influenced. The effectiveness of grass roots party activity has also been empirically demonstrated.[27] Heretofore, the success of precinct work has been taken as evidence for the traditional models of machine support. In this book, a series of hypotheses is derived from these models and subjected to empirical test by a combination of quantitative and qualitative methods. As I have already indicated, the results point to the alternative model outlined above.

Two Setting and Method

During most of this century, political parties in the United States have been distinguished from their counterparts in other countries by their comparatively loose structure at the national level and their tight organization at the local level.[1] Unlike highly-organized, mass-based parties that have existed in other countries, the strong urban parties of America's industrial age were structured around patronage rather than ideological concerns. Thus it was that Harold Gosnell could present his 1937 study of Chicago's machine as typical of party politics in urban settings across the nation.[2]

Over the course of this century, however, the American party system has undergone considerable change. Not only has the strength of partisanship declined among American voters,[3] but the nature of partisan politics has changed as well. Samuel Eldersveld gives a succinct description of this evolution:

> On the way out, presumably, is the "old-style" local politics, with its discipline, personal loyalty, spoils system, welfare services, the deliverable vote, and continuous year-round attention to precinct affairs. On the way in, presumably, are "leaders" instead of "bosses," more visibility in party activity, a looser organization, less discipline, more sporadic vote-getting activity, and more reliance on the mass media.[4]

 If this transition to "new-style" urban politics has taken

place in most cities—and there is a good deal of evidence that it has[5]—then Chicago offers a marked deviation from the trend. For the struggle for office in the Second City continues to be fiercely partisan, and the dominant party is organized much as it was in Gosnell's day. Often touted as "the last of the big-city machines," the city's patronage party remains the most formidable in the nation despite its widely publicized failure to return Mayor Bilandic to office in 1979. And the Chicago machine is not nearly so anachronistic as casual observation would suggest. In fact, patronage-based party organizations continue to play an important role in many large cities and many more smaller ones.[6] As the present study will attempt to show, it has been possible for some "old-style" party organizations to adapt to changing conditions, surviving in a modified form still clearly recognizable as that of the political machine.

Chicago Politics

The Democratic party has dominated Chicago politics since the elections of 1932, when Republican officeholders at all levels of government were swept out of office in a massive realignment of voter loyalties caused by the collapse of the national economy. This was not the beginning of machine politics in the city; before the Depression both Republican and Democratic factions were traditionally organized around favors and patronage.[7] However, the capture of the bulk of local offices and patronage, together with the continuing concentration in the central city of population groups with lasting loyalty to the "party of the New Deal," allowed the Regular Democratic Organization of Cook County to consolidate its power into a virtual one-party rule that remained in force through the 1970s.[8]

Throughout this period the party structure has remained strong, hierarchical, and essentially unified. It is through this formidable organization, rather than through the formal powers of municipal office, that party leaders have effectively and consistently influenced both election outcomes and governmental decision-making in Chicago and, to a lesser extent, in

Cook County. When Richard J. Daley was elected mayor in 1955 the position of the Democrats was further solidified, for Daley retained his position as chairman of the Cook County Democratic Central Committee until his death in 1976 during his sixth consecutive term as mayor. Holding both the powers of the mayoralty and the powers of party leadership, Daley was able to control the city council and departments completely, and thereby to work his will in city affairs to an extent unmatched by any big-city mayor of his time.[9] Upon his death, these powers were once again split among several party leaders, a fact which no doubt contributed to the ineffectiveness of the succeeding administration.

Daley left his mark on the party's structure, for throughout his tenure he worked at consolidating control of patronage, slate-making, and other party decisions under himself and a trusted few within the party. This centralization was one factor that made possible the rather smooth transfer of power which followed his death; it also spawned resentments within the party which later threatened its unity. Nevertheless, the fundamentals of party structure today remain unchanged from what Gosnell described in the mid-thirties. The city is still divided into fifty wards, each of which elects an alderman who sits on a formally strong but practically weak city council. Aldermanic elections are nominally nonpartisan, but aldermen maintain public partisan affiliations nonetheless, and at no time during the Daley era were fewer than forty of the fifty aldermen firmly in the Regular Democratic camp. In a primary election, each ward also elects a committeeman from each major party, who sits on the central committee of his party together with committeemen elected from suburban townships. The Democratic committeeman, who in many cases also holds a government office, is the "ward boss." Virtually immune to defeat at the polls,[10] the Democratic committeeman has a voice in slate-making, dispenses patronage jobs to people who vote in his ward, and leads a ward-based party organization. The committeeman appoints a precinct captain and other workers to represent the party in each of the ward's precincts—districts of between four and six hundred registered voters—and picks Democratic judges of election for each precinct polling place at election time. In contrast, the Republican committeeman usually controls no patronage, offers virtually no services to citizens, and appoints few precinct captains.[11]

The patronage system has been kept strong in Chicago governments, despite the encroachments of the Civil Service and other reforms. Since the system operates in secret, the number of patronage jobs and the exact procedures by which they are dispensed are difficult to determine. The total number of politically controlled jobs in all Chicago governments is probably around twenty thousand.[12] Not all of these jobs are controlled at the ward level, and the number of jobs controlled by a single ward committeeman probably varies from one to four hundred. Although the patronage system operates *sub rosa,* it is not an informal system, for the central committee keeps careful account of who controls which jobs, and allocates patronage according to a complex formula based on each ward's Democratic voting strength. Thus the Democratic ward organizations in Chicago continue to be staffed primarily by persons holding publicly-funded jobs which are under the political control of their ward committeemen.

One indication of the long-term stability of Chicago's machine is its performance in generating votes. The city committeemen and their patronage organizations are able to turn out consistent numbers of voters for the party's candidates in election after election. Figure 1 shows the trend in Chicago voting over the last 47 years. There are sharp fluctuations in the Democratic vote totals for regular elections in Chicago as a result of the cycle of presidential and off-year contests, nationwide trends in voting turnout and party identification, and the strength and weaknesses of particular candidates relative to their opponents. But there is far less fluctuation over the same period in the vote total for Regular candidates in Democratic primaries. Whether the primary is uncontested or hotly fought, the Organization regularly produces around 300,000 votes citywide—an average of 6000 votes per ward.[13] Some instability in

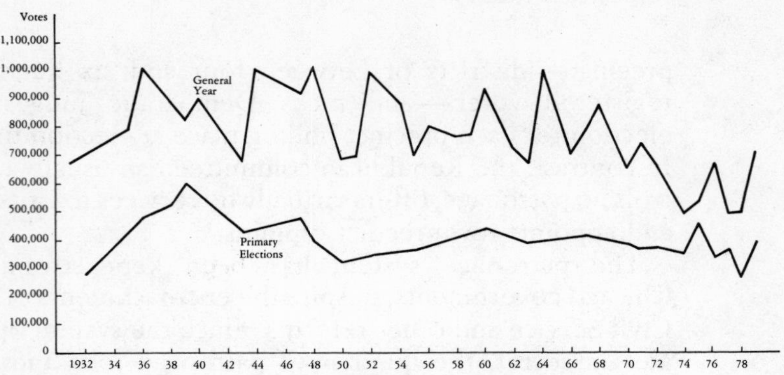

Votes
1,100,000
1,000,000
900,000
800,000
700,000
600,000
500,000
400,000
300,000
200,000
100,000
0
General Year
Primary Elections
1932
34
36
38
40
42
44
46
48
50
52
54
56
58
60
62
64
66
68
70
72
74
76
78

Fig. 1. Number of votes for the Democratic candidate in general elections and the Regular candidate in Democratic primary elections, City of Chicago, 1931–79

NOTE: For list of primary election candidates, see note to fig. 2. General election vote counts are plotted for the following candidates:

Year	Office	Democratic Candidate
1931	mayor	Cermak
1935	mayor	Kelly
1936	senator	Lewis
1939	mayor	Kelly
1940	governor	Hershey
1943	mayor	Kelly
1944	state's attorney	Touhy
1947	mayor	Kennelly
1948	state's attorney	Boyle
1950	sheriff	Gilbert
1951	mayor	Kennelly
1952	state's attorney	Gutknecht
1954	senator	Douglas
1955	mayor	Daley
1956	state's attorney	Gutknecht
1958	sheriff	Sain
1959	mayor	Daley
1960	state's attorney	Ward
1962	sheriff	Spencer
1963	mayor	Daley
1964	governor	Kerner
1966	senator	Douglas
1967	mayor	Daley
1968	governor	Shapiro
1970	sheriff	Elrod
1971	mayor	Daley
1972	state's attorney	Hanrahan
1974	sheriff	Elrod
1975	mayor	Daley
1976	governor	Howlett
1977	mayor	Bilandic
1978	senator	Seith
1979	mayor	Byrne

the primary vote is discernible after Daley's death, but even in his 1979 defeat Mayor Bilandic received the normal vote for a Regular candidate.

Seen in historic perspective, then, the ability of the Regulars to influence election outcomes has never been complete, but it is substantial and has not declined greatly in the last half-century. Contested primaries and losses to popular non-organization candidates for county and statewide office have occurred occasionally throughout this period. In contests for city office, Democratic victories in the regular elections are virtually assured; in the wards, only a handful of Republican and Independent aldermen and state legislators are elected. It is not easy to account for the continued strength of the Regular Democrats in Chicago, especially if we start from the assumptions of the traditional models of machine support. In later chapters we shall address this question of persistence; for now it is sufficient to note that patronage politicians are very much in control of both the citywide political system and the local subarea in which this study was conducted.

The Ward

This study focuses on one of the City of Chicago's fifty wards. It is an area of distinctive character with which I became intimately familiar in the years I lived there. In order to preserve a certain degree of anonymity in reporting my research, I will limit my description of the ward to an account of its broad social and political characteristics. These characteristics can be made clear by defining the place of this ward in the social geography of the city as a whole.

Ernest W. Burgess considered the spatial pattern of Chicago in the 1920s to be typical of rapidly growing industrial cities at that time.[14] He noted the existence of a "Zone of Transition" which then extended for a mile or two in all directions around the city's central business district. It was an area in which invasion by commercial land use was imminent, the housing stock was obsolete and deteriorated, and a succession of poor ethnic groups made their first settlements in the city. Around this band of slums was a ring of modest, wood-frame houses and flats which Burgess called the "Zone of Workingmen's Homes"; here somewhat better-established ethnic groups were housed. The next zone out was the "Residential Zone" of better residential hotels, newer apartment houses, and brick bungalows. At the time Burgess wrote, the ward I studied lay roughly on the inner fringe of this prosperous zone, encompassing some of the better parts of the workingmen's zone.

In the fifty years that have passed since Burgess published his schematic, the Chicago metropolitan area has retained its concentric form to some extent, but the size of the zones has vastly expanded as the city has grown and decentralized.[15] The blight and poverty which Burgess observed in the Zone of Transition have now spread over much of the inner third of the central city. In the ward I studied, the residential hotels and apartments of the 1920s and the pre–World War I houses still stand, but they are for the most part shunned by the middle-class and working-class families they originally housed. And like Burgess's Zone of Transition, the area is undergoing the blighting and disruptive effects of anticipated ecological succession, for land in the ward is steadily being converted to institutional, commercial, and high-density high-rent residential use. The area differs in several respects, however, from the immigrant slums which Burgess observed: its residents, while poor by today's standards, enjoy real incomes well above those of the urban poor of the 1920s; there is no single predominant ethnic culture in the area, and the ward is comparatively uncrowded, as it succumbs gradually to the cycle of abandonment that plagues our inner cities.

Social Characteristics

Because wards are required to have equal numbers of inhabitants (ca. 60,000) and because of political gerrymandering, their boundaries rarely coincide with those of the city's officially recognized community areas or informally defined neighborhoods.[16] This particular ward comprises sections of several adjacent community areas; for descriptive purposes it can be divided into three ecologically distinct subareas. First, there is a long strip of high-rise apartment buildings, occupied by a white upper-middle-class childless population, a large proportion of whom are Jewish. Behind this glittering facade is the second area, a bleak district of deteriorating three-story apartment buildings and rooming houses, where the one common denominator is poverty. A few square blocks here have a long history of black occupancy. For two decades, Southern whites dominated the remainder of this district, but by the time of this study many of them had moved to better housing outside the ward. Those who remain now share their territory with native Northern whites, Mexican-Americans, Puerto Ricans, Cubans, American Indians, South Asians, and Orientals. A disproportionate number of area residents are disabled, elderly, or both. Mental illness, alcoholism, and crime rates are high. Institutions of poverty are visible on the commercial streets: cheap barrooms, flophouses, day-labor hiring halls, welfare agencies, and secondhand stores. Some blocks are total slums. The population density has declined, leaving some abandoned buildings and many vacant lots. Yet some blocks still have carefully maintained old buildings with stable residents.

The remainder of the ward is an area of old two-flats and single-family homes populated by white working-class families of varied ethnicity. This area did not become part of the ward until 1971. A generation ago it was part of a large German and Swedish area of second settlement which grew up around a commercial center located just outside the ward. Now the ethnic character of the population is changing, but the area remains more closely linked to the old commercial center than to other parts of the ward. Some Mexican-Americans, Puerto Ricans, Filipinos, and Koreans have moved into this district in the last decade, but ethnically it is still predominantly European. It is an aging neighborhood with some seriously deteriorated blocks, but it is not a slum.

The diverse character of the three areas is reflected in the census statistics shown in table 1. The high-rise apartment district houses few children and many elderly

Table 1 1970 Census Characteristics of City of Chicago and Three Areas of the Ward

	High-rise Area	Central Area	Working-class Area	City of Chicago
Approximate population	20,000	35,000	12,000	3,370,000
Percent under age 18	9.7	29.9	28.7	32.1
Percent age 65 and over	18.9	11.1	14.1	10.5
Percent of occupied housing units occupied by owner	4.1	5.1	26.2	34.8
1969 median family income	$13,370	$7,460	$9,940	$10,240
Percent of population age 25 and over with 4 years high school completed	67.1	37.2	42.6	43.9
Percent of population age 5 and over who lived in same house in 1965	34.9	28.3	47.9	52.3
Percent of native-born population born in the South	6.1	22.6	9.1	14.7
Foreign stock as percent of population	39.9	27.1	41.6	29.7
Russian origin as percent of foreign stock	28.2	2.4	2.6	6.4
German origin as percent of foreign stock	9.1	7.8	22.3	9.9
Spanish-speaking as percent of population	4.0	17.6	10.4	7.3
Negro as percent of population	1.2	4.2	0.2	32.7

SOURCE: City of Chicago Department of Development and Planning, *Chicago Statistical Abstract,* Part II (Chicago: City of Chicago, 1973).
NOTE: Area statistics are aggregates for groups of contiguous census tracts nearly coincident with areas of the ward.

persons. Income and educational attainment are high, but nearly two-thirds of the residents have moved during the last five years. There is little home ownership. The sizable percentage of foreign stock includes many of the Jewish residents, the largest proportion of whom are of Russian origin.

The central area is more familistic. It houses as many elderly persons as the high-rise area, but they constitute a smaller proportion of the population. Like the high-rise area it is primarily a rental district, but incomes and educational attainment are low and transiency is high.

At the time of the 1970 census, this was still considered a "hillbilly" neighborhood with a high proportion of Southern whites, but the presence of other minorities was already discernible at that time and became increasingly apparent during the 1970s.

The age distribution of the population in the working-class area reflects its family-oriented but aging character. Home ownership and stability are higher than anywhere else in the ward, although still somewhat lower than the rates for the entire city. Income and educational attainment are moderate. The number of persons of German origin is still noticeable, as is the increasing number of Spanish-speaking residents.

Voting Behavior

The three areas are as different politically as they are demographically. The central area is a Democratic stronghold. The high-rise strip tends to vote selectively for liberal candidates, although it also houses some staunch Republicans and a tradition of Democratic voting persists among the Jewish residents. Until recently, the working-class area was dominated by the Republican party. When the boundaries of the ward were changed to include this area, the local Regular Democratic Organization set about building Democratic strength there. Although Republican support has diminished, the area is still essentially conservative and fails to back liberal Democratic candidates.

The outcome of the 1972 general election (table 2) provides a good illustration of the voting patterns in the ward. The conservative incumbent president, Richard Nixon, headed the Republican ticket. The Democratic ticket included liberal presidential candidate George McGovern and incumbent Cook County State's Attorney Edward Hanrahan, a man who had become identified with conservative, anti-black, law-and-order sentiments. Hanrahan's Republican challenger, Bernard Carey, was endorsed by liberal anti-machine forces. This election was a true test of party loyalty: to vote for one party's candidates for both offices would require that a consistent liberal or conservative position be aban-

Table 2 1972 General Election Outcome in Areas of the Ward

Area	McGovern and Hanrahan (consistent Democrat)	McGovern and Carey (Liberal split)	Nixon and Hanrahan (conservative split)	Nixon and Carey (consistent Republican)
	Percent of Precincts Which Carried for:			
High-rise area	5%	86%	0	9%
Central area	100%	0	0	0
Working-class area	20%	0	60%	20%

NOTE: Each area comprises 10–20 geographically contiguous voting precincts.

doned. In every precinct in the ward's central area, both McGovern and Hanrahan received a majority of the votes cast. Six out of every seven precincts in the high-rise area split in favor of the liberals, McGovern and Carey. In the working-class area, most precincts split in favor of the conservatives, Nixon and Hanrahan, but a few voted straight Republican and a few voted straight Democratic.

In general elections the Democrats usually carry the ward, but there are exceptions. Carey won the ward by a few hundred votes in 1972; in the same election, incumbent United States Senator Charles Percy, a Republican, won easily over a machine-endorsed challenger. This ward is not one of the Chicago machine's most "deliverable." But Regular Democrats do prevail most of the time, and they do so more frequently in this ward than in adjacent wards with similar demographic characteristics. Their strength in this ward is demonstrated by their consistent success in primary elections. In the March 1974 primary, for example, the ward supplied 1.7 percent of the votes cast citywide for Thomas Tully, the Organization's candidate for the Democratic nomination for county assessor. Since 1.7 percent of the city's registered voters lived in the ward at that time, the ward supplied its share of the machine's citywide vote. Figure 2 compares the ward and citywide

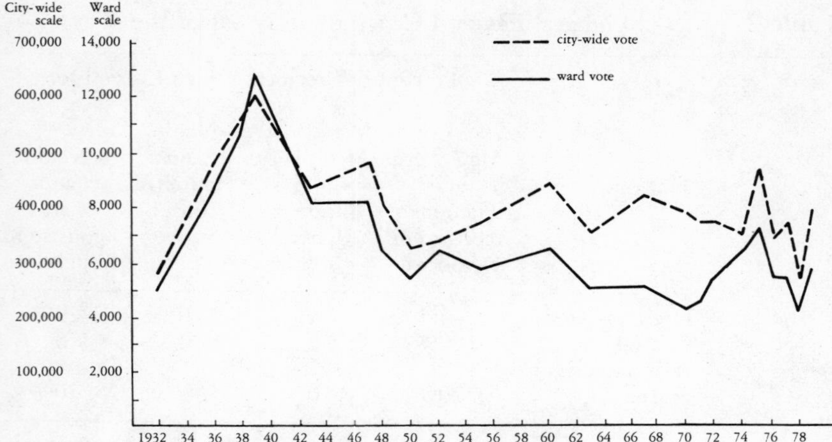
City-wide scale
Ward scale
700,000
14,000
600,000
12,000
500,000
10,000
400,000
8,000
300,000
6,000
200,000
4,000
100,000
2,000
city-wide vote
ward vote
1932
34
36
38
40
42
44
46
48
50
52
54
56
58
60
62
64
66
68
70
72
74
76
78

Fig. 2. Number of votes for the Regular candidate in Democratic primary elections, for the ward and the City of Chicago, 1932–79

NOTE: Ward vote for years through 1971 is the average of the vote in two wards which contained the territory of the ward studied. Vote counts plotted are for the following candidates:

Date	Office	Regular candidate
April 1932	governor	Horner
April 1936	governor	Bundeson
April 1938	senator	Igoe
February 1939	mayor	Kelly
April 1943	mayor	Kelly
February 1947	mayor	Kennelly
April 1948	state's attorney	Boyle
April 1950	sheriff	Gilbert
April 1952	state's attorney	Gutknecht
February 1955	mayor	Daley
April 1960	governor	Kerner
February 1963	mayor	Daley
February 1967	mayor	Daley
March 1970	senator	Stevenson
February 1971	mayor	Daley
March 1972	governor	Simon
March 1973	assessor	Tully
February 1975	mayor	Daley
March 1976	state's attorney	Egan
April 1977	mayor	Bilandic
March 1978	senator	Seith
February 1979	mayor	Bilandic

primary totals for Organization candidates from 1932 to 1979. The ward has consistently held its own, and during the time of this study supplied an increasing proportion of the Organization's citywide vote.

How much of the ward's Regular Democratic strength is attributable to the efforts of party agents? One indication of their efficacy is the outcome of a 1972 special election to select a local advisory council for a federally funded city program. Although this was a nonpartisan election, the Regulars unofficially backed a slate of candidates, and the Democratic committeeman instructed his precinct captains to expend every effort on behalf of the slate, because several Independent and radical candidates were also running. Unaided by any other mobilizing forces,[17] the captains "delivered" 7 percent of the ward's registered voters. We should not assume, however, that their influence is limited to this low level in highly publicized major elections.

Political Organization

Regular Democrats completely dominate political decision-making in this ward. The Democratic committeeman, alderman, and local state senator are all Regulars. At the time I began my research, one of the two Democratic state representatives[18] serving the ward was a Regular and one was an Independent Democrat; the latter was replaced by a Regular in 1974.

Local and federal human services programs are administered by appointees of the Regular Democrats, and the community representatives elected to oversee the operation of such programs are, for the most part, Organization loyalists. There is, however, some organized opposition to these decision-makers.

One source of opposition is the "amateur" political club movement.[19] Locally the movement comprises several groups with overlapping membership, including the ad hoc campaign committees of Independent candidates. These groups have no year-round precinct organization. They are organized around commitment to issues of good government and social justice, not patronage. In this ward, their natural territory is the precincts of the high-rise strip, where their candidates often outpoll the Regulars. But the Independents do poorly in other areas of the ward. Often they have too few campaign workers to canvass all precincts.

Another source of opposition is radical organizers. Like the Independents, they stress issues in their organizing efforts, but they do so from a more class-conscious, conflict-oriented, and ideological point of view. Several radical factions are intermittently active in the ward's central area, although their success there has always been limited. They have little impact on election outcomes, but they do have some effect on local decision-making processes. Their views are occasionally represented in the community press, and they distribute their own newspapers and pamphlets. They organize meetings and demonstrations in which they confront local decision-makers with demands. Although the outcome rarely accords with their demands, their activities certainly cause those in power to avoid confrontation with them.

The ward's Regular Democratic Organization (which I call the ward club, a term not used by its members) is more effective in maintaining its political power than clubs in nearby wards with similar population characteristics. The ward committeeman has control over some 150 patronage jobs, and if he continues to produce favorable election results, his patronage power will rise. However, the ethnic identification of the club leadership limits its power. The committeeman, alderman, ward sanitation superintendent, and most of the leading precinct captains are Jewish. Their ethnicity prevents their wholehearted acceptance into the inner circle of citywide party leaders, almost all of whom are Irish. Moreover, Jewish residents of the ward are concentrated in the area which is least supportive of machine candidates. Thus, the fundamental tie of ethnicity is lacking between most ward residents and those who govern them.

There is little evidence that strong sentiments of solidarity exist between local residents and ward club members. Only about a third of the club's precinct captains live within the boundaries of the precincts to which they are assigned; less than two-thirds of them live within the ward. This absentee political control is particularly evident in the ward's central area, where only a quarter of the precincts have a resident precinct captain. The club's dingy, unattractive storefront office, the ward office, is an administrative outpost, not a community center. Club members do not spend their idle hours there, and non-members enter only on business. The club is the principal seat of local political power, but local networks of friendship do not center around it. Yet, overall, the ward club is effective, for it wins most elections, controls most important decisions, and continues to block the growth of opposition movements in the territory it serves.

Method

My research combines participant observation with an interview survey of a sample of ward residents.[20] My contact with the ward club began in February 1972 while I was a graduate student at the University of Chicago sociology department. At that time an alderman approached the department with the idea of using a student intern to help him with legislative research. I expressed interest in the assignment and soon found myself the unpaid part-time assistant of a Regular Democratic alderman. In June 1972, I moved into the working-class area of the ward. I worked as the alderman's full-time assistant that summer. From the beginning, he knew that I helped him not out of political conviction but as a means of gathering data for sociological research. However, I did not reveal this to other members of the ward club. They treated me at first with the suspicion and reserve that Regulars typically show young liberal intellectuals. As I continued to work there, the club leaders and the ward office staff accepted me as "one of the alderman's people," and the precinct workers treated me like an office staff member. After a few months, I found I was no longer called upon to account for my presence. Club leaders never considered me an insider, but they trusted me as much as they trusted other members of low rank in the club. They regarded me as dependable and discreet, but not as someone who knew anything about practical politics.

I remained active through 1973 and resided in the ward until 1975. I kept extensive field notes on what I observed. I spent the largest part of my time helping to handle requests for service from the alderman. I supervised two college student interns recruited by the alderman and helped train a succession of paid aldermanic assistants. I went to scores of neighborhood meetings, occasionally as the alderman's representative. I regularly attended meetings of the ward club's membership and served for a time on the committee which produced the club newsletter. I served with twenty Regular Democrats on the advisory council of a federally-funded community development program. I accompanied the alderman to city council meetings, to housing court, to meetings with city administrators. I stood with him in the corridors of City Hall where politicians meet and converse. Each election day, I went with him as he made the rounds of the precincts to greet election workers. I attended the club's annual fund-raising dinners, the annual picnics, the alderman's fund-raising parties, and the election night victory celebrations. However, I did not canvass voters in the precincts or take an active part in any political campaign. By 1974, I had cut down my involvement in club activities and local political life so as to devote more time to other phases of this research.

In the fall of 1974 I completed brief, structured interviews with 160 ward residents. These interviews were designed to reveal the extent of use of party services and the causes and consequences of use; the survey instrument is reproduced in appendix A. The respondents were drawn from two random samples: a systematic sample of the ward's registered voters (the voter sample) and a smaller sample of persons whose names were on file at the ward office as having requested assistance from the alderman (the client sample). The sampling methodology and interviewing technique are detailed in appendix B. I completed most of the interviews by telephone, but I interviewed in person many of those who could not be reached by phone, achieving thereby an overall completion rate of 79 percent. The distribution of responses to each item on the interview schedule is shown in appendix A.

This combination of methods makes it possible to contrast the voter's view of the ward club's activities with the club members' view of what they do. The qualitative data I collected as participant-observer provide insight on how the ward club secures the support of its members, and how members go about performing services for voters. Office records to which I had access provide additional information on party services. These findings are discussed in Part Two of this book. The survey interviews provide data on the extent of use of party services, the causes of use, and the effects of use on voter loyalty to the party. With these data, analyzed in Part Three, the exchange models outlined in the preceding chapter will be tested. Data based on observation of the interaction between ward politicians and community groups, presented in Part Four, provide evidence for the alternative model of machine support I have proposed.

Part 2 Inside the Ward Club

Three Defended Venality: Commitment and Compliance in the Ward Club

To understand the nature of machine politics in the ward I studied, we must begin at its center, the ward party organization. There exist within this political club certain social mechanisms by which members are influenced to behave in ways that accomplish organizational goals. Such a system of relationships is part of any sizable task-oriented group; we can refer to any such system, as Amitai Etzioni does, by the term *compliance structure.*[1] Because the ward club is part of a patronage-based political party, it confronts unusual problems in protecting its image of legitimacy in the community upon which it depends. Because of this problem of securing necessary support from a hostile moral environment, the club has developed a complex compliance structure which I shall refer to as a system of *defended venality.* The task of this chapter is to analyze this distinctive system of social control, based on the events I observed as a participant in the activities of the club.

The System of Defended Venality

In the subcommunities of a large city, political power comes both from above and from below. Powerful groups organized on a citywide (or larger) scale use their political resources to accomplish their own purposes in local affairs, and to generate support and contributions of resources from local residents. On the other hand, the local area can, under favorable circumstances, become the site of a network of personal relationships that aggregates many local residents into a political force that can accomplish its purposes in citywide affairs and generate contributions of support from large scale organizations.[2] One of the continuing issues in the study of machines is whether the local patronage party organization is primarily an instrument of power from above, or an expression of power from below.

We may resolve this issue by recognizing that the nature of the patronage party in a given area is an outcome of the interplay of power from above and power from below, and that each of these varies from place to place. The availability of power resources from above varies within the city of Chicago since some committeemen control more patronage and have greater influence over decision-making in city agencies than other committeemen do. Power from below varies because community attachments and the political effectiveness of grass roots groups vary greatly, depending on such factors as the territorial distribution of distinct population groups, the stability of settlement patterns, the strength of local institutions, and the age and status of an area and its residents. Whatever the balance of these powers may be in a particular ward, the ability of the citywide party organization to generate local support must not be taken for granted. The party's use of material incentives to influence local actors can easily backfire, causing antagonism rather than support. Where power is imposed from above, its legitimation in the community and in the ward club itself is problematic.

In the ward club which I studied power comes primarily from above. Ninety-seven percent of the club's 150-odd members hold patronage jobs.[3] The government jobs under the ward committeeman's political sponsorship pay an aggregate annual salary of over $1,000,000. The committeeman makes all significant decisions in the club, with the advice of a handful of trusted insiders. He in turn is constrained to follow the directions of his superiors in the citywide party hierarchy. Lines of communication and authority are strictly vertical in the club. The club is clearly not organized around charismatic personalities, a coherent ideology, or some high moral purpose. It is a highly secretive organization in which most members know very little about what happens at the party's higher levels and show little emotional involvement with each other or with the club. The club is not constituted of strong primary groups, or even of representatives of important primary groups in the community. Its importance in ward political life stems from its nature as the local outpost of the city's most powerful political organization.

The people whom this outpost recruits into service naturally vary in their motivations. We may usefully distinguish two kinds of club members according to their personal stakes in compliance. One group is the *strongly motivated members,* consisting primarily of people who aspire to citywide political office or position and see participation in the ward club as the means to achieve it. These are the professional politicians and those who would like to be professionals. For these people, the stakes are high, since their self-esteem and their economic careers are seriously bound up in the club's success and their own success in the club. The majority, however, who can be termed *acquiescent members,* have no real prospects of rising to high positions through the ward club. Their careers depend at most on the politically sponsored jobs they hold in local government, and their concern is to maintain their political sponsorship, not to make a life out of politics itself. If all the club members were strongly motivated, then compliance would not be problematic in the club. But inevitably there are too few openings in the party hierarchy to staff a whole ward organization with hopeful aspirants to leadership. In a ward with limited citywide "clout," the number of aspirants is further restricted.

The ward club is like many another voluntary association in that it offers only a limited number of leadership positions. Unlike many successful groups, however, it cannot offer its members and potential recruits enhanced social standing in the eyes of the larger community. Club members make strong and invidious distinctions between members and nonmembers, but the Regular Democratic Organization is hardly a prestigious group. Although there are a few professional-level government employees among the club members—for example, an attorney in the office of the Corporation Counsel and an electrical engineer in the Bureau of Electricity—lower-level clerical and manual workers predominate. The median income for patronage employees in the club was just over $8,000 in 1972. As shown in table 3, which is based on data from the club's

Table 3 Average Annual Salary of Ward Club Patronage Workers, 1972

	All Precincts	High-rise Area	Central Area	Working-class Area
All workers	$8,815	$ 8,986	$ 8,750	$ 9,093
Precinct captains	$9,675	$10,500	$10,108	$ 9,675
Noncaptains	$8,411	$ 8,921	$ 8,237	$ 9,365
Number of patronage workers per precinct	2.4	2.3	2.7	2.1
Estimated 1972 median family income in area	—	$15,777	$ 8,803	$11,729

NOTE: Five precincts that include parts of both the high-rise and central areas are excluded from calculations for each of those areas. Family income figures for 1972 are 1969 figures shown in table 1, adjusted for the intervening rise in family income. Adjustment is based on ratio of 1973 to 1970 median income for white families in the United States, taking into account the difference between Illinois and the nation in rates of increase in median family income 1959–69. From U.S. Bureau of the Census, *Statistical Abstract of the United States: 1976,* 97th edition (Washington, D.C.: U.S. Government Printing Office, 1976), tables 647, 659.

internal records, the salary level of patronage workers varies somewhat from one part of the ward to another, and precinct captains generally have somewhat higher-paying positions than other club members. However, with but one exception—the precinct captains in the ward's poorest area—the income level of the party workers is lower than the median family income of the residents in their part of the ward. On the basis of general occupational prestige, then, ward residents have little reason to look up to members of the ward club. This difference in status is exacerbated by the bad image of local government workers in general and patronage employees in particular: many people view them as dependent, devious, and incompetent to hold down a job in the private sector. I can offer no quantitative evidence on the prevalence of this negative image, but it is certainly widespread and is not restricted to middle-class members of the community.

With avenues for advancement limited, and with the larger community holding club members in no special esteem, most of the club's members have limited stakes in the party's future, and therefore will not reliably contribute to its efforts out of self-interest alone. Yet the ward club is able to get its job done despite the lack of involvement on the part of acquiescent members. All the precincts are staffed with a captain and several workers. For the most part they make the financial contributions which the club unofficially requires. They register voters, canvass their precincts before elections, and bring out the voters on election day. On the rare evenings when the club meets, the storefront meeting hall office is filled to capacity. And, as I have already observed, the party has a good record of success in ward elections. It might appear, then, that the material inducements offered by the party's local leadership are sufficient to elicit the necessary contributions of time and money from all club members. Are the latter an unusual group of politically amoral people who do not demand legitimation of the party's power? It is my contention that they are not, and that to posit a distinct "style" or "ethos" as an explanation of their compliance is to seriously misunderstand the moral basis of the patronage party and overlook some of the club's most distinctive aspects.

The patronage party is not an isolated or self-sufficient collectivity with a monopoly on authoritative judgments of good and bad. It depends on continuous and intensive outreach into the community at large where values inimical to it are thoroughly institutionalized. These values dictate that public officials should seek to achieve community goods by democratic methods and that it is wrong for self-interest to dominate the political scene. The existence of these widely shared values does not necessarily prevent the patronage party from succeeding, but the party certainly cannot succeed by seeming to be and do what it actually is and does.

The need to preserve a legitimate image increases the complexity of the ward club's internal structure for two reasons. First, it is essential to the party's effectiveness that its members portray the party to outsiders in positive terms—as an organization seeking community goods through democratic means. Beyond contributions of time and money, then, the ward club must secure its members' adherence to a set of norms which facilitate control and prevent the disclosure of the party's hidden activities. Second, the members themselves are recruited from an environment which is opposed to the use of material incentives in politics. Their work for the party brings them into continual contact with that environment. To the extent that the members share the value that venality in politics is wrong and have low personal stakes in the club's success, it is not possible for the party to secure their genuine commitment through the use of patronage alone. Lack of strong commitment in turn makes it more difficult for the club to secure adherence to the party norms that protect its public image. Accordingly, the club must be organized in such a way as to secure compliance and to create and preserve commitment without subverting its utilitarian goals. As a patronage party, the club uses appeals to the material motives of its members, but to be effective the club must defend itself against potential repudiation of these appeals by voters and by the club members themselves.

Hidden Activities

The ward club has many things to hide from the public. Some of the party's activities and relationships are illegal; others violate no law but are at variance with widely accepted standards of good government and fair play. Disclosure of these activities would damage the credibility of the party's claim that it seeks to achieve community goods through democratic methods.

What things are concealed by the ward club which I studied? First, there are the illegal aspects of job patronage, the extraction of money dues and political work from sponsored jobholders by threatening to "vise" them (withdraw sponsorship and cause them to be fired). The deficient qualifications and job performance of some sponsored jobholders are kept secret because they could invite accusations of disregard for the public good. Some club members who hold federally funded jobs are politically active, a violation of federal law. Some are involved in corrupt practices of public administration, such as illegal payoffs, and others have close ties to government officials who have been publicly disgraced for corrupt practices. A few political workers engage in illegal election-day practices, and many used vote-getting techniques which are manipulative or dishonest. In dispensing favors and rewards, the club follows patterns of political favoritism, nepotism, and ethnic particularism. On occasion, club leaders announce decisions as their own when they are actually following the directives of party leaders downtown. The club enjoys the close cooperation of some local organizations and agencies which pretend to be independent or non-political. There are also attempts to secure the cooperation of organizations by covertly placing party loyalists into positions of leadership. Finally, many decisions affecting the club and the community are made privately by a few club leaders. The public deliberative processes which give legitimacy to these decisions are planned in advance and regulated by party loyalists so as to accord with the preordained outcome.

The preceding list is not intended to be exhaustive. Undoubtedly patronage parties at other places and times have been engaged in other types of clandestine activity. The central point here is that a patronage party, by definition, pursues goals which are at variance with the public good by methods which conflict with the ideals of liberal democracy. In a system where suffrage is broad and public office is attained by direct election, the defense of venality requires that these facts be protected from disclosure.

The Regular Ethic

The party's secrets can be concealed because its members generally adhere to a distinctive set of norms institutionalized in the party. The Regular ethic is based upon two central principles: loyalty and discretion. The attitudes and behavior considered proper for a Regular Democrat vary with his role, but at all levels, these two principles underlie the prescriptions. Here are some of the unwritten rules which apply to a person with a high ward-level position—a committeeman or alderman, for example:[4]

1. Be faithful. Obey your leader, and stand by him in all conflicts.
2. Take care of your own. Repay those who are faithful to you.
3. Support the whole ticket. Vote for the party, not the man or the program.
4. Show respect. Treat government and party leaders as worthy, their activities as consequential.
5. Don't be ashamed. Defend the party proudly to all.
6. Don't be absent. You are not loyal if you are not there.
7. Don't ask questions. The party lets you know all you need to know.
8. Shun outsiders. Communicate with Independents only when absolutely unavoidable.
9. Keep out of the papers. You don't need publicity, the party will take care of you.
10. Stay on your own turf. Never involve yourself with territory outside your district or issues not of exclusive concern to your constituency.
11. Don't be first. Initiative entails unnecessary risk.
12. Don't get caught.
13. Leave your spouse at home. Gatherings of politicians are for business.

These rules consistently set the party's interest over that of the individual member. They are based on the axiom that the Regular Democratic party is the means to all valued ends, both individual and collective. For the strongly motivated member whose stakes in the party are high, adherence to party norms follows naturally.

For the acquiescent member, this basic commitment is lacking. The party's reliance on face-to-face contacts for mobilization of the electorate makes it impossible to insulate members from hostile people and ideas. Almost every active member of the ward club must regularly canvass voters in the precinct. There is a constant round of neighborhood and community meetings, some of them in the ward office, at which opposition leaders are often present. Club members are thus directly confronted with the disapproval and contempt of those who oppose machine politics. This may be reflected in a condescending tone of voice, a silent frown, a door slammed in the face, a verbal attack on the party, or a direct denunciation of the club member himself.[5] Open disapproval is also frequently expressed in the mass media. Nobody affiliated with the Regulars can be unaware that there are many persons, including some of stature and power, who think their way of doing politics is wrong. The Regular Democrat is always potentially subject to direct challenge, and where his stakes in the party are limited, his commitment to the party and his compliance with the Regular ethic are threatened. We therefore find in the club a complex compliance structure which uses sanctions to promote compliance even in the absence of commitment; controls sensitive information to preserve commitment and minimize the damage that breaches of compliance might cause; and builds commitment over time by resocializing participants. Let us now examine each of these aspects of the club's compliance structure in greater detail.

Sanctions

The ward committeeman has formal authority over the patronage jobs by which most club members earn a living. He is entitled at any time to vise a patronage worker. The political job is the fundamental benefit which the ward club extends to a member, and taking the job away is the ultimate sanction. In practice, however, this sanction is almost never used. In my three years with the ward club, I heard of no patronage jobholder who lost his job for inadequate political work. The word *vise* is hardly ever used, although most party members seem to understand its meaning. When addressing a club meeting, the committeeman occasionally says, "After the election we're going to weed out the ones who aren't working."[6] But these threats are made almost as rarely as they are carried out. Despite his formal role as job sponsor, the committeeman's actual control over the economic welfare of his jobholders is limited in several ways.

First, since the 1970 "Shakman decision," it has been illegal to fire a public employee for failure to make political contributions or to do political work.[7] This makes vising both risky (the fired jobholder might resort to the courts) and troublesome (the actual firing has to be subtly handled so no violation of the law can be proved).

Second, withdrawal of sponsorship might result in the loss of the job for the committeeman as well as for the jobholder. Some political jobs require technical qualifications which the committeeman cannot expect to find among the jobseekers in his ward. If he cannot promptly fill an available job, he may be obliged to relinquish it to the committeeman of another ward in exchange for a job which is easier to fill. The new job is likely to have a lower salary and therefore bring in correspondingly lower annual dues. Control of patronage jobs is the committeeman's principal power resource and a mark of his status in the party. It is better for him to tolerate non-compliance than to jeopardize his control over an important job slot.

Third, some jobholders are protected from being fired even though they acquired the job with the help of the committeeman. They may be "departmental," enjoying a special relationship with the department head who would block any attempt to dismiss them. They may fall under the protection of the State Personnel Code or the Hatch Act. Skilled craftsmen are often immune because they are protected by strong unions.

Fourth, the jobholder may not value his patronage job enough to fear its possible loss. Patronage jobs often have low prestige compared to non-patronage jobs involving similar work. The value of the job to the jobholder depends upon his age and skills and the strength of the private job market—in short, on the availability of other opportunities.[8]

In most cases, then, the strongest sanction which the committeeman can apply is a less formidable one than vising: he can sever his relationship with the club member. The ward club does not issue membership cards, but there is a membership list kept current by the committeeman's secretary. Notices of meetings, the ward newsletter, and other mailings go only to those on the list. When a member fails to contribute money or work, or otherwise shows unmistakable disloyalty, his name disappears from the list. He is no longer welcome at club meetings. The committeeman may refuse to meet with him. His requests for favors will be scornfully dismissed. Casting an intransigent member out of the club does not bring him into compliance, but it serves as an example to others of what may happen to them if they should fail to comply.

This practice helps to maintain a strong insider-outsider distinction in the club. While members are not particularly emotionally attached to one another, they do have a strong "we-feeling." They refer to other Regular Democrats as "one of our people," "one of us," "a guy who's with us"; and to politically active non-Regulars as "not with us" or, simply, "them." Although commitment to the club varies as it does in any voluntary organization, the leaders make clear that being Regular is a matter of identity: either one is a Regular or one isn't. There is no middle ground. The key question which the committeeman puts to persons who seek his sponsorship for a job is: "Are you 100 percent Democrat?" The only acceptable answer is yes. Divided loyalty is considered disloyalty. Partial compliance is labeled unacceptable, although in practice it must often be tacitly accepted. Though the vising power is almost never used and the expulsion of club members is not frequent, the maintenance of a sharp insider-outsider distinction helps keep all members aware that full compliance with the Regular ethic is expected of them.

Even if the committeeman's control over the economic well-being of club members were more complete, it would still not be sufficient to ensure compliance. The committeeman lacks a differentiated set of sanctions which he can selectively apply to offenses according to their gravity. If a club members fails to do what is expected, the committeeman can express his disapproval or get angry. He can vise the worker or expel him from the club. But he has no intermediate punishments at his disposal. If the member is not strongly motivated, the committeeman's expressions of disapproval are likely to have little impact on his behavior.

A further difficulty with the application of negative sanctions in the ward club is that standards of acceptable performance are vague. The monetary contribution expected from patronage jobholders is clear enough: a fixed rate, usually 3 percent of the annual salary, which may be reduced in hardship cases. But what constitutes satisfactory precinct work? The committeeman is familiar with the various precincts and how they have voted in the past. He hopes for improvement in the vote returns, but how is he to tell what effect the precinct workers' efforts have had in a particular election? What constitutes an unacceptable result? The committeeman's evaluation of the results are tempered by his impression of the voting history of the precinct and the amount of effort the worker has expended. But his information is limited. He cannot actually observe the canvassing activities in the precincts; he must rely on the reports of precinct captains who color their reports to protect their people and enhance their own image. Even the vote counts reported to him on election night are sometimes falsified to look better than the actual results.[9] If a club member does no precinct work, the committeeman will eventually find out about it. But if the bare minimum is done, the committeeman cannot accurately determine how hard the member really worked. The uncommitted member can easily get by without incurring disapproval if he attends club meetings, pays his dues, and stuffs a few leaflets in the mailboxes in his precinct. But the party expects—and usually gets—more than this.

Club leaders use some positive sanctions to reward members, but these are not of great material value. In the typical ward club, positions of responsibility and prestige are few; they are held by strongly motivated members of long seniority. Most committeemen avoid the creation of formal levels of authority above the rank of precinct captain, for fear of granting others in the club a base of power which might eventually be turned against them. For the most part, then, promotion within the club is not available for use as a reward.

An exception to this rule took place in the ward I studied, when a new committeeman took office in the club. He inaugurated several appointive positions which were meant to increase vertical differentiation and opportunities for promotion. He appointed six "area leaders," precinct captains who were each given supervisory authority over eight other captains. These supervisors were assigned scattered precincts, instead of a contiguous territory, so as to diminish the threat to the committeeman from below. New standing committees were created (among them, finance, entertainment, and publicity committees), each of which had a chairman who was to sit on an executive committee. Every member was expected to join at least one committee. New statuses were created at the precinct level also. Each precinct captain was asked to appoint an assistant captain, a female aide, a senior citizen aide, and a "young Democrat" aide. But the attractiveness of the new positions was diminished by the committeeman's deliberate failure to delegate real authority. Club members reacted to the innovations with their usual apathy, because they seemed to involve greater contributions without extra remuneration. The standing committees never met, except for those which, as before, organized fund-raising and social events for the club. Vertical communication was not improved and the discretionary authority granted to the committeeman's subordinates was not increased. As the new committeeman became more secure in his position, he dropped the rhetoric of democratization, and no one in the club seemed to miss it.

The new committeeman also attempted to provide more material incentives for good performance. During a pre-election voter registration drive he instituted a raffle in which each new registration of change-of-address obtained by a member would count as an entry, with ten Thanksgiving turkeys for prizes. He made it clear that only bona fide changes-of-address would be accepted.[10] However, in the majority of the ward's precincts there were no new registrations. The few workers who did obtain many new registrations were the ones who always had brought in the most new registrations. The failure of the raffle to improve participation illustrates the limited effectiveness of positive inducements where motivation is low.[11]

Club leaders do grant some purely symbolic rewards to good members. For example, they frequently flatter members of moderate competence by introducing them to outsiders as "one of our best workers." There is a raffle at the club's annual fund-raising dinner, and club leaders call on individual members to select each winning ticket from the box. This ritual is one of the few opportunities for good members to be honored before the whole membership. The fact that the club leader knows a member by sight and calls his name announces to all present that this is a good club member. But for those who are so recognized, the value is in having the committeeman's approval; the respect of the other members, the majority of whom remain a mass of nameless faces, is far less important.

Clearly, the committeeman's limited ability to produce compliance through the use of sanctions is a reflection of the nature of his authority. He exercises one-man rule through distribution of material incentives. Although this appeals to material motives of members, it does little to foster normative commitment.[12] The committeeman's jealous monopoly of authority in the club limits the practical value of the rewards he is willing to make available. The purely symbolic rewards he grants have limited appeal to acquiescent members. But crude sanctions applied from above are nevertheless a significant component of the compliance structure of the club, ensuring from most members at least the minimal contribution that will ensure continued sponsorship of their patronage jobs.

Control of Sensitive Information

The Regular ethic, with its stress on discretion, dictates that party members should keep to themselves all information about the party's hidden activities. The defense of venality requires that, insofar as possible, this information also be kept from club members. The careful control of sensitive information by the leadership serves two functions. It minimizes the potential damage that indiscretion by weakly committed members might do. What members do not know, they cannot reveal. It also serves to preserve the commitment of party members. The Regular ethic is predicated on faith in the party, and this faith is based in part on what is known about the party.[13] The less a member is committed to the party, the less able he is to accept negative information about it without damage to his allegiance. Where information is controlled so as to maintain a close correlation between commitment and knowledge of sensitive matters, both secrecy and commitment can be preserved.

It is typical of formal organizations that participants' authority, commitment, and knowledge are intercorrelated. But organizations differ in the way these things are distributed. The ward club is extraordinary in the degree to which it is centralized. It would be detrimental to the functioning of any organization if role incumbents were consistently denied information which was necessary to the adequate performance of their organizational roles. Generally, members of the ward club have access to the minimum information they need to do their jobs. But because the club's decision-making authority is so highly centralized, the duties of most members involve the execution of directives without the opportunity to exercise their own judgment. Club members are told what to do and how to do it, but not why.

Joe, who had dropped out of junior college after a year or two and still lived with his mother in the ward, had been looking for work for a long time. He had helped his precinct captain at election time and had spent many hours trying to help out at the ward office. His precinct captain prevailed upon the committeeman to see if he could find Joe a job. Interested in the mechanics of job sponsorship, which were always kept well concealed, I chatted with Joe after he emerged from his conference with the committeeman.

"Where you headed, Joe?"

"Going downtown. The committeeman said he's gonna try to get me a job."

"What kind of job?"

"He didn't say."

"What'd he tell you to do?"

"He said take this letter down to Room ___ at City Hall and give it to Mr. Able."

I asked Joe what the sealed letter said; what office he was being sent to; what Mr. Able's position was; what department he might be referred to. Joe knew none of these things. He was not prevaricating—he simply had not been told and had not asked.

Joe, of course, was a raw recruit, but the same peremptory style is used when club leaders give directions to long-time members. Because they are not granted discretionary authority, subordinates enjoy no legitimate claim to the knowledge upon which decisions are based. As Gosnell has pointed out, from the party's point of view, one characteristic of the ideal precinct worker is that he does not ask too many questions.[14] The loyalty expected of good members is unconditional. To ask questions would be to suggest that the subordinate might not obey if the answers were unsatisfactory or were not forthcoming. The leadership not only withholds information from subordinates but makes those who express curiosity feel that they are doing something wrong.

Communication within the party tends to be strictly vertical, following lines of authority. Cooperation and communication between persons at the same level are minimal. The club as a whole cooperates very little with other ward clubs, even those in adjacent wards. Precinct captains stick to the business of their own precincts. When mobilization of the club is necessary, as in the days before an election, the committeeman holds a series of small conferences with individual precinct captains or with a few workers from one precinct. In the privacy of his office, the details of precinct work are discussed and worked out: whom to select as an election judge, how large a turnout can be expected, how much money will be needed on election day. Discussion of job patronage and money contributions also takes place only in private conversations. Sometimes the committeeman's close lieutenants are present. When club members wait outside the committeeman's office, they rarely talk about their business. There exist, of course, informal communication channels between friends, and even people who are not well acquainted will try to obtain information from each other when there is no alternative. But there are no formal means of horizontal communication, no cliques or interest groups (other than the group closest to the committeeman) which routinely share information received, and very few opportunities for informal peer contact.

Control of information is markedly different in the patronage party than in political clubs which stress membership participation. In what Wilson calls "amateur" clubs,[15] the social contract between leaders and members is much clearer. Members possess the ultimate decision-making power. Leaders rule at their behest. Members participate in the decision-making process; they discuss club goals and tactics and they vote on important questions. They feel they have both the right and the duty to inform themselves and are quick to disapprove reticence or evasiveness in their leadership. As Wilson has pointed out, in the agenda of goals that amateur clubs pursue there are inherent conflicts which militate against the supposedly central norms of participation and openness.[16] But the treatment of information in the amateur club is always more open than in the patronage party club, for two reasons. First, in the absence of patronage and other material inducements, access to inside knowledge is one of the most attractive incentives a club can offer. Second, since material incentives are not crucial to the functioning of the amateur club, there is less damning information to damage commitment if revealed.

Secrets and Status

Although inside information is not distributed to ward club members as a general inducement to participation, it is used infrequently as a reward for strong commitment. It has both material and symbolic value for the club member. When granted access to it, he knows that he is looked upon with favor. He can tell others that he is so privileged, thereby elevating his status in the club. Thus he enjoys an advantage in the competition within the club for status and its rewards.

Since information which confers status is sensitive, there are few situations in which the holder of such information can display it to confirm his status. The opportunity sometimes arises when secrets are made public, as in the following situation:

The man who was ward committeeman when I first began participant observation had held a prestigious elected office for many years. He knew that he would be appointed to a judgeship after the November 1972 election. Nevertheless, he ran for reelection in the primary, because it seemed doubtful that any other Regular Democrat could defeat the strong Independent candidate who also sought the nomination. After winning in the primary he withdrew from the race, and, in accordance with the state law, a new candidate was picked by the Democratic committeeman of the area. This replacement candidate (a Regular) was assured of election because of Democratic strength in the district. The Independent candidate had anticipated this strategy, publicly warned of it throughout the primary campaign, and stood ready to go to court to demand a special primary if the committeeman were to withdraw. It was therefore necessary for his withdrawal to be delayed until just before the election. His campaign was de-emphasized, but most club members took this as a sign of confidence in his reelection.

In the second week of September, there was a meeting for all members at club headquarters. Instructions were given for registration and canvassing drives, literature was distributed, and several prominent candidates on the party's countywide ticket made speeches. The committeeman presided and commented at length on what each of the speakers said. His own candidacy was not mentioned until, at the end of the meeting, the alderman was called upon to say a few words. Like the other speakers, he stressed the fact that the whole ticket must be supported, including presidential candidate George McGovern, who was not popular with the Regulars. He continued: "And let's not forget that our own great committeeman is running again. I predict a great victory for him; he's going to get the biggest plurality he's ever received!" This declaration was met with hearty applause.

Ten days later the committeeman announced to reporters that he was withdrawing from the race. I was in the ward office with the office secretary when the news was made public. Several astonished club members phoned in for verification of the report. Sue, the secretary, confided to me that she had known for some time that he would not run. The committeeman's executive aide had told her more than a month earlier. She had kept the news from everyone. Sue then asked that I not tell others that she had known, "so they won't be jealous." Thus she made known to me her superior position in the club. Later in the day the alderman arrived at the office and I told him that I suspected that he had had advance knowledge of the withdrawal. This was a delicate situation. Since only the committeeman's top lieutenants had had advance knowledge of the withdrawal, the alderman would be admitting low status if he replied that he had not known. If he confirmed that he did know, he would be admitting that he had deliberately misled the entire club in his remarks at the meeting and that he had kept the information from me. "I bet it was a big surprise to you, you bastard," I said. He winked as if to say, "That's for me to know and you to find out." He did not state whether he had known beforehand, and if so, for how long. A few days later I again asked him to tell me the inside story of the decision to withdraw; he said he would tell me sometime, but he never did. I heard no complaints from any member that the withdrawal decision should have been disclosed to the membership earlier, although I am sure others felt chagrined because they had not had individual access to the secret information.

Sensitive information, then, is truly privileged information. It is told to those who can be trusted not to tell. Those who are told do not disclose the information because to do so would violate that trust and jeopardize their future access. To give away information about a secret also tends to deflate the status value of knowing the secret. Thus attaching privilege to secret knowledge helps keep it secret, and secrecy makes access to it a privilege.

The importance of this principle to people in the patronage party was underscored one day as I stood with the alderman in the lobby of City Hall. The alderman was greeting the politicians who happened by. Some paused to chat with him, and several times he took one or another aside. They would put their heads together and speak so as not to be overheard. I later asked the alderman about these private conversations. He told me what they had talked about. It was not a matter of great sensitivity. He added, "But if you don't act like something's a big secret when you tell it to these guys, they don't listen to you."

Information Control and Contact With Outsiders

The control of sensitive information is furthered by norms that limit opportunities for interaction between club members and outsiders. We have seen that Regulars draw a sharp distinction between themselves and outsiders and that affiliation with the party is viewed as a matter of identity, not just ideology. The boundary is made sharper by the expectation that as little communication as possible will take place across it. Some contact is inevitable since the party communicates with most of the electorate in its efforts to mobilize support. There are some grounds for interaction with Independents which Regulars accept as legitimate. Interaction which cannot be justified calls into question the club member's identity as a Regular. Even justifiable interaction is acceptable only if the club member makes it clear that he feels repugnance for the Independents he confronts.

The demand that the opposition be shunned is not expressed in a subtle way. One evening about twenty tenant-union members with Independent ties came to the ward office and met with the alderman to discuss code violations in their building. There were some middle-aged people, a few young blacks, and several hippies. Since they could not all be seated in the alderman's office, he met with them in the public area of the ward office. Marty, one of the top precinct captains, came by while the meeting was in progress. "What the hell is the alderman doing with all those longhairs?" he asked. "Who the hell are they?" It was necessary for the office staff to assure Marty that the alderman had not initiated the meeting.

On another occasion, the head of the local McGovern campaign office came to see the alderman. She was a liberal, upper middle class woman who had long been a leader of Independent Democrats in the area. She did her best during the presidential campaign to secure the cooperation of the Regulars and had frequent conferences with the committeeman. She brought with her to the office a woman who sought the alderman's assistance in fighting eviction. The alderman was busy, so I asked the two women to wait, invited them to be seated near his office rather than in the crowded waiting area, and offered them coffee from the staff coffee pot. As we sat sipping coffee and discussing the eviction problem, Billy, a senior member of the ward club, came over and said, "What do you think this is? Coffee isn't free around here, you know." Billy was well aware of the campaign organizer's identity and he did not make these comments in a joking way.

Later in the 1972 campaign, a storefront office for Independent candidates opened within a block of the Regulars' ward office. There was a party to celebrate the occasion on a night when the ward office was also open. Curious to meet some of the "opposition" workers, I went over for a visit. I introduced myself, picked up some literature, and got a few cookies to take back to the ward office. The committeeman was alone in his office. I asked him if he would like some "Independent cookies." "What the hell were you doing over there?" "Getting something to eat." He looked displeased but said nothing more. I was careful not to commit a blunder of this kind again.

When the community organizers from the Catholic parish started a number of block groups in the community, there was almost no involvement of precinct captains in any of these groups. This was more than a reflection of the captains' failure to exert real local leadership. The precinct captains were well aware that block groups were being formed. But the organizers were outsiders. Therefore the block group meetings had to be avoided.

The captains' feelings about Independents are also evident in their vociferous complaints to club leaders each registration and election day that Independent poll watchers are "interfering" with the smooth operation of the polling place. The anger and frustration do not only stem from the occasionally intrusive behavior of the poll watchers, or annoyance at being observed and thus prevented from questionable conduct in the polling place. They reflect the tension of spending twelve hours with someone with whom one feels constrained not to interact in a friendly way. And to some extent the captains adjust their expression of displeasure to accord with what they think club leaders expect them to feel.

Thus the relationship of insiders to outsiders is combative rather than congenial. Independents are not treated as the loyal opposition but as aliens bent on illegitimate conquest. Preexisting age and class cleavages work in concert with the party's norm of communication avoidance, since Independents tend to be younger and wealthier than Regulars. But these cleavages alone do not explain the avoidance. Even when cooperation is in the patronage party's interest, as in the McGovern campaign, close working relationships are not permitted to develop. In most campaigns, the Independents have no chance of victory, yet the Regulars shun them as if the Organization's fate hung in the balance. This avoidance makes sense as a part of the system of defended venality. Communication with persons who do not subscribe to the Regular ethic is prevented. Dissemination of sensitive information to the party's enemies is blocked. And club members whose commitment may be incomplete are protected from the challenge of informed and articulate criticism of the party.

Socialization

We have seen that the behavior of club members is rewarded and punished by club leaders, and that control of sensitive information constitutes an additional organizational defense. But adherence to the Regular ethic rests most securely on commitment to the party. We have noted that motivations of members differ in strength, and that a primary determinant of commitment is the member's aspirations for advancement through the party. But normative commitment rests not only on self-interest, but on a person's political attitudes and beliefs, which are subject to the influence of groups. An important element in the club's system of defended venality is its ability to foster commitment to the party and internalization of the Regular ethic as the member continues his or her participation. This is not to say that most new members are successfully transformed into strongly motivated insiders. Rather, it points to the learning processes that produce behavioral conformity to party norms, and the moral framework that encourages willing, if not always enthusiastic, acquiescence in the defense of venality.

Several forces operate to convince the new club member of the legitimacy of the party's means and ends. First, he is in a new social position, involving new tasks and the opportunity to observe things of which he was previously unaware. His new position subjects him to a new set of expectations for proper behavior and his new point of view helps justify these expectations. Second, the people who work with him, his peers and immediate supervisors, know that he is a novice and actively seek to teach him appropriate attitudes and behavior by example, encouragement, and admonition. Third, the club leaders provide authoritative rationalizations for the party's activities in their indoctrination talks at club meetings. The effect of these forces is enhanced by the adroit manipulation of symbols of legal and moral authority to make the club's activities seem proper.

Learning from Precinct Work

Most club members initially become involved in politics as a means of securing a patronage job. Little or no advance political work is required. The applicant needs only a recommendation from the precinct captain for the committeeman to write a letter of sponsorship. The committeeman satisfies himself that the new jobholder understands his or her obligations to the ward club: come to all meetings, contribute a percentage of salary, help in the precinct at every election, and be a "good Democrat." On the job, the new worker finds that politics are seldom discussed. He knows he is not the only political jobholder in his place of work, but patronage is not mentioned at all. Then election time comes and the learning begins.

It is in the precinct that much of the political reeducation of the new club member takes place. The precinct captain assigns him canvassing duties and on election day has him passing out leaflets, keeping track of who votes, or contacting reliable voters who have not yet voted. In performing these tasks he spends hours in the company of experienced Regulars as they interact with other insiders and with outsiders. Different precincts require different electioneering techniques, but in every precinct the new political worker is taught the tricks of the trade.

Tim, an attractive, middle-aged bachelor with a strong taste for liquor, is precinct captain in one of the skid row sections of the ward. Just before the start of the fall 1972 campaign, he took the time to explain his vote-getting techniques to a group of new club members:

> You've got to knock on every door. You can't go by the voters' list, because these people move around too much. Take good care of your building managers—they hold the key to success. If they won't cooperate, then you may have to hit them with some kind of

> inspection; just make sure you get them to cooperate. Be careful to check up on the Rooming House Affadavits and see that everybody listed has gotten registered to vote. If some guy moves out after registration to a nearby precinct, bring him in and vote him anyway.

A prolonged and ill-informed debate about the legality of this advice ensued, after which Tim continued:

> They're going to close all the taverns on election day this year, so I'm arranging for free drinks to be given out at a tavern near the polling place. We'll have a limit on the number of drinks a guy can have, and if he hasn't voted, he doesn't drink. But you've got to be careful. Last year I had all kinds of goddamn Independents and city lawyers all over the place in my precinct, just looking for something to nail me on. They should have been there during the primary: I had one guy who stood in front of the polling place hollering to see the precinct captain, yelling that he wasn't going to vote unless he got paid!

Tim left the impression that he does pay some of his voters if necessary.

Joel, a twenty-eight-year-old law student who captains a precinct in the high-rise area of the ward, offered quite different advice:

> When I go out canvassing in the apartments where the singles are, I wear my flared pants, an ecology button, and a peace button. My generation is the least tolerant there is, you have to look like them and use their language in order to be accepted by them. I tell 'em to open the damn door and cut the bullshit, and sure enough, they'll open up for me. But in the high rises where the older couples live, I wear a coat and tie. When I call on those young so-called Independents, I've even said 'I'm the man from Dicky Daley's rip-off machine.' They think that's really cool and open. But with the old ladies, I'm as gentle as they come. If they open the door on a chain I step back from the door and say '*Please* don't open the door.' They always open the door when I say that.

He told of an encounter with a "very rich University of Chicago law student" in his precinct, who expressed disdain for the Regular Democrats. As Joel was leaving, he overheard the student say to his unemployed wife "I'd vote his way if he could have found you a job with the city." Joel reported with pride that he flew into a rage at that: "I went back and told the guy, 'You're no better than the people you condemn, the winos who vote for a bottle of Muscatel.' When I saw him the next day at the polling place, that guy said hello to me just as friendly as could be. And you know what? I'll bet you anything he voted my way." The new worker not only witnesses and hears about these practical techniques; he sees them validated in the victory of "his" candidates.

I was not able to observe directly the learning process which takes place in the course of doing precinct work in this particular ward. But based on my own previous experience in precinct work and the fact that most workers have little contact with the ward office, I have no doubt that important changes in attitude occur as the novice becomes a seasoned precinct worker. He becomes more aware of the average person's ignorance of politics and indifference toward it and more confident of his own persuasive power. He begins to view vote-getting as an end in itself.[17] He learns that many criticisms of the patronage party are exaggerated or unjust. He is more conscious of the party's positive efforts on behalf of his neighborhood. And he loses any naive idealism he may have had about the electorate.

Learning from Service Activities

Most club members do not become involved in the day-to-day activities of the ward office; those who do are usually experienced and highly trusted. But the alderman of this ward recruited outsiders for his office staff, most of whom were young, liberal, well educated, and from other parts of the city. The presence of these outsiders, myself included, was a great strain on the committeeman's small staff of Regulars. The outsiders had to be prevented from observing hidden activities, or at least from understanding what they observed. Since they were novices, they needed to be assisted in the execution of even the most elementary tasks. They threatened to upset the existing distribution of tasks and authority in the office. Their presence also placed a strain on the office's limited operating resources. Tension between the committeeman's staff and the aldermanic assistants who stayed more than a few months lessened over time, not only because accommodating arrangements were eventually worked out, but because "the alderman's people" became resocialized as the Regulars made clear what was expected of them. The experience of the aldermanic assistants is unusual in that they were recruited from sectors of society in which antipathy to patronage politics is traditionally strong and immediately placed in positions from which they could observe the club's day-to-day operations. Yet they were socialized into some compliance with the Regular ethic by the same forces which act upon the typical novice in the club.

In the months I spent working as the alderman's assistant, I learned new orientations toward the residents of the ward. Each of the other volunteers and paid assistants with whom I worked underwent a similar transformation as he or she dealt with requests for services. Each of us started with the assumption that all service clients were equally worthy. Since they were all voters or potential voters, every attempt was to be made to win their support. They were also citizens in need and hence deserved adequate help even if it was inconvenient or unpleasant for us to provide it. If they were poor or incompetent in some way, this was not to be held against them. As the alderman's representatives, we felt we should remain polite and accommodating at all times. We disapproved of the rude and arrogant manner which the Regulars adopted toward some clients and some of us interpreted it as unfair discrimination against unjustly oppressed people.

Gradually our orientations changed. We learned that helping people was time-consuming and nerve-wracking work which interfered with other office duties. As I investigated complaints, I frequently discovered that the client had misrepresented the circumstances. I found out that clients sometimes rewarded my best efforts not with gratitude, but with anger and further complaint. I learned that, for the most part, other agencies were cooperative and seemed sincerely interested in righting any real wrongs that come to light. As time went on, I noticed that some of my clients were chronic complainers who expected help with one problem after another. I came to understand that one cannot expend too much effort on a single exasperating case without depriving others of help. I discovered that "problem" clients were readily silenced if I pointed out ways in which they themselves were to blame for their situation. I realized that gentle prodding is not always the most effective means of securing the cooperation of other agencies; occasionally I had to berate or threaten them. In short, I learned not to be too nice.

The more experienced office staff helped me and the other novices to arrive at this less charitable point of view. For example, when Sue, the office secretary, would see a client enter the office whom she knew to be troublesome, she would let one of us deal with the problem. She would feign intense involvement in a task, and sometimes she would simultaneously warn and taunt me, "Here's one for you, kid." Sue thus intensified the pressure to toughen up. If I allowed a troublesome client to rave on and on, she would complain pointedly that she was being disturbed. When I or another novice eventually showed signs of a harder orientation, more experienced staff members would reinforce the new attitudes with praise and the appropriate rationalizations. Sue reassured me after I had lost my temper with an irksome chronic complainer: "When I first started working in the office, I tried to help these people, just like you've been doing. But it was pointless, they come back again and again. We're here to help people, but some people just don't want to be helped. We can't have people like that in here all the time and still do our work."

Learning from Political Conflict

Similarly, the new club member is introduced to new orientations toward the party's principal opponents, the

Independents. As we have seen, he is discouraged from having any unnecessary contact with Independents. When he does see them, it is usually in situations of conflict, such as when protest groups meet with club leaders. As a party worker, he is aware of the efforts his leaders have made on behalf of the protesting groups. He notices that Independent leaders take pains to prevent his party from getting credit for any progress that is made. Since the protest organizers use tactics designed to intensify conflict,[18] the new worker begins to perceive them as seekers of political advantage, not community goods. The pettiness of some committed Independents angers him; they may tear down his election posters or treat him with overt contempt. He hears the private judgments of committed Regulars, which, accurate or not, carry the weight of years of experience in politics.

"These liberals always want to work on the immediate problem rather than the important issues you don't see at first glance."

"These guys want everything done yesterday. What do they think we are?"

"If the Independents ever got control of Model Cities, they'd look at that $80 million and sit there with their fingers up their asses wondering what to do with it."

"Independents base their arguments on emotion; they aren't rational. If you understand the issues and know the candidates, there's no way you can vote any way but Democratic. They love statistics, but they don't know any more about the facts than anyone else."

"The only difference between what they call a machine and their own organization is that our organization wins elections."

"This guy claims to be such a big Independent now that he's running for state rep, but he's worked for the Republicans all his life."

"Most of them aren't from our ward anyway."

Learning from Club Leaders

During the formal club gatherings, considerable time is spent persuading the members to act and think like good Democrats. Meetings are called for several evenings during the two months preceding each election, and candidates are sent by the Cook County Democratic Central Committee to address the club. Attendance is mandatory. Most candidates talk about themselves only in passing and devote most of their time to praising the other Regular candidates, the Democratic party, the mayor, precinct workers in general, and the workers of this ward in particular. As the guest speakers arrive and depart, the committeeman and his aides fill in with speeches reiterating these same themes. Support for the entire ticket is urged, and each candidate is described as an outstanding and highly qualified person. Members are exhorted to work hard for a big victory. The Democratic party is described as the party of the people; it is credited with sole responsibility for "every progressive program introduced by the federal government since 1932." The ward club's service activities are glowingly described:

> We're here every day of the year helping people, election or no election. The committeeman and alderman are often here until 11:00, 12:00, 1:00 at night working to take care of people's problems. When you call on the voter, you have something to offer him, because you represent the party that's helping him every day.

Pride is a recurring theme, almost always negatively or defensively expressed. "Remember, you have nothing to be ashamed of." As Joel explained to a group of new members: "When they hear you're a precinct captain, the Independents expect you to be a dummy, a street sweeper or a garbage collector, to say 'dis' and 'dat' instead of 'this' and 'that!' He hunched his shoulders, stuck out his chin, and scratched his ribs in illustration. "But it's you, the precinct captain, who has the information. You've read the material, you know the issues. Don't ever be ashamed you're a Democrat!"

Occasionally a direct appeal is made to the self-interest of club members. At a meeting in which the new committeeman had exhorted the members to purchase more tickets to the club's annual fund-raising dinner, one of the senior club members asked to be recognized. Somewhat hesitant about adding to the committeeman's statement, he said, "I hope you don't mind if I point out to everybody that this is our first dinner under our new committeeman. The mayor and everybody are going to be watching. If we fill that hall with people, they're going to know that this is a strong organization, and that's good for our new committeeman. And what's good for him is good for us, because it means he can get things done for us downtown." Usually statements at meetings leave implicit the congruence of interests between the club and its members.

Critics of the party are dismissed in these talks as misinformed or badly motivated. Said one candidate: "People are getting wise to these newspapers; they know who runs them. They endorsed my opponent because they said I was too loyal to my party. Since when is being a good Democrat something bad? It isn't, unless you're a Republican who runs a big newspaper." When the local McGovern campaign people suggested that the party should be more open, the committeeman replied: "There isn't a single person in this ward who can honestly say that this office and this organization aren't open to everybody in the ward, regardless of their being Republican, Independent or whatever. We're here every day, and anyone at all can come in here and we help them."

Of course, this statement neatly evaded the issue which the McGovern forces intended to raise—that of participation. It illustrates that fairness and rationality are of secondary importance in these speeches. The object is to give an answer to every criticism which might trouble members and point out the bases for positive assessment of the party. The leadership demonstrates how to respond effectively to the disapproval of others. As William Foote Whyte suggested in his analysis of appeals used in grass-roots politics in Boston, "The words used by the politician furnish ammunition to his supporters."[19] These responses are useful to all members in their assigned task of soliciting support. Over time, some come to sincerely believe these ideas, which, although too disconnected to constitute an ideology, serve as an adequate rationale for normative commitment.

The Appearance of Propriety

The persuasiveness of the socializing forces at work in the ward club is enhanced by the fact that activities visible to the whole membership conform with the outward proprieties of legal and democratic rule. The club is legally constituted as a non-profit corporation under state law, with a president, secretary, and treasurer. The committeeman acts as treasurer, a trusted senior advisor to him serves as president, and his administrative aide is the secretary. At club meetings the president calls the meeting to order, asks the aide to call the roll, then yields the floor to the committeeman, who presides. The alderman and any honored guests also sit at the rostrum. On the rare occasions when questions come from the floor, the committeeman recognizes members one at a time. Here the resemblance to a parliamentary proceeding ends—there are no motions from the floor, no debates, and no votes. A large diagram of the formal structure of the club hangs behind the rostrum. It is an imposing chart, but nothing constrains the club leadership to adhere to it. There is no written constitution or book of rules. Many of the positions exist only on the chart. Others are filled but have no duties. For example, the dummy post of committeewoman was created on order from the central committee as a gesture toward the women's rights movement. The woman selected for the post was the club president's wife. She was personable and active in charity work but had no interest in politics or women's rights. This kind of manipulation of symbols helps legitimate the committeeman's one-man rule in the eyes of the members without decentralizing his authority.

The appearance of propriety is also obtained by control of information about the proprieties themselves. We have seen that the average member's access to information about the club is severely limited and that no written rules exist. The leadership is therefore able to establish new norms to suit its purposes, assuring the members that "this is how it is done." The administrative aide's accession to the post of committeeman was legitimated by this means.

When a committeeman vacates his post before the end of his four-year term, a successor is elected by the precinct captains of the ward. Since the precinct captains are appointed by the committeeman, the practical meaning of this rule is that the committeeman names his own successor. The outgoing committeeman chose as his successor his administrative aide, who had been a diligent but undistinguished party worker for almost twenty years. However, both the alderman and a senior precinct captain had hopes of gaining the post by securing the support of precinct captains who were unenthused about the committeeman's choice. When the committeeman announced his resignation and a date was set for the election meeting, these contenders tried to line up support, but they found they were too late. They learned that immediately following the resignation, the outgoing committeeman's lieutenants had visited precinct captains in their homes and asked them to sign "nominating petitions" for the committeeman's choice. There was no formal requirement that such petitions be circulated, but they were easily made to seem proper. They were contrived as a vehicle by which the lieutenants could confront each captain and put individual loyalty to the test. As signatures accumulated, it became easier to secure additional support. By the time the election meeting was held, all opposition had capitulated. The aide was nominated by the alderman and elected unanimously. The nominating petitions were not necessary to assure the aide's victory, but without them the appearance of sovereign choice by the captains would not have been so well preserved.

Being a Regular Democrat

To be a good member of a Regular Democratic ward club one does not simply adopt the practice of announcing one's partisan loyalty in all public situations. The system of defended venality depends on discretion, which means not only concealing party secrets, but making strategic use of other people's ignorance of one's party membership. On the job and in most community activities, club members are expected to avoid outward expressions of partisan loyalty. A somewhat nervous new club member, who had just learned that she had been accepted for employment at City Hall, asked Marty what her new job would be like. His response was, "Just don't talk politics in the office." Indeed, open discussions of politics among city workers are infrequent, and they are usually about "safe" political questions—for example, criticism of a Republican administration in Washington, which offends neither Independents nor Regulars. The discussion of politics is avoided because local politicians have substantial influence over hiring, promotion, and decision-making in these agencies. Politics is a sensitive area because the agency has an interest in concealing those outside influences from a disapproving public, and because agency officers have an interest in concealing these influences from the employees over whom they exercise authority. In practice, of course, these issues *are* discussed among patronage workers, but only in private and on the basis of mutual trust.

In community affairs people's partisan affiliations are sensitive matters because Regulars who are active in local agencies and voluntary organizations can act most effectively on behalf of the party if they maintain an appearance of being nonaligned. Their opinions and decisions will not be taken as seriously if they show themselves to be recipients of patronage. Of course, it is helpful to the party agent if he is able to identify other Regulars among the people around him. Since Regulars are not immediately distinguishable from other participants, club members become adept at managing political expression according to their awareness of the loyalties of those with whom they interact.

After a meeting of the advisory council of the local anti-poverty agency which I attended as an observer, a young man who had also been in the audience apparently recognized me. He introduced himself and then asked carefully, "Where do I know you from?" I sensed that he wanted to find out if I was "with" the Regular Democratic Organization, and I could not remember who he was, so I said merely "I work with the alderman." He then said "I know now—I've seen you at the ward meetings. I'm with the organization too. Do the folks around here know who you're with?" I responded that I had not mentioned it to anyone, but that it was well known that I worked with the alderman. "Well, I have to kind of keep it under my hat, because of my job here at the Agency." Since his job was federally funded, he had to be discreet about his political activity, which is restricted by federal law.

The acquiescent members of the ward club, who may be ambivalent about their party ties, become doubly adept at managing political expression. Once a Regular determines that someone works for the city or is "with" some Democratic ward club, he knows that they share specialized political knowledge. Each can assume the other is acquainted with patronage procedures, precinct work, and the internal hierarchy of the party. They can talk shop, exchange gossip about their wards and city departments, and pass on information in terms outsiders may have difficulty understanding. But each will attempt to conceal from the other any lack of commitment to the party. Only with the passage of time and the development of mutual understanding and trust will either dare to suggest that he resents having to contribute to the ward club, shirks his precinct work, or secretly supports some Independent candidate. Alienation is not considered attractive among Regulars. Affiliation with the party is taken by others inside and outside the party to be a matter of identity, a measure of one's value as a person. One does not reveal one's affiliation lightly, and having done so, one is not quick to reveal one's private view of being a party member. The resocializing forces at work in the party may or may not succeed in instilling genuine commitment. But they do succeed in teaching that the appearance of loyalty is a very serious matter.

Commitment and Compliance

The patronage party organization in the ward I studied derives its power from material incentives, controlled from above. It seeks to achieve influence in a moral environment that is hostile to such power. Hence the compliance structure of the club is a system of defended venality. Do the members comply with the Regular ethic? Most behave in accordance with it. Are they committed to the party? A few are intensely committed, a few are alienated, and most are acquiescent or mildly committed. Members pay high membership costs: not only money and time but the psychic costs of demeaning subservience. They are kept uninformed about most party affairs and sometimes they are baldly deceived. They frequently find themselves looked down upon and must carefully manage their expressions of loyalty. It is certain that they would not pay these high costs if they did not get the benefits of patronage in return. But the reliable compliance and widespread acquiescence of club members cannot be wholly attributed to the ability of club leaders to apply material sanctions to their behavior. Although few members strive for excellence as it is defined by party norms, most do regard the party as a legitimate organization, because their leaders take care to make it appear so. The same pervasive secrecy which denies members the full participation that could breed stronger commitment protects the members from knowledge that could threaten their commitment. Through participation in club activities, contact with other members, and indoctrination by club leaders, members develop an adequate rationale for the loyalty and discretion which the party expects of them. The club's complex compliance structure does produce conformity to the Regular ethic, and thus the system of defended venality permits the club to secure from local residents the political support upon which it depends.

Four Aldermanic Service Activities

Chicago's Regular Democratic Ward organizations devote a great deal of effort to the delivery of services to individual voters. Precinct captains and workers solicit requests for help from people in their precincts. Each ward committeeman spends several evenings every week at his ward office seeing people who come to him for help. In most ward clubs, it is the alderman who is given chief responsibility for handling the steady stream of service requests to the ward office. In the ward I studied, the alderman aggressively pursued this role, and established himself as the chief broker of government-connected citizen services in his ward.

This chapter will deal with the way in which the alderman and members of his staff perform service activities. Our central concern will be to establish the purpose of these club members in providing services. Are they primarily trying to serve the needs of their community or are they mainly interested in winning votes for their party? To answer this question, we shall first consider the traditional role of the Chicago alderman, his power resources, and the constraints under which he works.

Role of the Alderman

As legally defined, the duties of a City of Chicago alderman are legislative. He represents his ward on the city council, the branch of municipal government to which the city charter grants the greatest formal authority. Traditionally, aldermen have also been expected to answer complaints from their constituents and to expedite the allocation of municipal services to the residents of their wards. In practice, the provision of services has become their primary function.

The service function is of great political importance to Chicago aldermen because the existing political structure prevents most of them from establishing a record of effective legislative activity in the city council. Since over four-fifths of the aldermen belong to the Regular Democratic majority, they are able to vote on the winning side of every issue. However, these Regulars are tightly controlled by the citywide party leaders, who sponsor and take credit for all significant legislation. The important decisions are made within the party, and power within the party is wielded not by the aldermen but by the ward committeemen. The alderman must run for office in a nonpartisan general election, and is thus more vulnerable to defeat than the committeeman. Unable to stand on a personal record of legislative initiative or accomplishment, the incumbent alderman endeavors to secure the favor of his constituents by careful attention to their requests for service. The importance to the alderman of his service function is recognized in the ward club. Club members channel complaints and service requests to him and refer to the varied favors the party performs for individual citizens as "aldermanic services."

The Alderman's Powers

The Regular Democratic alderman is able to provide services to his constituents partly because of the power resources he possesses. These resources are little different from those available to legislators in other governments. They include official authority, expertise, personal ties, and party ties.

Official authority. By virtue of his office, the alderman has the legal authority to introduce ordinances in the city council which grant certain privileges. Among these are loading zones, stop signs and other traffic controls, exemptions from certain licensing and inspection fees for charitable institutions, and street closing permits for fairs and parades. By long-standing tradition, no alderman will introduce such ordinances for territory outside his ward, so each maintains an effective local monopoly on these privileges (subject to veto by party-controlled city council committees). In addition, the alderman is informed of pending actions by the city's executive departments that affect his ward, such as proposed zoning changes and permits for driveways and overhanging commercial signs. While the alderman himself cannot grant or deny these privileges, he may delay them by raising objections and demanding administrative review. The alderman's official powers also make available to him resources which he may use to influence delivery of services over which he lacks direct control. He has a statutory right to inspect the internal documents of all city departments. Since as a legislator he votes on the annual city budget, each city office endeavors to cooperate with his wishes as far as possible. Some aldermen control additional official resources by virtue of their chairmanship of important city council committees.

Expertise. The alderman has experience in handling all kinds of service requests. He knows which departments have jurisdiction over each kind of service, what information they require to efficiently provide the service, what criteria are applied in deciding if the service will be provided, and who exercises decision-making authority within each department. He knows how to get past the gatekeeper to the decision-maker, how to make himself understood on the telephone and in writing, and how to apply pressure without causing service to be denied. When he confronts a new problem in providing service, he has access to written directories and knowledgeable informants that help him to find a solution quickly. Even when he lacks the authority to demand service, personnel in other agencies immediately sense that he knows his way around and assume it would be unwise to displease him.

Personal ties. These may be preexisting family, ethnic,

religious, or friendship ties. Most aldermen pursue occupations outside politics, such as law or insurance, that bring them into association with a wide circle of important people. Bonds of acquaintanceship generally develop between the alderman and the agency personnel whom he regularly contacts for service. Some persons who have contact with the alderman find him congenial. He may solicit their friendship with such tokens of esteem as greeting cards and personal visits to their offices. These bonds may be strengthened if the alderman helps the bureaucrat by providing him useful information, covering up his shortcomings, or commending his work to superiors. The alderman actively cultivates these personal ties for they can be important even if they are not strong attachments. They are part of an intelligence network that enhances the alderman's expertise and allows him to use his power resources wisely.

Party ties. The alderman who is a loyal Regular Democrat has extra leverage in negotiating with city agencies. In most cases, the bureaucrats with whom he deals are political appointees of the same party. They understand that their departments and their individual careers flourish at the pleasure of the party. They strive to keep party notables such as aldermen satisfied. Their cooperation is more than an attempt to curry favor and avoid negative sanctions from the party. As loyal Regulars, many of the agency personnel feel obligated to ensure that the elected politicians of their party receive adequate support from the executive branch in their efforts to deliver services.

The ability of the alderman to influence administrative decisions on behalf of his constituents derives not only from the power resources he commands, but from certain properties of the larger system in which he acts. Chicago's political structure and political culture both support the continued influence of the alderman. The institutionalization of the alderman's service function may be understood partly as a natural process in which appropriate attitudes and practices gradually gathered the weight of tradition during the long decades of Republican and Democratic machine rule in Chicago.

Traditionally, aldermen have had few functions other than aldermanic service, citizens have contacted politicians to secure city services, and city departments have been open to service requests from party agents. More important, the machine has of course used its political power to block reforms that would alter the established relationships and legal arrangements which strengthen the alderman's service-broker role. Small single-member districts, city council authority over permits and fees, and the legislative courtesy that gives each alderman control over his own territory have all been preserved. The preservation of the patronage system has been of prime importance for the alderman's role, for it transforms the alderman's status within his party into a power resource that is effective in every branch of local government.

The powers of the alderman are not without their limits. He has formal authority over very few services. He can influence the delivery of most services only to the extent that he can petition or cajole public agencies, or use his power resources to subject them or their employees to informal sanctions. His influence thus depends on the voluntary cooperation of government employees. In persuading agencies to give priority to his requests, he must compete not only with the demands of the general public, but with forty-nine other wards whose aldermen and committeemen also demand special service. If he is highly placed in the party hierarchy, he can expect to receive privileged treatment, but he cannot expect other politicians to be entirely excluded from access to favors. At least one city department (Buildings) has regularized the allocation of political privilege by channeling all aldermanic complaints through a single employee whose full-time assignment is to keep the politicians satisfied.

Other limits are imposed by the operating resources at the alderman's disposal. The city budget grants him his salary, a salary for one assistant, and a modest sum for office expenses.[1] He may have access to funds or other resources from a private job or a city council committee chairmanship. The office space and telephone of the ward club are usually at his disposal. A few aldermen also recruit volunteer help. But the resources are always finite and seldom allow the flow of service requests to be handled with ease.

Aldermanic Services in the Ward Office

The limitations on the alderman's resources were evident in the day-to-day operations of the ward office in which I worked. The flow of complaints to this office was sometimes more than the alderman's staff (a paid assistant plus one or two volunteers) could handle. Service requests came into the office at an irregular rate. Some days the phones seemed to ring constantly, and a backlog of requests would rapidly accumulate, since many could only be resolved by an extended series of phone calls and letters to city agencies. On some days there would be only one or two routine requests, but these would often have to be set aside while the staff performed other tasks for the alderman.

The caseload not only strained the office's manpower but other available operating resources as well. There were only two phone lines at the ward office for conducting the business of both the alderman and the committeeman. The one good typewriter was reserved for the committeeman's secretary. There was no copying equipment. The alderman refused to expand the operating resources at his own expense, and the committeeman refused to use club funds for additional facilities which he felt would primarily benefit the alderman. This disagreement was one manifestation of a long-standing tension between the two men.[2] If they had resolved their differences, the caseload could have been handled more smoothly.

Despite these limitations, the alderman actively solicited requests for service. When addressing meetings of the ward club he would remind members, "We're here to help you do your job. If there's anything in your precinct that needs doing, or if one of your voters has a problem, just call me or my assistants. We've plenty to do now, but we're always looking for more." Each year the alderman mailed a newsletter to all voters in the ward describing his accomplishments and inviting requests for service. At meetings of neighborhood and block groups the alderman ceaselessly urged citizens to let him know of their needs. The effort which he expended to increase the flow of service requests is strong evidence of the importance which the alderman assigned to doing favors.

Defended Venality and Aldermanic Service Activities

Why do aldermen and other party agents devote such great effort to providing services to people? The party agents themselves would like outsiders to believe that they are motivated by selfless devotion to the duties of their office and the welfare of their community. It seems unreasonable, however, to ascribe pure altruism to these politicians. Is it not possible that they are pursuing the goal of public service—delivering important services which satisfy the legitimate needs of their constituents—in the hope that the public will approve of their performance in office and give them support? Such motivations of enlightened self-interest would be compatible with what the public expects of elected officials in a competitive democracy. But in reality the service activities of patronage politicians are aimed more directly at a somewhat different goal, that of creating relationships of indebtedness that will generate political support for the party and its candidates. This goal of winning votes at times calls for different actions than does the goal of public service. The members of the ward club believe in the exchange models of machine support, and their actions are guided by that belief. While their goal is more to help the party and themselves than to help the residents of the ward, they of course do not announce these venal motives. Like other hidden activities of the ward club, the real nature of party services must be defended from a hostile moral environment.

Party agents must disguise their motivations partly because of the nature of social exchange itself. An important property of relationships of social exchange is that the supply of services "is not contingent on stipulated returns, though there is a general expectation of reciprocation."[3] Even if we were to assume that the recipients of party services are unconcerned with any notion of the public interest, we would not expect party agents to explicitly announce that their services are offered on a *quid pro quo* basis. But we cannot assume that the clients are private-regarding. Explicit stipulation of returns for favors is particularly inappropriate for incumbents of public office, for under widely shared democratic norms they are expected to give selfless service to their constituents. The party is careful, therefore, to manage expressions of its motives according to these institutionalized expectations. The motto on the ward club's letterhead reads: "Dedicated to Public Service."

Commitment to the public service goal is even expressed in the private statements of members of the office staff. On one occasion, a mentally unstable client visited the office and was dissatisfied with the service he received. As he left he cried out angrily, "I'll show you! I won't even vote this time, since you think you can treat me like this!" The committeeman's aide shook his head when he heard this and said quietly to the others behind the counter: "That really gets me. That's not what we're interested in, that's not what it's all about." I do not doubt that the aide sincerely meant what he said about the primacy of altruistic goals. Such authoritative statements about the party's purpose help affirm the appearance of propriety which, as was shown in chapter 3, is important for the maintenance of members' commitment. But the fact that winning votes is the more important organizational goal is evident from the manner in which key aspects of service delivery are managed by the office staff. The pattern of allocation of services demonstrates the essential venality of the alderman's service activities. And the techniques by which he and his staff manage credit for services are best understood as mechanisms for the defense of venality—ways of getting the most out of the doing of favors without revealing selfish motives. We turn now to an analysis of these aspects of service delivery.

Service Allocation

Requests for service are treated differently by the ward office according to the nature of the request and the identity of the client. Obviously some service requests require faster action than others. Some are related to human needs which require immediate satisfaction: a family has been evicted and must find housing, an old woman has run out of food, a water main has burst. Others are not so fateful, but must be promptly handled nevertheless: a parade permit is requested at the last moment, a surprise inspection of a construction site is needed. A few services must be delayed. For example, permanent paving repair, curb and gutter work, and tree planting can only be done at certain times of the year. Timing is not crucial in the delivery of most services, and the promptness of service can be determined by the staff member according to his own criteria. He can give the service request high priority, expending extra effort to assure prompt action. He can give it routine treatment (mediate it), deliberately delay it, or not honor the request at all. In delivering favors, then, the staff member allocates not only substantive services, but the benefits of more rapid receipt of service. Because not all requests of the same type can be given equal priority, priority is distributed among like requests according to the status which the staff member assigns to the client.

The ward office does not use a formal system of categories or even a uniform set of labels to designate the status assigned to clients or the priority appropriate to their requests, but the pattern of allocation is nonetheless clear. Allocation is made on the basis of, and communicated in terms of, four perceived characteristics of clients: (1) their worthiness as human beings; (2) the likelihood of their future support of the party; (3) the degree to which the party is obliged to them for past support; and (4) the potential political importance of their support. These four variables have an ordered, cumulative effect on the status assigned to a client.

As illustrated in table 4, the four ordered criteria yield five status categories into which most clients can be placed. In the lowest category are the *undeserving.*

Table 4 Ward Office Client Statuses

Criteria				
Worthiness	Future Support	Past Support	Importance	Status Categories
–	–	–	–	Undeserving
+	–	–	–	Outsiders
+	+	–	–	Citizens
+	+	+	–	Good Voters
+	+	+	+	Top Democrats

These are persons whom the staff judge to be of insufficient worthiness. This status is assigned to clients who demonstrate obvious mental imbalance or senility; also included are drunks, panhandlers, and disreputable-looking members of minority groups. Clients may be judged undeserving when they first contact the office, or they may be assigned that status after making several unreasonable service requests. The following excerpt from my field notes describes one such client:

> (Monday) Irv came in again today, with his wife(?) Gloria, who doesn't talk much but appears to be as crazy as he is. He claims she was born in 1952, although the woman appears to be about 45. He was very softspoken, almost polite today; perhaps they have put him on tranquilizers. Irv explained in somewhat garbled language that he had had to go back into the mental health center for a few days, and while he was gone "somebody stole the yellow checks" (the ones redeemable for food stamps). "Besides, my welfare check hasn't come; y'know, the green one." I called Irv's caseworker over at Public Aid. He asked if Irv had filed a police report on the stolen checks; of course he had not. I told the caseworker I would call him back, since I still had no firm grasp of what the problem was. While I was still vainly listening to Irv, Gloria found the missing checks in her purse. I reprimanded Irv mildly and he left.
>
> (Wednesday) Irv and Gloria came in again today; this time Irv was angry and loud. He said he couldn't

> cash his check because he didn't have his I.D. (His wallet was still at the County Jail, where he had spent a day last week and forgotten to recover his personal property.) I told him to go down to the jail and pick up the stuff, which they were holding for him as we had arranged last week. He said he had no money for carfare. I glanced at the papers he had handed me. There was a crumpled Medicaid I.D. and an envelope containing thirty-five dollars in cash. I started to yell at Irv: "What do you mean no money?" "That's for food! I'm not going all the way down to that jail! It's not my fault they put me in there. Why should I have to go back down there?" In a very loud voice, I cut him off: "Get off your high horse, Irv, get the hell off your high horse, get the stuff, and don't come back here until you do!" The two left angry, not to reappear for several days.

The ward office is located in a storefront on the main thoroughfare of the ward's poorest district. Thus the number of undeserving clients attempting to obtain service is significant even though the standards of worthiness are hardly stringent. The usual disposition of requests from the undeserving is to ignore them if unreasonable and treat them routinely if they involve little effort. Sometimes a complainant will insist on an unreasonable request, and the staff member must go through the motions of helping him so as to avoid an unpleasant confrontation. If the unworthy client is unreasonably persistent in his demands, he may be ejected from the office by threats of police arrest.

Those clients who are not unworthy but who are deemed unlikely to support the party in the future are *outsiders.* These are persons known to be radicals, Independents, or Republicans. Usually they are persons whom the staff can identify as having been in open conflict with the party in the past. Of course such persons do not often request service from the Regular Democrats, but when they do their requests are ignored or assigned low priority. Outsiders are not, however, subject to overt retaliation. For example, if an Independent leader wants a tree trimmed, the office staff will not attempt to prevent the Forestry Bureau from carrying out the task. Persons who reside outside the ward boundaries are also refused service. They are courteously referred to the party office in their own ward.

Clients are placed in the third category when little is known about them. Clients not known to be undeserving or hopelessly opposed to the party are treated as *citizens,* and their requests are given routine priority. Sometimes a citizen's request gets extra attention because a staff member takes a personal interest in the delivery of a certain service, or because it comes at a time when it can be handled along with a similar request from a high-status client. But a simple request by a decent ward resident about whom nothing is known usually gets routine treatment.

In the fourth client category are those who are worthy, known to have supported the party in the past, and likely to give future support. These are the *good voters,* and they are given priority treatment. When precinct captains request priority service from the ward office on behalf of a voter, they say, "See what you can do for this gal, she's one of my best voters." The same justification is used by the office staff in requesting priority service from agency personnel. Members of the ward club and people who work closely with them[4] are also accorded this high status. A person in this category is referred to as "one of our people."

The highest status is given to clients whose support is important to the reputation of the ward club within the citywide party structure. These *top Democrats* include officers of the ward club, circuit court judges, elected officials, mayoral appointees living in the ward, and their relatives. Requests by financial backers of the party also get highest priority. These are usually the people most able to help themselves in obtaining service, but the office staff will expend extraordinary effort to fulfill even their trivial requests.[5]

There is more to the allocation of priority than mere calculation of the maximum potential political return. There is also a sense of obligation on the part of party members to repay those who have supported the party. The precinct captain asks for special treatment for a "good voter," rather than for "a voter whose support I will need." The perceived process of exchange works both ways, placing both party agent and client under obligation. Clients sometimes attempt to activate the staff's sense of obligation by dropping names or volunteering other information about themselves meant to demonstrate their long-standing loyalty to the Regulars.

However, failure to support the party does not necessarily exclude a person from receiving favors, for the party agents endeavor to extend over a wide compass the network of voters who are obliged to them. Most precinct captains claim that they help anyone who asks them, regardless of politics. We have seen that requests by citizens whose party affiliation is unknown are given normal priority by the ward office staff. A few precinct captains privately advise members not to "waste time" doing favors for Republicans. The most common practice among captains is to offer freely those services requiring relatively little effort and allocate the more difficult favors to good voters. Clearly, the pattern of allocation of services, which systematically passes over many persons with genuine needs, shows the basic goal of party agents to be winning votes, rather than public service.[6]

Management of Credit

If service activities are to win votes, then clients must be made to believe that the actions of the party agent are the cause of the delivery of the service. Obviously, a political organization seeks to maximize the benefits it derives from service activities by claiming credit for things which people think of as desirable and avoiding blame for undesirable things. The adroitness of credit management[7] by the ward office staff is a reflection of the primacy of its goal of winning votes, and its need to keep that goal disguised.

Certain characteristics of politics at the ward level facilitate effective credit management and enable it to substitute at times for actual service delivery.[8] The ignorance of the average voter about the inner workings of city and party bureaucracy serves as the fundamental basis for credit management. Also helpful is the fact that the actual responsibility for the accomplishment of a goal is often widely distributed among agencies with different purposes and spheres of control. A claim of credit by one actor is not incompatible with similar claims by other actors. The diffuse mandate of the alderman's office allows him to claim credit for actions by almost any arm of government, while the limitations on his official power allow him to avoid blame. He is aided in claiming credit by the tacit support of other political actors, who hesitate to refute his claims even if they know them to be exaggerated. If the alderman is careful, he can adjust his claims of credit to his audience, making the more modest boasts when in the presence of those who are more apt to know the true situation.

Most of the credit management techniques employed by the ward office staff differed little from those which all street-level bureaucrats employ in the interest of maintaining a satisfied clientele. The staff members would try to lower the expectations of clients who made impossible or difficult requests. Many complainants acted as if they believed the allocation of municipal services was solely in the province of the alderman. Staff members would explain, usually truthfully, that firm agency rules, limits on city resources, or limits on the city's jurisdiction were to blame for the failure to produce a requested service. They would also point to mistakes by the client which could be blamed for the failure. Where no service could be delivered, they attempted to secure credit for having made an honest effort or for having provided helpful information. They might even insist that someone from the relevant agency contact the client directly to explain the decision to refuse service.

Because it is necessary to uphold the appearance of legitimacy, party agents do not reveal to low status clients the real reason that services are denied to them. For example, a woman asked the alderman to help her obtain renewal of her apartment lease. He recognized her as a participant in a recent neighborhood meeting at which he felt he had been unfairly attacked. The alderman was a friend of the attorney representing the realty company which wished to terminate the woman's lease, but he did not disclose this fact to her. He told the woman that the realty company was within its rights and could not be forced to renew her lease. He offered to write a letter on her behalf, adding that it might not be of any help. After she left, he called his friend to tell him that he would be writing a letter of inquiry and that he wished only to receive written clarification of the decision to let the lease lapse. He made it clear that he was not asking for a reconsideration of the case. The prearranged exchange of letters was completed, the woman was made to feel that an effort had been made on her behalf, and the alderman's grudge against her was satisfied without being revealed. Had the client been a Regular, the alderman would certainly have attempted to use this personal tie to get the lease renewed. He made no such effort for this outsider, but he was careful to maintain the appearance of dedication to the goal of public service.

Some rather elaborate techniques of credit management were part of the established routine of the ward office. Clients were always asked for their name and address.[9] The alderman insisted that every telephone inquiry by the ward office to a city agency be followed up in writing, with a carbon copy to the client. The text of the letter varied with the nature of the service request, but it always asked for a reply in writing. If the request was of a type which was likely to be satisfactorily delivered by the agency, the alderman asked for a written reply to his office, with a copy to the client. The agency's letter reporting the delivery of the requested service would thus have the alderman's name and address typed at the top and would make direct reference to his request. If the request could probably not be delivered, the alderman asked for a written reply to the client, with a copy to his office. The letter explaining the rejection of the client's request would show the alderman's name only in the lower left-hand corner, and it would be clear that the agency, rather than the alderman, had rejected the request. Requests were often sent to agencies for reply with full knowledge that they would be rejected. The alderman thereby avoided having to say no. Copies of all correspondence were also sent to the captain of the client's precinct.

This procedure was costly in terms of both operating and power resources. Before the alderman with whom I worked took office, it had been the practice to handle requests with a minimum of written work. A request would come in, someone in the ward office would jot it down on a scrap of paper, relay the request by phone to the appropriate agency, and discard the scrap of paper. Doing favors that way was hardly a full-time job. The credit management procedures introduced by the new alderman consumed many man-hours and much postage without substantially increasing the quality of services delivered. Undoubtedly, more requests could have been handled if fewer letters were written. The stream of written demands also burdened personnel in the city agencies. Department heads were not pleased with the alderman's attempts to shift blame to their agencies. The new procedures created friction between the alderman's staff and agency personnel. The Department of Police refused to answer requests for abandoned car removal in writing. The Bureau of Streets could not be persuaded to put the name of the complainant on its replies, or to write separate letters for each individual request. All the departments balked at sending copies of correspondence directly to constituents; some cooperated by enclosing a carbon which the alderman could forward. Some requests were never answered in writing, and when they were, it was often weeks after the service itself was delivered. Yet the alderman's interest in credit management was sufficient for him to continue with the cumbersome procedure despite this resistance.

The alderman sometimes employed an even more extravagant means of claiming credit for services. For example, after a stop sign was installed at a previously unmarked intersection in the ward, he sent a letter to every registered voter in the precincts near the sign, crediting himself, the committeeman, and the precinct captains, and inviting further requests for service. The mailing was made practical by a contribution to the alderman of free time on a computer which could generate the mailing labels for selected precincts. The alderman's letter made no mention of the local block groups which had originated the stop sign request and gathered signatures to support it.

The alderman's attempts at credit management were limited by the need to avoid embarassing exposure of false claims. His claims were also limited by internal competition among party leaders for public credit. Fortunately, the credit could usually be shared,[10] and this sharing of claims of credit is a fundamental element of party loyalty. The party politicians pool their accomplishments so that the legitimacy of all in the party is enhanced. This requirement of loyalty conflicts with the ambitious politician's natural inclination to claim exclusive credit for his achievements. As a Regular Democrat, the alderman was constantly at odds with other party leaders because he tried to claim too much credit for himself and failed to give sufficient credit to others in the party. Continued support from superiors and subordinates in the party hierarchy was contingent on his sharing of some credit with them. This is why he provided precinct captains with copies of his correspondence with their voters and occasionally included the committeeman in his public accounts of how certain services had been delivered. He had a natural claim to exclusive credit for some services which were clearly delivered through his official aldermanic authority or through his personal contacts. He was sometimes able to achieve exclusive credit by publicizing his efforts in citywide media to which other party politicians had poor access. But credit for most favors cannot be claimed exclusively by any one party agent. This diminishes the effectiveness of the delivered services in creating strong feelings of personal obligation to the alderman.

In summary, the party agent's attempts to manage credit are aimed at maximizing the voter's sense of obligation to him. But he is limited in the claims he can make by the ability of his clients to detect invalid claims, by the generalized norms that regulate exchange transactions, by the imperatives of party loyalty, and above all by the need to preserve the appearance of commitment to the goal of public service.

Conclusion

The provision of services to individual voters remains an important arena of activity for the alderman and other members of the ward club. The alderman's official authority, expertise, personal ties, and party ties provide him the power resources he needs, and his influence over service delivery continues to be supported by Chicago's political structure and culture. The techniques by which services are allocated and credit is managed in the ward office are clearly purposive. The aim of doing favors is to win votes, although, as part of the system of defended venality, this goal is carefully concealed from the public. Party agents actively solicit requests for favors, allocate favors to those they judge to be most likely to reciprocate, and do their best to gain credit for service delivery.

While the goal of the party's service activities is unmistakeable (when viewed from the inside), the constraints on its ability to deliver service and manage credit must lead us to wonder whether its efforts at generating obligations among voters are really successful. These efforts to build voter support through processes of exchange can only be successful if many voters make use of party services and the actual services which they receive are significant. The next task, therefore, is to assess the quantity and quality of the ward club's services to local residents.

Part 3 Favors and Votes

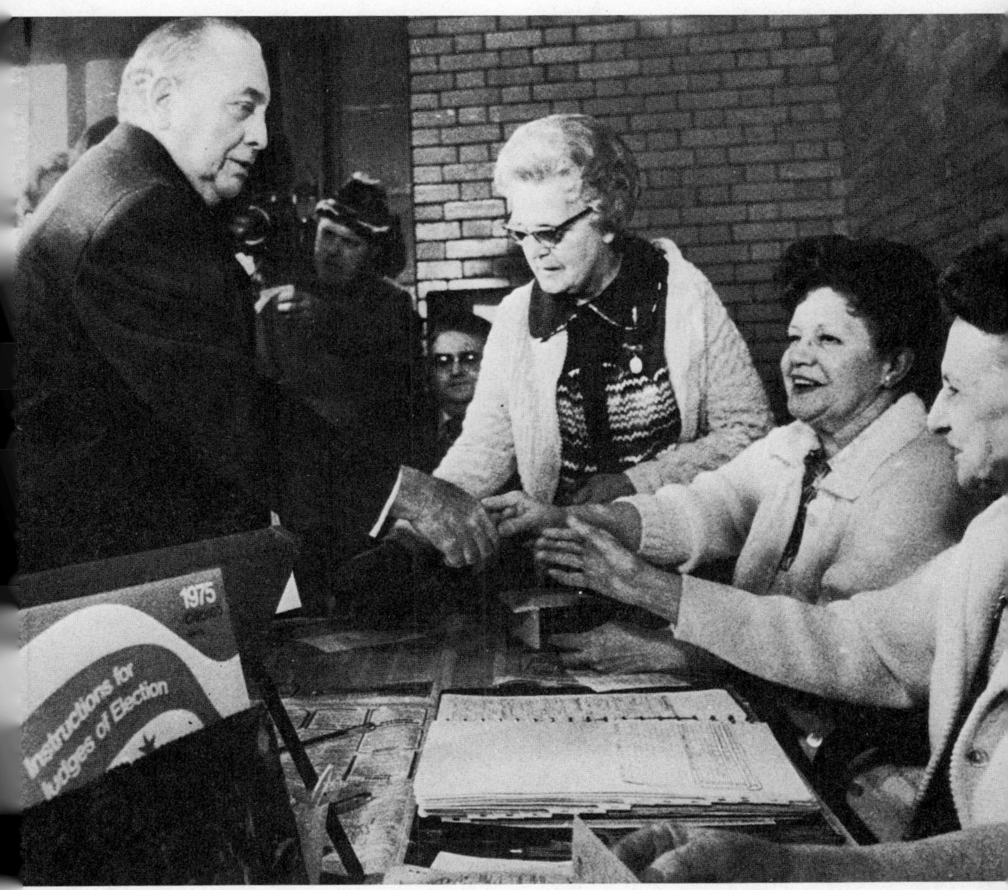

Five The Changing Level of Party Services

Numerous writers have suggested that during the last half-century large-scale social changes have reduced both the public's demand for political favors and the machine politicians' ability to supply them. In this view the decline in the market for the party's services accounts for the shift from "old-style" to "new-style" urban politics.[1] Since the traditional models of machine support have stressed the importance of the party's service activities in generating votes, the alleged decline in services has accordingly been accepted as an explanation for the decrease in power of machines in most American big cities. Conversely, the strength of Chicago's machine during and after the Daley era is often viewed as indicating that the local market for political favors somehow survived in that city.

Since the exchange models of the machine link machine support to the market for favors, we can subject those models to an initial test by determining the extent to which voters in Chicago make use of party services. If there has been substantial decline in the delivery of services, then the continued vigor of the patronage party in Chicago casts the exchange models into doubt. We should bear in mind that if significant party services are widely distributed they still may have little influence on the electoral choices of the public. If party services are not widely distributed, however, they cannot plausibly be the primary source of the widespread support Chicago's machine continues to receive.

This chapter seeks to establish the extent to which voters in the ward I studied are aware of the services of the Regular Democrats and, more importantly, the extent to which they actually make service requests. The data come from the files of the alderman with whom I worked and from my sample survey of the ward's registered voters. The levels of awareness and use of services revealed in data from this ward are assessed by comparisons with recent data from other complaint-taking offices and from other sample surveys. The present data are also compared with available descriptive data on the service activities of Chicago's party agents over the last half-century, to see how the type of service the machine delivers has changed over the long term.

The Alderman's Caseload

It is impossible to determine exactly the number of service requests which agents of Chicago's patronage party handle. Most aldermen do not keep systematic files on their service activities, and most precinct captains keep no records at all. Fortunately, the alderman with whom I worked devoted considerable effort to the maintenance of good records. He made his files available to me, and these suffice to provide an approximate notion of his caseload.

In calendar year 1972, 609 discrete service requests were recorded by the alderman and his staff,[2] an average of 2.4 requests per working day. These recorded requests probably represent the bulk of the ward club's service activities for the period, but an unknown number of service requests do not find their way into the alderman's files. Some of the helpful actions of the alderman and other party agents are too trivial to be put in writing. Some complaints are handled by precinct workers without the alderman's help, and thus without being recorded. Requests for those favors requiring the most political pull (such as patronage employment or relief from jury duty) are channeled to the ward committeeman, bypassing the alderman. On the other hand, the 609 requests were not all direct requests from citizens to the alderman: 103 of them were received by precinct captains or other club members who channeled them to the alderman for action. In any case, since the alderman energetically solicited service requests and vigorously pursued them, his caseload was probably above the average for other Regular Democratic aldermen.[3]

Other Complaint-Taking Agencies

How does the alderman's caseload compare with that of competing complaint-taking agencies in Chicago, and equivalent agencies in other cities? The Mayor's Office of Inquiry and Information in Chicago is a centralized agency which receives citizen service requests and forwards them to the city's executive departments. The agency records thirty to fifty thousand service requests each year, averaging about 725 complaints per ward each year.[4] Thus the alderman's caseload (relative to the size of his constituency) is comparable to that of a competing bureaucratic agency established to mediate between citizens and the city's specialized service bureaus.

In other cities offices with similar purposes are reported to have caseloads of the same general order of magnitude. The City of Houston's central office for processing citizen service requests records 35 to 50 citizen-initiated contacts per working day, including those initially transmitted to elected officials and individual city departments, which are eventually routed through this agency.[5] This works out to one complaint a year for each 80–120 citizens, compared to one service request to the alderman for each 100 citizens in the ward I studied. In contrast, the Complaint Bureau of Detroit's Office of the City Clerk in 1973 processed only 2,638 citizen contacts concerning "environmental enforcement," a broad category including problems with litter, noxious weeds, rodents, and pollution.[6] This works out to one complaint for each 600 citizens, a low request rate that reflects the somewhat specialized nature of the bureau.

It hardly needs to be stated that there are great problems in reliability and comparability between the counts of service requests reported by these several agencies. Record-keeping by any organization, be it a large-scale bureaucracy with a full-time staff or an informally organized crew like the alderman's staff, is subject to both random error and systematic biases which we cannot fully assess. Agencies use diverse criteria in deciding which communications they will count as discrete service requests. There is no simple way to discover from a count of service requests the number of individuals who initiated the requests. The flow of requests to the centralized complaint-taking agency tells us nothing about the requests that go directly to the specialized service bureaus, or those which are mediated by elected officials on behalf of their constituents. Nevertheless, it seems safe to conclude that the flow of service requests which was received in the ward office where I worked was comparable to the flow which American citizens generally direct at their major local government complaint-taking agencies. This conclusion is strongly supported by the attitudes and behavior reported by the voters whom I interviewed.

Survey Results

The ward residents whom I interviewed in 1974 were drawn from two systematic samples: a sample of the ward's registered voters and a sample of persons whose names were on file at the ward office as having requested assistance. Since the purpose of this section is to assess the extent of awareness and use of party services among the electorate, only the responses of the voter sample will be considered at this point. As these responses will be used to infer population characteristics, it is important to consider the limitations of the sample. Of the valid names sampled from the list of registered voters, 79.1 percent were successfully interviewed for a total of 106 interviews. Completion of four out of five attempted interviews is a good rate for surveys of this kind; it was achieved by combining telephone and in-person interviews, and persevering in attempts to contact potential respondents.[7] Nevertheless, it is probable that those voters who could not be interviewed include a disproportionate number of people who fail to participate in local politics. In other words, the interviewed sample probably has somewhat higher rates of awareness and use of party services than the electorate as a whole. Unfortunately, there exist no other data on the characteristics of the ward's registered voters, against which the characteristics of the interviewed sample might be compared and the degree of bias assessed.[8] However, the sample is sufficiently large and the completion rate sufficiently high for these data to clearly answer the question at hand: do party services reach a substantial proportion of the electorate?

Awareness

The decline in the market for machine services is thought to be a result of several factors: a decrease in the "clout" of party politicians, an increase in the importance of competing sources of service, the development among city dwellers of values and aspirations which make them skeptical of blatant political intervention, and a decrease in their need for outside help because of their rising standard of living.[9] Of these factors, only the last would produce a decline in the overall propensity of citizens to seek help from political and governmental institutions. The other factors, together with the growth in size and scope of governmental service bureaucracies since the New Deal, will simply produce an increased tendency for citizens to contact government agencies directly instead of seeking the mediation or intervention of patronage party agents. The vitality of the market for machine services must therefore be assessed in relation to the propensity of citizens to contact local government agencies directly.

In order to make this comparison, each respondent was asked, near the beginning of the interview, to name the service resources he or she would call upon to secure some frequently-needed services: bulk trash cleanup, street repair, removal of an abandoned car, and information on city services. Note that these are services which citizens do not normally provide for themselves or purchase on the private market; they are the legitimate province of specific city agencies. Therefore the responses tell us whether citizens are able to procure services of this kind without some kind of help, and indicate which sources of aid they turn to when they need help. With reference to each service I noted whether the respondent cited (1) the *correct* service resource—i.e., that which a citizen would need to choose for the most rapid and direct service, (2) a source of aid within the citywide government, (3) a source of aid within the local patronage party, and if so, whether a precinct worker or a ward-level party agent was mentioned, or (4) a non-governmental and non-political source of aid, either institutional (phone company, newspaper service bureau) or personal (neighbor, relative, building manager).[10] Part A of table 5 gives the wording of the questions and lists some of the responses from the voter sample.

The results show that most citizens would need some help in making known their need for these mundane services, for knowledge of correct service resources was not widespread. However, the great bulk of the voters identify various governmental and political institutions as potential sources of aid. When we examine whether voters cite local political service resources or official citywide resources, we find that over half the voters mentioned local resources, while 45 percent mentioned downtown agencies. Of those who mentioned any political or governmental resource, two-thirds mentioned at least one local resource.[11] The ward-level party agents were more frequently mentioned than precinct workers, but precinct agents were mentioned by

23 percent of those who mentioned any political or governmental resource and by 19 percent of all voters. Clearly, there is among voters of this ward extensive awareness of the services offered by the local patronage party, which has by no means been overshadowed by awareness of the services of official citywide agencies.

The foregoing results are based on responses of voters to open-ended questions that do not suggest politicians as a service resource. Later in the interview, respondents were asked directly if they viewed Democratic party agents as potential sources of aid (table 5, part B). Almost three-fourths of the voters thought that party agents would help them.

Several other interview items reveal that voter awareness of Democratic party agents is extensive. Thirty-seven percent were able to recall the name of their alderman or Democratic ward committeeman when asked (table 5, part C). More than a third were able to name the alderman. The Democratic ward committeeman was less well known: only 11 percent could remember his name.[12] In contrast, only two of the voters interviewed could name the G.O.P. committeeman.

We have noted that 19 percent of the voters spontaneously named precinct agents as service resources. A far larger proportion were aware of the existence of Democratic precinct captains (table 5, part D). Over three-quarters of the voters knew that there was a Democratic captain in their precinct of residence.[13] Almost 60 percent of the electorate claimed to know the Democratic precinct captain (or a Democratic precinct worker) at least by sight (table 5, part E). Of these, half characterized the relationship as one of acquaintanceship or better. However, less than 5 percent of the voters referred to the precinct agent as their "friend." Precinct agents clearly maintain extensive contacts with the electorate, but apparently not on intimate terms. They do work on a face-to-face basis, but their ties to the voters are not highly personal.

If we assume for a moment that these sample data represent population proportions with complete accuracy, we can calculate, for illustrative purposes, the

Table 5 Institutionalization of Party Services
(Responses of Voter Sample [N = 106] to Selected Interview Items)

A. Question 3: Whom would you call or go see if:
a) there was a big pile of boards and trash in your alley?
b) a big hole in the street in front of where you live?
c) an abandoned car on the block?
d) If you weren't sure whom to call or go see, who would you ask?

Response	Number	Percent
Named precinct captain once or more	20	18.9
Named alderman, committeeman or ward superintendent once or more	41	38.7
Named any of the above once or more	55	51.9
Named mayor's office or other downtown city department once or more	48	45.3
Named none of the above	20	18.9
Named no "correct" service resource	39	36.8
Named one "correct" service resource	44	41.5
Named two or more "correct" service resources	23	21.7

B. Question 8: Do you think any of the people in the Democratic party would help you out with a problem if you asked them to?

yes	76	72.4
depends, don't know	20	19.0
no	9	8.6

C. Question 11: Do you happen to know the name of your: *a*) alderman, *b*) Democratic ward committeeman, *c*) Republican committeeman?

Identified alderman correctly	37	34.9
Identified Democratic committeeman or his predecessor	12	11.3
Identified either of above correctly	39	36.8
Identified Republican committeeman correctly	2	1.9

D. Question 9*a:* Do you have a Democratic precinct captain in the precinct where you live?

yes	82	77.4

E. Question 9*d:* How well would you say you know the Democratic precinct captain (or worker)?

Just by sight	23	21.7
By sight and by name	7	6.6
Acquainted	21	19.8
Know well, but not friends	7	6.6
Friend	5	4.7
Know by sight or better (sum of above)	63	59.4

F. Questions 13–17: Did you ever have occasion to ask your alderman for assistance with anything? Democratic ward committeeman? Republican ward committeeman? Democratic precinct captain? Republican precinct captain?

Asked precinct captain	14	13.2

Table 5 (*con't.*)

Asked alderman	22	20.8
Asked Democratic committeeman	7	6.6
Asked any of above	35	33.0
Asked alderman or Democratic committeeman, but not captain	21	19.8
Asked Republican committeeman	1	0.9
Asked Republican precinct captain	1	0.9

number of contacts the average Democratic precinct worker in this ward maintains. We can estimate that 21,600 registered voters actually reside in the ward.[14] From my own experience as a participant observer, I estimate that 100 of the ward club's 150-odd members are active precinct workers. The average active worker, then, is assigned 216 voters, of whom 111 know him at least by sight, 44 are at least acquainted with him, and 10 say they are his friends. Obviously the ward club's precinct workers have effectively carried out their task of contacting the voters, and thus the widespread awareness of their services is not surprising.

Extent of Use

The foregoing data on voter awareness show a high potential for citizen contacts with local party agents. To what extent is this potential realized in actual behavior? Each voter was asked whether he or she had ever had occasion to ask for assistance of some kind from the alderman, Democratic committeeman, or precinct captain. The results, displayed in part F of table 5, show that a full third of the interviewed voters report having requested service at some time from one of these party agents.

It is probable that some discrepancy exists between the reported rate of use of party services and the actual rate. This discrepancy would largely be due to some respondents who fail to remember their use of services or who consciously evade reporting it.[15] Since use is somewhat under-reported, 33 percent is a conservative estimate of the proportion of the electorate that has used party services.[16]

How are requests for service distributed among party agents? The alderman is clearly the chief broker of party services. A majority of the persons who contact the party for service go through the ward office. Most of the service requests received at the ward office are channeled to the alderman.[17] Yet a significant proportion of the electorate has requested service at least once from a precinct captain or worker: 13 percent of all voters and 40 percent of the voters who report use.

It is noteworthy that these data on service use closely parallel the data on voter awareness discussed above. The number of voters who cite each type of party agent as a potential source of aid is naturally greater than the number who actually have used the services of that type of agent. However, the ratio of voters who cite ward-level agents to those who cite precinct agents is identical to the ratio of ward-level users to precinct-level users—about two to one. Thus both kinds of data indicate that provision of party services is somewhat centralized at the ward level, and that service activities at the precinct level have by no means disappeared.

To assess the extent of use of local party services in this ward it would be useful to compare these findings with data from national samples or from other large cities. Unfortunately, directly comparable data are scant. Several major national sample surveys have gathered information on citizen contacts with government officials, but they fail to distinguish issue-related contacts from requests for services, and/or they fail to distinguish contacts with official service agencies from contacts with more political agents. For example, a 1973 poll by Louis Harris found that 24 percent of the nation's adult population have "gone to their local government to get them to do something." The percentage who had made such contact was only 19 percent among residents of central cities in urbanized areas.[18] The percentage would doubtless be higher if the sampling universe had been limited to registered voters as in the present study. But taking into account the wording of Harris' question, which is highly inclusive of both issue-related contacts and service requests to official agencies, the extent of contact with local officials seems quite low compared to the level I found in this ward.

Another large-scale survey of the American public, conducted in 1967 by the National Opinion Research Center, found that "slightly less than 20 percent [of the adult population] report ever having initiated a contact with a local government leader about some issue or problem." In their extensive analysis of these data, Sidney Verba and Norman Nie classified these reported contacts according to the type of problem involved: 13.2 percent of the respondents made local contacts that had a "group or social referent," and 6.2 percent made contacts with a "particularized referent."[19] No distinction is made between party agents and government service bureaus, and nonvoters are included in the sample, yet the reported extent of contact is even lower than that found in the Harris poll.

Samuel Eldersveld's 1956 study of political parties in Detroit was more directly concerned with citizen contacting of local party agents. He sampled the adult population of 87 precincts in Wayne County, Michigan. Only 29 percent of his 608 respondents knew that there were precinct leaders in their neighborhoods, 8 percent knew their precinct leaders "personally," and only 1 percent "reported they had consulted precinct leaders in connection with complaints about local governmental action or inaction."[20] The comparability of these data to those of the present study is limited not only by the differences in the samples and the wording of the questions, but also by the fact that some Detroit precincts had no precinct leaders at the time of Eldersveld's survey. However, even if a liberal adjustment is made for the inclusion in the sample of nonvoters and residents of precincts without leaders, no more than 42 percent of Wayne County voters were aware of their precinct leaders, 11 percent knew them personally, and 1.5 percent had used their services.[21] Precinct workers in the Chicago ward I studied would seem to be much more active than those Eldersveld studied: 77 percent of my respondents knew of their precinct captains, 31 percent said they were at least "acquainted" with them, 19 percent cited them as a service resource, and 13 percent had used their services.

Despite the limits on the present data and the lack of directly comparable survey results from other places, the evidence consistently supports the proposition that the services of party agents are used by a larger proportion of the electorate in the ward I studied than in other cities or in the nation as a whole. In addition, awareness of the party's personnel and services is very widespread among the voters I interviewed. Thus the intense activity I observed at the ward office and Chicago's national reputation as a city with "well-worked" precincts are not illusory; they reflect a volume of service delivery by the local patronage party that is in fact unusually high.

Change in Service Activities

The foregoing discussion has compared data from the present study with current data from other places. If these cross-sectional comparisons could be corroborated by data that show changes in the extent of service activities in Chicago over time, we could conclude with more confidence that the extent of party services has not declined. Unfortunately no longitudinal data are available on the caseload of the machine or the proportion of voters who receive party services.[22] Despite the lack of quantitative data, we can gain insight into the historical trend in party services if we make use of the qualitative data available in several earlier studies of Chicago politics.

Such qualitative data are of importance because the quantity of party services does not in itself reveal the extent to which the types of exchanges take place which are posited in the traditional models of machine support. Different services vary in value as objects of material or affectual exchange.[23] The value of a service depends in part on the amount of power that a politician must wield in order to provide it. A politician who is able to exert influence over administrative decisions which most people cannot affect will probably find much demand for his services, and the "price" or degree of obligation attached to such favors will be enhanced by the scarcity of actors able to supply them. That is, difficult favors should be more valuable as objects of material exchange. Certain other types of service activities will be particularly effective in strengthening the personal ties which the affectual exchange model identifies as the source of machine support. Still other types of favors are—for most recipients—insignificant as objects of either material or affectual exchange. We can assess historical change in the viability of the market for party services by applying to qualitative data from earlier studies and to data from the present study a typology of services that suggests their potential significance as objects of exchange.

A Typology of Services

There are six types of service which local patronage politicians provide to individual constituents. The first three involve the allocation of resources belonging to or under the direct control of the party agent. They are: (1) *provision of information* to the client, especially information that will help the client gain access to services from other agencies; (2) *grants of material value,* such as rent money, clothing, or the time and labor involved in running an errand; and (3) *involvement,* grants or displays of symbolic value, such as attendance at funerals, friendly guidance to youths, and gifts of trivial material value. The other three types of service involve the use of the politician's power resources (official authority, expertise, personal or party ties) to influence the delivery of services by other agencies. (4) *Mediation* occurs when a politician simply transmits a service request to an agency to be processed in the same manner as requests that have been directly submitted. (5) *Priority referral and ombudsmanship* occur when the politician uses his influence to assure unusual treatment of a request by an agency, without causing the agency to flout the law or professional standards in delivering the service.[24] (6) *Intervention or fixing* is when the politician influences an agency to produce a desired outcome that would not result if applicable laws and professional standards were followed.

Of these types of service, provision of information and mediation have the least significance as objects of exchange. Although these services may be of real help to the recipient, most people are aware that party agents have no monopoly on such services and that they can be provided with minimal cost in time or other power resources. Involvement is of greatest significance as a means of strengthening affectual ties between voters and party agents. Grants of material value and fixing are the types of service which most effectively generate a sense of obligation on the part of the voter, since they clearly represent a costly commitment on the part of the politician and may not be elsewhere available. Priority referral and ombudsmanship are types of service with an intermediate degree of significance as objects of either material or affectual exchange.

Historical Comparisons

The three most complete previous studies of the service activities of local party agents in Chicago are those of Sonya Forthal, Harold Gosnell, and H. Dicken Cherry.[25] Forthal interviewed 600 Chicago precinct captains in 1928; Gosnell replicated the Forthal study with 300 captains in 1936, and Cherry, using a similar interview schedule, interviewed 24 ward committeemen and 30 highly effective captains in 1951. Qualitative changes in party service activities since the 1930s are revealed when we apply the typology defined above to the results of these early research efforts and to data from my 1974 survey of voters.

Unfortunately, the quantitative results which the early researchers published do not give us the information we need to categorize the reported activities. Gosnell tabulated his results and those of Forthal according to a functional categorization of *what* was delivered or remedied ("government jobs," "tax adjustments," "trouble with the law," "funerals") rather than the way in which delivery was accomplished.[26] Cherry tabulated his 1951 interviews in a similar manner, showing the number and percentage of interviewed party agents who reported that they had engaged in each functional type of service activity. One cannot tell from the tables (or from the interview schedules as published) whether the party agent actually fixed a traffic ticket or merely answered a simple question about it, whether he attended many local funerals in his capacity as party agent or merely the number that any person would normally attend.

Fortunately Forthal, Gosnell, and Cherry included lengthy descriptive sections in their reports, including many detailed examples of service activity reported by their respondents. In tables 6 and 7 I have listed these examples and placed them into categories according to the typology discussed above. Since the examples were not always described in great detail,[27] I have had to make many subjective decisions in categorizing them. Therefore, these tables must be treated with caution. The length of the lists under each category are a function of the detail provided in the different reports and the degree to which I eliminated redundancy. The lists of examples under different headings should be compared for their content rather than their length. I have indicated in these lists whether each activity was still performed at the time of my research, based on my experience as aldermanic assistant, the alderman's files, and my survey of voters. The services which are listed as not performed today may not be completely impossible, but they are not regularly allocated to voters in the ward I studied. It is of course possible that other Chicago ward clubs with more powerful leaders do more fixing than members of this ward club. It is also possible that some precinct captains were involved in neighborhood activities of which I was not aware. But a few inaccuracies will not change the overall pattern: party agents performed many significant favors in former years that they cannot or do not perform today.

The diminished power of the party to perform significant services is even more evident when we compare these lists with table 8, in which are listed and categorized the service requests reported by the voter

Table 6 Activities of Party Agents Reported in Studies of Forthal and Gosnell

Activity, by Type	Activity Still Performed in 1970s?
I. Provision of information	
1. Give simple legal advice	yes
2. Explain enforcement practices, advise accordingly	yes
3. Give information about naturalization	yes
4. Act as interpreter	yes
5. Help fill out tax schedule	yes
II. Grants of material value	
1. Give children gifts; buy ice cream	yes; maybe
2. Distribute calendars	yes
3. Hire people for election day work	yes
4. Distribute Christmas baskets; Passover baskets	yes; no
5. Give away tickets to entertainment events	rarely
6. Distribute food	yes
7. Distribute coal	no
8. Help out with rent payments	no
9. Distribute clothing, children's outfits	used items only
10. Furnish bail	no
11. Maintain free soup kitchen	no
12. Allow free use of ward hall for weddings	no
13. Run errands	maybe
14. Lend money and tools	maybe
15. Convey to hospital	no
16. Provide transportation for funerals	no
17. Provide free lodging in flophouse	maybe
18. Fix a household fuse	maybe

sample surveyed for this study.[28] Even when we allow for biases resulting from the different methods used in the several studies,[29] it is clear that service activities today are very different from those generally attributed to the classic machine. Very few voters today receive grants of material value or report services that can be categorized as involvement. The largest proportion of the services the party provides are of the least significant types—provision of information and mediation—or they are priority referrals which expedite routine main-

Table 6 (*con't.*)

III. Involvement	
1. Promote better property maintenance and family supervision by neighbors	yes
2. Join and lead various voluntary organizations	yes
3. Bring voters to mass meetings	yes
4. Hold *Kaffee Klatsches* and picnics	yes
5. Hold dance to raise Christmas basket funds	tried unsuccessfully
6. Sponsor athletic teams	tried unsuccessfully
7. Organize ladies' clubs	no
8. Organize district clubs of 4–5 precincts	no
9. Give parties for men; for ladies; for mixed groups	no; no; no
10. Bring constituents to ward picnics	no
11. Attend funerals, send flowers, be pallbearer	no
12. Visit the sick	maybe
13. Adjust generational disputes	maybe
14. Adjust marital disputes	maybe
15. Act as matchmaker	no
16. Send Christmas cards to voters	no
17. Present American flags to new citizens	no
18. Raise bail	no
19. Raise funds for charity	maybe
20. Render neighborly aid, mend kites for kids	maybe

tenance services that have little significance for the fundamental welfare of the citizen.

Apparently the trends away from widespread fixing, generous handouts, and intimate neighborhood involvement have been underway for at least four decades. Comparing his results with the 1928 survey of precinct captains, Gosnell wrote of the decline in intervention and the increase in mediation: "The 1936 precinct committeeman in the city of Chicago was less of an employment broker, less of a tax-fixer, less of a traffic-slip adjuster, but more of a go-between for the relief agencies and the various branches of the federal government."[30] In turn, Cherry noted the similarity of the activities described by his 1951 respondents to those reported by Gosnell, but

Table 6 (*con't.*)

IV. Mediation	
1. Handle requests for sanitation and upkeep services	yes
2. Refer to private and public welfare agencies	yes
2. Act as interpreter	yes
4. Refer job applicants, public and private	patronage only
5. Take applications for permits	no
6. Refer tax adjustment requests	no
V. Priority referral, ombudsmanship	
1. Handle requests for sanitation and upkeep services	yes
2. Refer to private and public welfare agencies	yes
3. Help and hinder permit applications	yes
4. Direct client to lawyer	yes
5. Direct client to lawyer to win traffic court cases	maybe
6. Put in a friendly word for court defendants	only for club members
7. Take tax schedules to Board of Review for reconsideration	no
8. Get dogs out of the pound	no
9. Help in getting police, fire department, janitor jobs	no
10. Help widowed mothers get pensions	no
11. Help with adoption, birth certificates, work certificates	no
12. Prevent under-age children from getting work permits	no
13. Arrange hospitalization	no
14. Arrange transfer from one hospital to another	no

he found that they included less distribution of free coal, food, and rent money, and less fixing of court cases. Thus, despite the continued high volume of service requests to party agents, the provision of potentially valuable party services has steadily declined in Chicago as it has in other cities.

Reasons for the Decline

Why has the ability of the alderman (or other party agent) to do important favors diminished over time? As

Table 6 (*con't.*)

VI. Intervention	
1. Handle requests for sanitation and upkeep services	yes
2. Get release from jury duty	yes
3. Arrange zoning variance	yes
4. Give out jobs as park life guards	yes
5. Adjust taxes (and sometimes collect fee)	no
6. Obtain permits	no
7. Fix criminal cases	no
8. Fix traffic cases	no
9. Fix fire code violations	no
10. Adjust juvenile misdemeanors	no
11. Intercede in eviction and dispossess cases	maybe
12. Reinstate student dismissed from school	no
13. Get transfer of child from one school to another	no
14. Help get pensions	no
15. Help get work certificates	no
16. Get government to pay funeral expenses	no
17. Send private doctor to tend for needy	no

discussed in chapter 4 above, this ability is linked to the alderman's control of power resources and to the properties of the larger political system which he seeks to influence. These have changed significantly during the past several decades.

Chicago's aldermen gave up some of their official powers to the executive departments during the first years of Mayor Daley's administration. For example, in 1956 the city council turned over to the Department of Streets and Sanitation the power to grant driveway permits.[31] At the same time party ties are less effective as a means of influence because of the Shakman decision and because of the gradual professionalization of government agencies. Clerical procedures are increasingly computerized and review processes streamlined. Despite the continued strength of Chicago's patronage system, unobtrusive intervention in rationalized administrative procedures by the ward politician or the patronage workers he sponsors has become more dif-

Table 7 Activities of Effective Party Agents Reported in 1952 Study by Cherry

Activity, by Type	Activity Still Performed in 1970s?
I. Provision of information	
1. Give simple legal advice	yes
2. Tell about available welfare services	yes
3. Recommend private clinics to the sick	maybe
4. Inform jobless of private job openings	maybe
5. Pass the word on housing vacancies	maybe
6. Give advice on making and financing investments	maybe
7. Provide information on veterans benefits	no
8. Help fill out FHA loan applications	no
II. Grants of material value	
1. Distribute Christmas baskets	yes
2. Distribute coal	no
3. Provide auto(s) for funeral procession	no
4. Pay for traffic tickets	no
5. Provide lawyer for court cases	no
6. Make small short-term loans	maybe
III. Involvement	
1. Have friendly chats with neighbors	yes
2. Buy tickets for various charity events	yes
3. Serve as witness for naturalization	maybe
4. Intercede in marital dispute (if local opinion clearly favors one side)	maybe
5. Adjust generational disputes	maybe
6. Hold annual ward dance and raffle at Thanksgiving or Mardi Gras	no
7. Sponsor boxing bouts	no
8. Sponsor bunco and bingo parties	no
9. Organize boys' clubs in neighborhood	no
10. Conduct naturalization classes	no
11. Attend funerals, send flowers	no
12. Attend weddings	no
13. Send flowers to seriously ill (paid for by ward organization women's club)	no
14. Raise bail	no
IV. Mediation	
1. Help with naturalization problems	yes
2. Refer to welfare agencies	yes
3. Take applications for permits	no
4. File FHA home loan applications	no

Table 7 (*con't.*)

V. Priority referral, ombudsmanship	
1. Handle requests for sanitation and upkeep services	yes
2. Help and hinder permit applications	yes
3. Help get building department and zoning approval	yes
4. Find temporary shelter for homeless	yes
5. Appeal to landlord not to raise rent	no
6. Appeal to landlords to discriminate in rentals and sales, help find alternate tenants	no
7. Get inexpensive lawyer for someone in trouble	no
8. Get medical aid at reduced rates	no
9. Help scholarship applications	no
VI. Intervention	
1. Handle requests for sanitation and upkeep services	yes
2. Give out jobs as life guards, summer park attendants	yes
3. Give out scholarships	no
4. Adjust taxes	no
5. Enforce segregated housing	no
6. Get landlord to postpone rent due date	no
7. Get medical aid at reduced rates	no
8. Secure admission to TB sanitoria, mental hospitals, public clinics	no
9. Fix traffic tickets (only to prevent revocation of license)	no
10. Talk policeman out of making an arrest	no
11. Arrange safe jumping of bail	no
12. Get criminal charges dropped or lessened	no

ficult. In addition, those who do intervene are increasingly vulnerable to public exposure and criminal prosecution, because since 1972 the offices of United States attorney, Illinois attorney general, and Cook County state's attorney have not been held by Regular Democrats. It would be foolish to suppose that the fix has disappeared from Chicago politics; but it would be equally unrealistic to ignore the steady tightening of the limits on the ability of Regular Democratic politicians to

Table 8 Service Requests Reported by Cross-Section of Voters in Ward, 1974

Request, by Probable Type of Service Received	To Whom
I. Provision of information	
1. Get mother into senior citizens' project	ward committeeman
2. Real estate tax problem	precinct captain
3. Child care facilities	precinct captain
4. Sidewalk repair	precinct captain
II. Grants of material value	
1. Loaned etcher for identification of values	ward committeeman
III. Involvement	
1. Help arrange wine and cheese party for candidate	precinct captain
IV. Priority referral, ombudsmanship	
1. Get new school park	alderman
2. Maintain funding for educational program	alderman
3. No hot water or heat	alderman
4. Unruly tenants	alderman
5. Tavern complaint	alderman
6. County hospital lost valuable X-rays	alderman
7. Accident claim	alderman
8. Street repair	alderman
9. Sewers backing up	alderman
10. Trash in alley	ward committeeman
11. Pile of trash in street	alderman
12. Abandoned car	alderman
13. Abandoned car	alderman
14. Abandoned car	alderman
15. Abandoned car	alderman
16. Abandoned car	alderman
17. Bad building next door	precinct captain
18. Remove debris after fire	precinct captain
19. Take down and replace trees	precinct captain
20. Fix curbs	precinct captain
21. abandoned truck	precinct captain
22. Abandoned car	precinct captain
VI. Intervention	
1. Got job for son (unspecified)	alderman
2. Got job as life guard	ward committeeman

Table 8 (*con't.*)

3. Stop sign	alderman
4. Stop sign	alderman
5. Building inspection to aid striking tenants	alderman
6. Stopped challenge to voter registration	precinct captain
7. Helped get driver's license (took payoff)	precinct captain

NOTE: Some respondents mentioned more than one service request. A few service requests are not listed above because their nature was not specified by the respondent, or because no service was rendered in response to the request. Specific information about the procedures followed by party agents was not solicited from respondents. The classification by type of service reflects the kind of treatment each request typically received in the ward studied. N = 106.

get things done for their constituents. The patronage party in Chicago survives in spite of, rather than because of, the degree of significance of the services it delivers.

Conclusion

This chapter has assessed the quantity and quality of services delivered by the ward club. Despite some limits on the available data, there are many indications that the volume of requests received by party agents is high—higher than in most places outside Chicago. The annual flow of requests processed by the ward office staff rivals the caseload of centralized complaint-taking agencies of government in Chicago and other cities. The awareness of party services and acquaintance with precinct workers among the ward's voters are astonishingly high. One in three of the ward's voters has at some time contacted a local party agent to request a service. However, the available data indicate that the services which these voters request are not the kinds which have the greatest value as potential objects of exchange. Apparently there has been a long-term decline in the quality—but not the quantity—of patronage party services.

Our assessment of the level of party services was meant as an initial test of the traditional models which see the machine's political strength as being derived from its service activities. The results are equivocal. If we had found that party services reached very few voters, we could have dismissed the exchange models out of hand. We found instead that use of party services is widespread in the ward. Our task now is to discover the impact of these services on the political loyalties of the voters. We have already touched on this issue in our categorization of services according to their potential value as objects of exchange. The finding that the value of services has been declining is an indication that their political impact is limited. In order to measure the impact of party services more directly, we must now shift the focus of study from the party agents and the services they offer to the residents of the ward they serve.

Six Users of Party Services

Who asks for help from the machine? This chapter examines the characteristics of people who request favors from the patronage party organization in the ward I studied. Establishing these characteristics serves two purposes. The first purpose is descriptive, for knowing what the clients are like will help us to build an accurate image of the Chicago machine's service activities. The second purpose is analytical. The traditional models of machine support imply that the users of party services have certain distinctive characteristics. By determining whether they have these characteristics, we subject the traditional models to further empirical test.

Four Hypotheses

Previously published evidence on the machine's clientele is fragmentary and for the most part anecdotal. The traditional models of machine support have regarded the users of party services as its principal supporters; thus descriptions of users vary according to the model of machine support which different observers employ. Based on the alternative models outlined in chapter 1 and what we know about patterns of political participation, we can identify four competing hypotheses about the characteristics of users.

The Political Participation Hypothesis

Citizen contacts with elected officials can be viewed as one important means by which people influence their governments. Social scientists who have studied the workings of democratic systems have gathered vast amounts of data on the various forms of political participation—voting, discussing candidates and issues, following political events, campaigning, seeking public office, etc.[1] These data consistently reveal that (1) people vary greatly in the degree to which they participate, (2) various forms of political participation are intercorrelated, and (3) levels of political participation are strongly determined by certain social characteristics and attitudes. In the United States (and to some extent in other countries) participation rates are higher among the better educated, persons of higher socio-economic status, members of dominant ethnic and racial groups, urban dwellers, and members of voluntary organizations. These differences in background and social position are accompanied by distinctive attitudes and orientations; political participants tend to be more interested in politics, better informed about issues, more committed to one side or another of current issues, and (at least until recently) more partisan. Underlying these orientations, or at least reflecting them reliably, is the citizen's attitude about his or her own ability to participate effectively in elections and public decision-making. Such attitudes can be measured with a variety of reliable and well-validated scales variously labeled "civic competence," "political efficacy," "political trust," and the like.[2] The ultimate determinants of political participation are certainly not completely understood, but it is clear that each of the activities by which citizens can influence the larger political system requires both psychological and social resources which are unequally distributed among members of the electorate.

We may theorize that citizen-initiated contacts with public officials require—or at least are facilitated by—these same resources. Citizens must be aware that a government official is able to deal with their problems; they must have knowledge of whom to contact; they need communication skills that allow them to get their message across; and they must believe, or at least hope, that the government will respond to their requests. These orientations are more likely to be found among somewhat privileged and active groups or classes. By this reasoning we can hypothesize that users of party services are overrepresentative of people who follow the news and are aware of current political issues, people active in voluntary organizations, and people with strong feelings of political efficacy; these may tend to be people with relatively high occupational status and educational attainment.

Citizen-initiated complaints are one form of political participation which has not been extensively studied. In the few studies based on national or metropolitan surveys which have included questions about real or hypothetical complaint behavior, the results have generally been supportive of the above hypothesis.[3] However, we should note that there are at least two important reasons to expect that levels of political participation may *not* be predictive of contact with patronage party agents. First, if requests for party services are based on people's degree of need, we would expect the people most lacking in resources to be the most frequent requesters of favors. Stated differently, it may be that the ability of privileged people to initiate complaints more easily may be offset by the fact that they less frequently have need for party services.[4] Second, greater ability to participate will result in higher rates of service use only if the bulk of requests for service are citizen-initiated. But urban patronage parties are distinguished by their efficient corps of grass-roots activists who systematically initiate contacts with citizens, soliciting service requests face-to-face. It would be a startling finding if the characteristics of the machine's clientele are simply those which facilitate most forms of political participation, for this would mean that—contrary to the party's claim of representing "the little guy"—the neediest members of the electorate are prevented from contacting the party by their lack of psychological and social resources, and the canvassing activities of the party's precinct workers fail to equalize the access of different classes to party services.

The Poverty Hypothesis

Most descriptions of the machine's clients stress their lack of economic resources. The overrepresentation of the poor among the clients is explained by the material exchange model of machine support, which assumes that requesting services involves the voter in a patronage relationship with a party agent. In this kind of relationship the user believes he has been granted favors for which he should feel grateful and beholden. A commitment of political support is expected of the user in return for favors granted.[5] Thus a request for services carries a potential cost for the voter. Those who can do so avoid this manifest cost by taking their requests for help elsewhere. But people who lack economic resources and political power will accept this cost, for they are in greater need of aid and have less access to alternative service resources. Poor people use the services of the machine for the same reasons that they borrow money from a pawnshop: they need what each institution offers and they accept the greater costs because cheaper alternatives are socially inaccessible to them. If the material exchange model of machine support is correct, then the user of party services is more a supplicant than a participant. In contrast to the political participation hypothesis, the material exchange model predicts that users of party services will be disproportionately low in socioeconomic status.

The Ethos Hypothesis

If the material exchange model describes service users primarily in terms of their access to resources, the affectual exchange model describes them primarily in terms of their cultural attributes. According to the latter conception, the culture of machine supporters and service users derives from that of immigrants from peasant cultures in Europe or the United States. To these urban villagers, ethnic and kinship relationships are the principal bases for interaction and for building trust; most of their dealings with people tend to be functionally diffuse and personal. It is difficult for such people to deal with impersonal and specialized urban service bureaucracies; in time of need they naturally turn to the more personal and affectively involved source of help: the neighborhood party worker. Moreover, these urban villagers lack any genuine commitment to the abstract and universal standards of equity upon which notions of "good government" are based. They therefore are less hesitant than "public-regarding" people to use personal connections to help themselves, their friends, or families.[6]

The "private-regarding" ethos is thought to have its historic origin in rural cultures and the ethnic slum, but in theory it can thrive in the absence of poverty. The full acculturation of ethnic populations into the public-regarding political culture may take far longer than does their integration into the occupational structure. Thus the affectual exchange model leads to the hypothesis that the descendants of poor urban immigrants are the more frequent requesters of favors from the machine. We should be able to identify these private-regarding groups by their ethnic heritage, by their religion (Roman Catholicism), or by attitudes they express that relate directly to the use of personal connections in dealing with problems.

The Community Attachment Hypothesis

Unlike the traditional models of machine support, the commitment model does not presume that the users of the machine's services are its most reliable supporters. The task of explaining degrees of machine support is recognized as different from the task of explaining rates of service use. The concept of community attachment is relevant to both tasks, but at this point we will restrict ourselves to the latter explanation.

In the commitment model, community attachment is not seen as a mere holdover of rural forms of social organization, essentially incompatible with modern urbanism and therefore common primarily among the underprivileged. Instead, community attachment develops voluntarily as an answer to the functional needs of certain people, particularly families in the middle years of the life cycle and people whose positions in the occupational structure lead to their extended residence in one locality.[7] Community attachment has both attitudinal and behavioral components: localism is seen in people's knowledge and sentiments about their neighborhoods, the proximity of the homes of their friends and relatives, the spatial patterns of their daily activities and organizational memberships, and the degree to which their own resources are locally invested, as in owning a home and supporting local fund drives. Because community attachment involves many aspects of life, there are a number of ways in which it can be linked theoretically to the use of party services. I find it useful to distinguish four such ways, each of which merits discussion in some detail.

Access. The first effect of community attachment operates quite apart from the material commitments, emotions, or value commitments of the local resident. Living in one area for a long time and developing social ties to people and groups in the area will enhance the citizen's chances for contact with the local party by integrating him or her into the local network of communication. Friends, neighbors, local leaders and neighborhood newspapers are good sources of information on what services are locally available and how to obtain them. Community attachment implies contact with these sources and hence greater likelihood of being exposed to the information. This information is normally a prerequisite for citizen initiation of a service request. Community attachment also increases the probability that a party agent will solicit a request from a citizen. This is partly because the canvassing efforts of precinct workers are directed primarily at registered voters and are somewhat more effective in reaching homeowners and established residents than in reaching transient or isolated people. In addition, the laws of probability dictate that long-term residents are more likely to have been reached by one or more of the party's recurrent canvassing drives than people who have lived in the area only a short time. Thus, community attachment involves enhanced access to the local communication networks which facilitate both contacts initiated by citizens and those initiated by party agents.

Need. The idea that service use is partly governed by the citizen's degree of need has already been suggested above in our discussion of the poverty hypothesis. There we simply equated poverty and need. The need for some kinds of services offered by the local party, however, is not related to sheer economic want, but stems from the economic investment patterns that constitute one component of community attachment.

Economic investment in the local area is most clearly typified in property ownership, particularly in home ownership. Such investment immediately generates obvious needs, since the investor has a direct material interest in the maintenance of his own property and in the control of all aspects of the adjacent locality which affect (or which the investor perceives as affecting) the market value of his holdings. Of course, it is in the nature of real property that its value is strongly determined by its overall locational advantage (which is affected by any change in nearby land uses) and by the amenities and social prestige of its immediate surroundings. Thus homeowners "need" a wide variety of services which in America are provided by city governments and in Chicago are subject to some influence by the local patronage party. Many of these needed services are mundane: removing bulk trash, dead animals, litter, and abandoned cars from the streets; maintaining light, sewer, and water services; and so on. The interests of property owners extend also to matters of less restricted impact which are surrounded by greater controversy: the control of deviant behavior, segregation of low-status minorities, control of zoning and development plans, and so on. These wider issues are of concern to nonowners as well, a fact which underscores the important point that material investment in a locality can take many forms other than property ownership and may involve economic resources other than money. People establish friendships in their neighborhoods, invest effort in the building of local institutions, build up credit with local businessmen: these are all investments whose maintenance and enhancement affect (among other things) the material well-being of the locally attached. Hence, on the basis of material needs alone, the locally attached are more likely to contact the party for services. To be sure, some nonmaterial motivations, growing out of community attachment, are involved in their requests for services. But some of the more routine and mundane services which the party offers are so directly tied to the economic self-interest of property owners that we can safely interpret any empirical linkage between requests for these services and community attachment as stemming primarily from the material needs of the locally attached.

Responsibility. The notion of community attachment goes well beyond considerations of material interest to include affectual and normative components as well. Localism involves emotional investments and moral obligations as well as narrowly rational self-interest. Localistic people may identify with their areas in the full sense of the word: they define themselves with reference to their neighborhoods or communities, so that what happens to the area affects their own identity. Insofar as this identification is manifested in actions intended to enhance or defend the citizen's individual social status, we might subsume this under the economic aspect of community attachment, thereby extending the notion of "need" to include nonmaterial goods which the citizen seeks to maximize. But community attachment involves altruism as well; the localistic citizen is emotionally attached and morally obligated to his neighborhood and the others who live there. The community is something to love, to help, to watch, and to watch out for. Whether these custodial sentiments are genuinely altruistic or are socially imposed is a matter for philosophical debate between exchange theorists and their normative critics; in any case, these obligations are social facts that present themselves in everyday life as important and widely shared expectations about "neighbors" and "good community citizens."

Community attachment thus increases the likelihood of service requests partly because it involves a sense of responsibility. People ask, for example, to have abandoned cars removed from the street not merely because their own safety and material well-being are thereby improved, but because they care about the safety and well-being of their neighbors. Community responsibility is probably only a small component of the motivation for requests for routine and specific services, but we can expect that it plays a far stronger role in requests for "general goods" that benefit the wider collectivity. Community attachment may not be a source of cosmopolitan attitudes, but it can expand the concerns of private-regarding people to include regard for the local community's interests along with those of family and friends. We may note in passing that this component of community attachment is what critics of "mass society" have in mind when they prescribe strengthened community ties as an antidote to the political irresponsibility of the atomized masses.[8]

Rights. If community attachment involves the responsibility of the citizen to show concern for the community, then it also involves the complementary obligation of the community to help the citizen. To some degree this obligation is borne by all members of the community to which the person commits himself, but it is most clearly carried by the community's political leaders, since (by definition) they have control over authoritative allocations of valuable things in the community. Therefore what we have been referring to up to this point as "requests" for "favors" are viewed by many in the community as claims or even "demands" based on a notion of rights.

The politician has a duty to serve his constituents, and the obligation to serve "good citizens" of the community is even more binding. Requests for services from the local party are thus publicly legitimated with reference to the informally defined rights of local citizenship. As was shown in chapter 4 above, ward office personnel deliver services to clients according to a set of unstated priorities based on the client's potential political utility for the party. Party agents give priority to the "good voter" and the "top Democrat" rather than the "good citizen." However, we need not assume that users of party services have the same ideas about their service contacts that party agents do. Persons with strong and longstanding commitment to the community will have a strong belief in their own legitimate claim on party services and will therefore be more likely to request them.[9] In contrast, people with little local affiliation or investment are likely to either call upon nonlocal sources of aid when the need arises, (judging them, perhaps unconsciously, as more likely than the "local hacks" to recognize the legitimacy of their claim on service) or to make no service request at all ("I figured nobody would be interested in my problem").

We can hypothesize that the notion of rights plays some role in the relationship of community attachment to all kinds of service requests, but certain kinds of request probably need stronger legitimation than others. The effect of the rights component of community attachment ought to be strongest in determining which people make requests for the most difficult and valuable favors that the party can perform for individuals.

It is important to view the notion of rights in historical context. Institutionalized rights of citizenship, which have continually changed with the growth of the modern state, are virtually definitive of the evolving nature of the state.[10] Indeed, today's advanced industrial states may be defined as "welfare states" in which citizenship rights have been broadened to include guarantees of access to resources well above the subsistence level.[11] This extension of welfare rights, which occurs partly by legal changes and partly by changes in informal expectations, implies the gradual disappearance of patronage relationships, as most people will no longer feel beholden to the politicians who give them help. This trend would tend to weaken political machines—if they secure their support through material exchange. Under the assumptions of the commitment model, however, the rise of the welfare state does not threaten the strength of the machine. The growth of welfare rights will also not diminish the use of local party services, if two conditions are met. First, as described here, a person's right to aid must be judged by reference to community attachment. This assures that services will be handled on the local level. Second, the public notion of the community citizen's rightful due must be broadened to include not only legally sanctioned rights of fair treatment from official government agencies according to universalistic standards, but also rights to unofficial help from the political party according to more particularistic standards. The latter condition seems to be fully met in the ward I studied, where a full third of the electorate had requested services from the local patronage party and over half mentioned party agents as a possible source of aid. This public redefinition of party services as being not only permissible but a matter of right is integrally related to the successful adaptation of Chicago's Regular Democratic Organization to changing attitudes of the citizenry.

Before examining the data, it would perhaps be helpful to recapitulate the four hypotheses about characteristics of users. The political participation hypothesis predicts that users will have the same attitudinal and social resources that typify those who engage in other kinds of political activity. The poverty hypothesis, based on the material exchange model of machine support, predicts that users will be drawn from the lower socioeconomic strata. The ethos hypothesis, based on the affectual exchange model, predicts that users possess a distinctive, private-regarding political culture. The community attachment hypothesis, congruent with the commitment model of machine support, predicts that users will be localistically committed—materially, emotionally, and/or morally. Service use is related to four distinct components of community attachment which I have referred to as access, need, responsibility, and rights. The survey findings allow us to test the validity of these competing explanations.

Results

The survey of ward residents I carried out in 1974 was specifically designed to explore the causes and consequences of use of party services. I anticipated that the sample of registered voters interviewed (N=106) would not include enough service users to make possible statistically reliable comparisons between users and nonusers. For this reason I drew a supplementary "client sample" of users from the alderman's office records of service requests. The combined sample of voters and clients (N = 160) contains enough users and nonusers to allow useful comparisons.[12]

The survey questionnaire included questions about service use and about the social position, background, attitudes, and political behavior of the respondents. Unfortunately, the questionnaire omitted some items which would help in testing the alternative hypotheses. The limited scope of the survey was partly dictated by cost and time considerations, which required that the interviews be short enough to be completed by telephone where possible. It was further limited by my expectation, based on the existing literature and my participant observation in the ward club, that the exchange models of machine support would be validated by the survey. The available data therefore are well suited for proving (or disproving) the exchange models, but provide somewhat unrefined measures by which to explore the community attachment hypothesis based on the commitment model.

The discussion of findings in this chapter will focus on the bivariate relationships between types of service use and selected predictor variables. We will examine not only the contrast between users and nonusers of party services, but the differences among users according to the type of party agent they contact and the type of service which they request. I also carried out multivariate analyses which indicate the relative importance of the four components of community attachment and the relative importance of the four alternative hypotheses about user characteristics. The latter results will only be summarized below; they are presented in more detail in appendix D.

Types of Users and Their Characteristics

Several different classes of service users were defined on the basis of the interview responses. Each respondent was asked about contacts with his or her alderman, Democratic committeeman, or precinct captain. A *user* is one who reported having contacted one of these party agents for help (or who was listed in office records as having made such a contact). All other respondents are *nonusers.*

Users may be divided into two categories, according to which type of party agent they have contacted for services—the precinct captain or worker on the one hand, and the alderman or ward committeeman on the other. Since the precinct agents regularly canvass the voters in their homes, we would expect their clientele to be more respresentative of the lower strata of the electorate than is the clientele of the ward-level agents who take phone calls and visits at the office. There might be a division of labor between ward-level and precinct-level agents, with each tending to specialize in different services.[13] Accordingly, respondents who have requested a service from their precinct captain or worker are defined as *precinct users;* those who have requested services from either their alderman or the ward committeeman, but who have never requested services from a precinct agent, are *ward users.* Precinct users and ward users are thus mutually exclusive groups that exhaust the set of all users.

Each respondent who reported having asked a party agent for assistance was asked to describe "the most important thing he ever helped you with." These descriptions are the basis for a classification of users according to the type of services they requested. The first of the three categories comprises requests for *general goods.* General goods are of potential benefit to a group, a neighborhood, or a whole community and cannot be granted to a single individual while being withheld from others in the collectivity. The remaining two categories are made up of requests for specific goods.[14] *Routine services* are those which can be provided by party agents with little effort, in the normal course of their service activities. The majority of these are housekeeping favors, such as abandoned car or bulk trash removal. Special favors are those which require greater skill or effort to deliver, or can be provided to only a few. Examples are requests for ombudsmanship, for jobs, or for fixing.[15] We can expect that these different types of service request tend to be made by somewhat different kinds of people, and exploring these contrasts will help make clear the factors which affect service use.

The classification of users according to type of agent contacted is not entirely independent of the classification according to type of service requested. Requesters of routine services are as likely to be ward users as are requesters of special favors. However, requesters of general goods work exclusively through ward-level agents, as one might expect since ward-level agents have a larger constituency and greater power to secure general goods. The ward users thus include persons who requested all three types of service; the precinct users comprise only requesters of the two types of specific goods. The reader should bear in mind that the contrast in characteristics of ward and precinct users is partly a result of the differences between requesters of general and specific goods.

Political participation indicators. Table 9 displays the percentages of nonusers and each type of user in the combined sample that have selected characteristics related to the political participation hypothesis.[16] The characteristics of the entire group of users are first compared to those of the nonusers. Users are somewhat more likely to have the behavioral characteristics of political participators. Higher proportions of users vote in minor elections,[17] are active in campaigns, and belong to voluntary organizations other than block or community groups.[18] However, users do not seem to be better informed about politics than nonusers are. They are more likely to read one of the metropolitan newspapers daily, but they are less well informed than nonusers about an important and well publicized metropolitan issue—the RTA proposal.[19]

Users appear to be no stronger than nonusers in their level of bureaucratic competence, "the attitudes, knowledge, and behavioral dispositions necessary to cope with bureaucracy."[20] Two items were used to measure bureaucratic competence. The first is taken directly from a study by Janowitz, Wright, and Delaney: "In general, if you had a problem to take up with a government bureau, would you do it yourself, or do you think you would be better off if you got the help of some person or organization?"[21] Users and nonusers had the same distribution of responses to this question. The second item was: "Sometimes big agencies like the phone company or the city government don't do what they're supposed to do. Do you think it does you any good to complain to them when this happens?" Users were only slightly more likely than non-users to think their complaints would be efficacious. This apparent independence of bureaucratic competence and service use does not necessarily cast doubt on the political participation hypothesis. Many of the services of the party consist of help with matters requiring the attention of large government agencies. Persons with low bureaucratic competence are more likely to require the party's help in coping with these agencies, and this may offset the fact that, given similar needs, persons with high bureaucratic competence are better able to call upon the party for help.

The questions used to measure attitudes of political efficacy are adapted from three items widely used in national sample surveys.[22] The only notable difference between users and nonusers on these items is that users are more likely to stress strongly the importance of the act of voting.

Overall, there are some substantial differences between users and nonusers in these indicators, as the political participation hypothesis predicts. But the differences are not very strong and are not consistent from item to item. The reasons for some of these inconsistencies will become clear as we examine the differences among types of users.

There are two important differences between ward and precinct users with respect to political participation. First, ward users initiate their own service requests, while many of the precinct users probably make service requests in response to the face-to-face solicitation of precinct workers. Therefore, precinct use does not require the same knowledge and abilities that facilitate ward use. Accordingly, we find that ward users are more likely than precinct users to belong to voluntary organi-

Table 9 Political Participation Indicators for Types of Users of Party Services

(Data are for combined sample of voters and clients, N = 160. Number of cases for which data were available is shown in parentheses.)

	Non-users	All Users	Type of Agent		Type of Services		
			Ward Users	Precinct Users	General Goods	Routine Services	Special Favors
a. Political behavior:							
Percent who have voted in recent minor elections	64.8 (71)	71.9 (89)	70.7 (58)	74.2 (31)	78.9 (19)	75.0 (36)	64.1 (39)
Percent who have campaigned or contributed to a campaign	18.3 (71)	38.2 (89)	37.9 (58)	38.7 (31)	57.9 (19)	41.7 (36)	28.2 (39)
Percent who belong to voluntary organizations of nonlocal scope	23.9 (71)	44.9 (89)	50.0 (58)	35.5 (31)	57.9 (19)	47.2 (36)	38.5 (39)
b. Political information:							
Percent who read a metropolitan paper daily	66.2 (71)	82.0 (89)	82.8 (58)	80.6 (31)	84.2 (19)	86.1 (36)	76.9 (39)
Percent who can describe the RTA proposal and know if it passed	69.0 (71)	53.9 (89)	62.1 (58)	38.7 (31)	63.2 (19)	52.8 (36)	48.7 (39)

c. Bureaucratic competence:							
Percent who would handle a problem with government on their own	45.7 (70)	44.3 (88)	52.6 (57)	29.0 (31)	52.6 (19)	48.6 (35)	33.3 (39)
Percent who think it is helpful to complain to large agencies	58.2 (67)	63.5 (85)	60.0 (55)	70.0 (30)	57.9 (19)	67.6 (34)	65.8 (38)
d. Political efficacy:							
Percent who disagree that politics is too complicated to understand	40.9 (71)	44.3 (88)	45.6 (57)	41.9 (31)	73.6 (19)	42.9 (35)	33.3 (39)
Percent who agree that election outcomes are important	48.6 (70)	48.2 (85)	40.0 (55)	63.3 (30)	38.9 (18)	54.2 (35)	48.6 (37)
Percent who strongly disagree that voting is not important	42.3 (71)	59.8 (87)	51.8 (56)	74.2 (31)	36.8 (19)	62.9 (35)	60.5 (38)
e. Summary score:							
Percent with score of 4 or more on six-item political participation index	35.2 (71)	48.3 (89)	58.7 (58)	29.0 (31)	73.7 (19)	50.1 (36)	35.8 (39)

zations and to be informed about the RTA issue. Ward users are much more likely to feel that they can handle their problems with government without outside aid,[23] and are slightly more likely to find politics understandable. Second, precinct users obviously include a disproportionate number of voters who are in frequent contact with their precinct captains. This frequent contact both stems from and reinforces a high level of involvement in the electoral process. The high involvement of precinct users is manifested in their strongly held beliefs that the outcomes of elections are important and that their own votes matter. It is manifested also in their behavior, for despite their relative lack of knowledge of issues and involvement in voluntary associations precinct users are slightly more likely than ward users to have voted in minor elections or been active in a campaign. The personal linkage of precinct users to precinct-level party agents may also be the cause of their high degree of confidence in the efficacy of making complaints to large agencies.

There are some important differences in the political participation characteristics of requesters of different kinds of service. Because general goods requesters are expressing to their local leaders concerns that extend beyond themselves, their families, or their friends, we would expect that they would have the characteristics that make possible responsible participation in community decision-making. Requesters of routine services need not have the same high-level understanding of politics and the same broad concerns, but they will tend to have most of the attitudes and resources that facilitate active participation. Requesters of special favors may not show the same characteristics, for their requests are based on special, pressing need for government action. This strong need may motivate requests even where the characteristics conducive to participation are lacking.

Accordingly, we find in table 9 that requesters of special favors are lower on most of the political participation indicators than the requesters of routine services, and are actually lower than nonusers on several of these items. The requesters of general goods score substantially higher than requesters of routine services on those items which probably relate most closely to informed and public-regarding participation: political campaign activity, voluntary organization membership, knowledge of the RTA issue, self-sufficiency in handling bureaucratic problems, and feeling that politics is understandable. However, the general goods requesters score lower than other users and nonusers on their perceptions of the efficacy of their complaints and the importance of elections and voting. This is partly the result of the underrepresentation among general goods requesters of precinct users, who, as noted above, tend to be most heavily involved in the electoral process. In addition the lack of electoral involvement by these issue-oriented service users may also bespeak a kind of informed cynicism about political realities in the city and the ward where they live.

It is useful to represent the chief political participation characteristics of the respondents by creating a summative index based on six of the items shown in table 9. The bureaucratic competence items are excluded from this index because their relationship to service use is theoretically and empirically ambiguous. The political efficacy items referring to the importance of elections and voting are excluded because they measure a kind of political involvement that is apparently independent of a voter's ability for informed and responsible participation.[24] The index thus includes all three political behavior items, the two political information items, and a single political efficacy indicator (belief that politics is understandable). As shown in table 9, high scores on this summary measure are more frequent among users than non-users; more frequent among ward users than precinct users; and occur among general goods requesters, routine services requesters, and special favors requesters with decreasing frequency.[25]

Socioeconomic status indicators. Table 10 summarizes the percentages among each type of user with characteristics relevant to the poverty hypothesis. The differences between users and non-users on these indicators are in the direction predicted by the poverty hypothesis: a higher proportion of users are in blue-

Table 10 Socioeconomic Status Indicators for Types of Users of Party Services

(Data are for combined sample of voters and clients, N = 160. Number of cases for which data were available is shown in parentheses.)

			Type of Agent		Type of Service Requested		
	Non-users	All Users	Ward Users	Precinct Users	General Goods	Routine Services	Special Favors
Percent with blue-collar occupations	33.0 (69)	40.7 (86)	39.3 (56)	43.3 (30)	16.7 (18)	50.0 (34)	39.5 (38)
Percent with no years of college education completed	51.4 (70)	56.8 (88)	56.1 (57)	58.1 (31)	31.6 (19)	60.0 (36)	61.5 (39)
Percent who receive public aid payments	11.3 (71)	13.5 (89)	8.6 (58)	22.6 (31)	10.5 (19)	16.7 (36)	10.3 (39)

collar occupations,[26] have attained no more than a high school education, or are welfare recipients.[27] However, the differences are quite small, and do not support the image of the patronage party as primarily serving a lower-class clientele; about 60 percent of all users are in white collar occupations.

Precinct users are somewhat lower in socio-economic status than ward users. The outreach activities of the precinct workers are an effective form of "downreach" that puts the party in contact with many who lack the resources to initiate service requests. Precinct workers are particularly successful in soliciting service requests from welfare recipients, a fact which probably results from the ease with which these unemployed people may be contacted at their homes, rather than from any peculiar needs or personality characteristics of welfare recipients. Nevertheless, the clientele reached by the precinct workers is far from being predominantly lower class.

There are notable differences in social status among users of different types of services. General goods tend to be requested by middle-class people; the special needs of the poor are apparently not expressed in requests of this kind. Poor people are somewhat overrepresented among requesters of routine services, which is remarkable when we recall that this group has rather high scores on political participation indicators. This underscores the theoretical distinction between the political participation hypothesis, which focuses on ability to obtain services, and the poverty hypothesis, which focuses on need for services. The requesters of special favors, in contrast, are more similar in social status to the nonusers, just as they were least different from nonusers in their political participation scores. Apparently the needs which these unusual and important services meet are not confined to poorer people.

Political ethos indicators. The ethos hypothesis predicts that immigrants from less modern states and their unassimilated descendants possess cultural attributes that encourage their use of party services. I tested this hypothesis using three indicators of ethos: ethnicity, religion and a scale of attitudes. Table 11 shows the results.

Respondents were categorized into broad ethnic categories according to the geographic contiguity of their countries of origin and the time of peak immigration from each country.[28] For the present discussion, it suffices to consider two categories that reflect relative ethnic status. The high-status category includes people who claim American ancestry or ancestry from western, northern and central European countries. The lower-status category includes persons with eastern or southern European ancestry, Latin Americans, and nonwhites. As table 11 shows, there were proportionately somewhat fewer members of the lower-status ethnic groups among users than among nonusers, in contradiction to the ethos hypothesis.[29] Precinct users included fewer low-status ethnics than ward users, perhaps because the poor population of the ward I studied included many southern whites who claim American or west European ancestry. The low percentage of low-status ethnics among users who requested general goods suggests that higher ethnic status is associated with public-regardingness; but there are not enough low-status ethnics among requesters of specific goods to lend support to the ethos hypothesis.

When we consider the religion of the respondents, the ethos hypothesis appears in a far more positive light. Roman Catholics are greatly over-represented among users of party services. Even more of the precinct users are Catholic than the ward users, which lends credence to the interpretation that being Catholic indicates a propensity for dealing with political institutions through personal channels. All the types of service requesters include high proportions of Catholics when compared to nonusers, but requesters of special favors are almost fifty percent Catholic, which suggests even more strongly the linkage of Catholicism to what Clark calls "nonideological particularism."[30]

This empirical relationship has been reported by other researchers working with data of various kinds,[31] but the nature of the linkage remains somewhat mysterious. In thinking about religious factors in behavior, it

Table 11 Political Ethos Indicators for Types of Users of Party Services

(Data are for combined sample of voters and clients, N = 160. Number of cases for which data were available is shown in parentheses.)

			Type of Agent		Type of Service Requested		
	Non-users	All Users	Ward Users	Precinct Users	General Goods	Routine Services	Special Favors
Percent with low status ethnic origins	38.0 (71)	33.7 (89)	36.2 (58)	29.0 (31)	26.3 (19)	41.7 (36)	33.3 (39)
Percent Roman Catholic	19.7 (71)	41.6 (89)	39.7 (58)	45.2 (31)	42.1 (19)	38.9 (36)	48.7 (39)
Percent with high scores on index of corruption	30.4 (69)	36.8 (87)	35.7 (56)	38.7 (31)	50.0 (18)	38.9 (36)	31.6 (38)

is helpful to distinguish (1) *group factors,* the distinctive social characteristics of groups which identify with a given religion in the setting being studied, and (2) *value-elements,* components of the religious belief system itself that may influence behavior.[32] One is hard pressed to "explain away" by group factors the religious effect in the present data. The effect is clearly more than a spurious result of the weak relationships with class and ethnicity which we have reviewed above. Doubtless the effect has something to do with the longstanding and well-documented tendency of Catholics in America to identify with and support the Democratic party, but this loyalty could be as much a result of service use as its cause. We could argue that being Catholic provides a basis for affinity and communication with others of the same religion and that Catholics contact the party more because many of its leaders and members are Catholic. However, this argument cannot be advanced with conviction inasmuch as the leaders of the ward party organization I studied were predominantly Jewish. A more plausible interpretation of the religious effect in terms of group factors is that Catholicism really serves as an index of a distinct type of ethnic heritage. Ethnic groups with this type of heritage are somewhat "spread out" along the present social hierarchy of ethnic group prestige. The private-regarding ethos survives among descendants of groups which emigrated from homelands which had weak democratic traditions, and these were primarily countries with largely Catholic populations. Because some of these groups, such as the Irish, have been able to achieve high socioeconomic status, private-regardingness is more strongly related to religion than to present ethnic group prestige. However, the importance of religion comes from the more general cultural characteristics of Catholic American ethnic groups, rather than from implicit or explicit theological elements.[33]

It is also possible to argue that the values and traditional practices of the Catholic religion itself create predispositions for the use of patronage services. Perhaps the Catholic church constitutes an institutional environment which predisposes its members to turn to similarly organized institutions for help with everyday problems. The ecclesiastical hierarchy and territorial organization of the church bear similarities to the structure of the patronage party. One might even draw a parallel between the mediated relationship of the lay person to what is sacred in the Catholic church and the mediated relationship of the user of local party services to the benefits of citizenship. If Protestantism has, in Seymour Martin Lipset's words, "contributed to individualism, self-reliance, feelings of personal responsibility for success and failure, and interpretation of social evils in terms of moral turpitude," while Catholicism "has tended to stress community responsibility, and does not emphasize individual morality,"[34] then the tendency of Catholics to use personal patronage more than do non-Catholics may reflect real contrasts in values. The present data cannot show whether the tendency of Catholics in this ward to use party services is the result of their national heritage or of religion itself, but the data do support the ethos hypothesis in that the religious effect cannot be attributed to causally prior structural variables. Cultural factors, associated in some way with religion, do have a significant effect on service use.

As a further test of the ethos hypothesis, I included in the questionnaire several items designed to measure attitudes that would predispose people to use personal connections as a source of help with their problems. Two of them were as follows: (1) "Sometimes people with 'connections' get better service from government agencies. Overall, how has this affected you—that is, do you think this has helped you or hurt you more?" (2) "If all Chicago policemen were honest and did their jobs strictly by the rules, what kind of service do you think that you personally would get from the police—better, worse, or about the same as now?" Those who answered "helped" or "neither hurt nor helped" to the first question, and "about the same" or "worse" to the second were given a high "corruption-acceptance" score on a dichotomous scale.[35] Table 11 shows the percentages with high corruption-acceptance scores among different types of users. Users are a bit more likely than nonusers to voice attitudes of high corruption-acceptance. Precinct users are a bit more likely than ward-users to score high on the scale, a finding which perhaps indicates some validity in the scale. However, the high proportion of general goods requesters who score high on this scale casts doubt on its validity as an indicator of the private-regarding ethos, since this ought to be the most public-regarding group. The questions I used to construct this scale do not tap the cultural differences among respondents that are reflected in the strong effect of religion on service use.[36] In the multivariate tests which will be discussed below, political ethos will therefore be indicated by religion.

Community attachment indicators. The questionnaires contained no questions that addressed actual sentiments about the local community, but as is shown in table 12 some indicators of behavior and social position that are directly related to community attachment are very strongly related to use of party services. This set of indicators is by far the most strongly and consistently related to service use of any set considered so far.

These data indicate that each of the analytically separable components of community attachment—access, needs, rights, and responsibility—is correlated with service use. Access to the local network of information is indicated by the responses to question 3, which asked whom the respondent would contact for certain routine services. Not surprisingly, users of party services were more likely than nonusers to cite as a service resource their precinct worker, ward committeeman, or alderman. To some extent, such knowledge of the availability of party services may be a result of prior service use, rather than its cause, but this is the best indicator for access to community information to be found in these data.

The needs component of community attachment is represented by home ownership, since homeowners have important material investments in the local area. Homeowners are overrepresented among all types of users, and most markedly overrepresented among requesters of routine services. Since routine services primarily comprise government "housekeeping" opera-

Table 12 Community Attachment Indicators for Types of Users of Party Services

(Data are for combined sample of voters and clients, N = 160. Number of cases for which data were available is shown in parentheses.)

			Type of Agent		Type of Services		
	Non-users	All Users	Ward Users	Precinct Users	General Goods	Routine Services	Special Favors
Percent of homeowners	7.0 (71)	33.7 (89)	32.8 (58)	35.5 (31)	26.3 (19)	47.2 (36)	30.8 (39)
Percent who belong to a block club or community organization	5.6 (71)	28.1 (89)	32.7 (58)	19.4 (31)	57.9 (19)	16.7 (36)	25.7 (39)
Percent who have lived in neighborhood 10 years or longer	35.2 (71)	68.5 (89)	70.7 (58)	64.5 (31)	47.4 (19)	72.2 (36)	74.4 (39)
Percent who read community press at least weekly	15.5 (71)	43.8 (89)	41.4 (58)	48.4 (31)	42.1 (19)	36.1 (36)	51.3 (39)
Percent aged 31–55 years	14.1 (71)	48.3 (89)	41.4 (58)	61.3 (31)	52.6 (19)	47.2 (36)	48.7 (39)
Percent with high localism score (2 or more of above 5 characteristics)	21.2 (71)	68.6 (89)	65.5 (58)	74.2 (31)	68.5 (19)	72.3 (36)	69.2 (39)
Percent who cite local party agents as a service resource	42.3 (71)	70.8 (89)	67.2 (58)	77.4 (31)	57.9 (19)	80.6 (36)	74.4 (39)

tions which preserve property values, this strong association illustrates clearly that need based on local investment is an important motivator of service use.

Members of block clubs and community organizations are overrepresented among all types of users. The proportion of members among requesters of general goods is conspicuously high, which suggests that membership in local organizations is a good indicator of the responsibility component of community attachment. Activism in local-advocacy groups can be both a cause and a consequence of responsibility; people join such groups because they feel the interests of the area are worthy of active support, and their activities in these organizations no doubt foster contacts and affiliations with other local people that enhance their sense of duty. Well over half the people who request general goods are members of community groups.

Length of local residence indicates the degree to which residents can claim the rights of community citizenship. Long-time residents of their neighborhoods are overrepresented among all types of users, but they are especially overrepresented among requesters of specific goods. These are the types of services which cannot be legitimated by reference to the common good, since they benefit primarily the individual who requests them. They are therefore legitimated by reference to the notion of community citizenship rights, which are most appropriately claimed by people who have lived in the area for many years.

Regular readership of the community press and being in the middle years of the life cycle are strongly associated with all types of service use. Neither characteristic has a marked connection to any one type of service use; each is apparently tied to several of the components of community attachment. We may presume that readers of the community press have access to a good source of community information, tend to have material investments in the local area, and may acquire an enhanced sense of local responsibility and rights. Age is linked with community attachment in that the middle years of the life cycle are most typically the time when families are raised, homes are purchased, and stable occupations are pursued. In this settled and productive time of life a person is more likely to become materially and sentimentally attached to the locality than in the comparatively rootless early years of adulthood, or in the older years which so often bring displacement and disaffiliation from local life.[37]

For the purpose of testing the community attachment hypothesis against the alternative hypotheses discussed above, it is appropriate to combine homeownership, local organization membership, length of local residence, community press readership, and stage in the life cycle into a single overall index of community attachment.[38] As shown in table 12, each class of users of party services is at least three times as likely as nonusers are to have scores of two or more on this index.

Multivariate Tests

In the foregoing discussion, the interdependence that exists among the components measured by indicators of community attachment has been ignored. To some extent the association of any one indicator of community attachment with service use is merely a reflection of that indicator's close association with other components of community attachment that also generate service use. The same sort of spurious effect on service use may be present for the indicators of political participation, status, and ethos, which are also somewhat correlated with each other and with community attachment. It was therefore necessary to apply to the data a method which reveals the effect of each predictor with other predictors statistically controlled. The method used was the loglinear approach developed by Leo A. Goodman, which outwardly resembles multiple regression analysis. This multivariate method was used to examine the effects of different components of community attachment on service use, and to test the four hypotheses of service use with which this chapter began. The method and results are described in appendix D; here it will suffice to outline the principal results.

The six components of community attachment were found to have about the same relative predictive power in the multivariate analysis as they do in the "zero-order" relationships displayed in table 12. Each of the simple correlations we examined above is partly a result of interrelationships among predictors (which are controlled in the multivariate analysis) but none of the simple correlations is wholly spurious. Indicators of access, need, responsibility and rights each have substantial independent effects on service use. It is particularly noteworthy that the effects of length of local residence and membership in local organizations do not disappear when homeownership and citation of the party as a service resource are controlled. This confirms the view that the moral and sentimental aspects of community attachment (responsibility and rights) are at least as important in determining use of party services as are the functional needs, specialized knowledge, and communications linkages that arise from local residence.[39]

In the multivariate tests of the four alternative hypotheses, political participation index scores and occupational status were found to have small effects on service use. They are not associated with all types of service use, and although the variations in their predictive power are instructive, these predictors contribute relatively little to the explanation of service use by the multivariate models. In contrast, being Catholic has a moderate effect and localism scores have a very strong effect on service use. These variables have strong independent effects on every kind of service use, far outweighing the other variables in predictive power. Localism is much the stronger of the two strong predictors. The multivariate results thus confirm what the zero-order associations suggested: the data give little support to the political participation and poverty hypotheses, moderate support to the ethos hypothesis, and very strong support to the community attachment hypothesis.

Conclusion

The foregoing data analysis allows an empirically based description of the clientele of the ward party organization I studied. Although the existing literature on the machine stresses that urban patronage parties specialize in services for poor and ethnic voters, a majority of the people who request services in this ward are employed in white collar occupations and a majority identify themselves with high-status ethnic groups. There is a slightly higher proportion of blue-collar workers among users than there is among the voters who do not use party services, which is but scant support for the poverty hypothesis. On the other hand, the users are not by any means an elite group of political activists. Their level of political participation is only slightly higher than that of nonusers. We find that the characteristics of different types of users vary somewhat: precinct agents reach a group of service users who participate in politics no more than nonusers, and users who make requests for general goods are as likely as nonusers to have white-collar status while being much more likely than nonusers to be politically active. Nevertheless, no group of users heavily overrepresents lower-status groups in the ward.

The outstanding characteristic of users of party services is their attachment to the local community. This is not to say that a majority of users have all the characteristics that indicate community attachment. Indeed, long local residence is the only such characteristic which more than half the users possess. However, the proportion of locally-attached people among users of every type is far higher than the proportion among nonusers. Users are more likely than nonusers to be homeowners, members of locally-based voluntary organizations, long-time local residents, readers of the community press, or persons in the middle years of the life cycle. Moreover, the multivariate analysis shows that the distinct components of community attachment have separable, direct and more or less additive effects on service use; the more attached a person is, the more likely it is that he or she will use party services. Thus, more than two-thirds of all the users have two or more of the five characteristics I used to indicate community attachment.

Another characteristic of users, weaker but nonetheless significant, is identification with the Catholic religion. Catholics do not constitute a majority of users, but there is a substantially higher proporition of Catholics among every type of user than there is among nonusers. The relationship of religion to service use is not a spurious result of religious differences in political participation, social status, or community attachment.

What is the significance of these findings? First, they cast doubt on the material exchange model of machine support. This model implies that users are poor people, a hypothesis for which we have found little support. Second, the findings give qualified support to the affectual exchange model, which implies the ethos hypothesis. The finding of a significant religious effect on service use supports that hypothesis, but we found no association between ethnic prestige and service use, and the attempt to measure attitudes toward corruption more directly also yielded no support for the ethos hypothesis. Moreover, the religion effect is overshadowed by the much stronger effect of community attachment.

Third, the results are congruent with the commitment model of machine support and a "systemic" conception of community attachment.[40] In the commitment model, support for the patronage party is not caused by use of its services; hence we need not predict that users have characteristics that permit them to be influenced by service use. Instead, we can consider the effects on service use of community attachment, conceived as a voluntary and functionally specific set of sentiments and behaviors characteristic of some modern urbanites under predictable circumstances. This complex of characteristics has several distinct components that independently and more or less additively increase the chances that a ward resident will make a service request, and jointly constitute the strongest predictor of who does so.

Although these data clearly tell us who uses party services, they can but suggest the validity of the competing models of machine support. Even though people who are poor or private-regarding do not form the bulk of the ward organization's clientele, it remains conceivable that the votes of such people are strongly influenced by the services they receive. The party may be generating support through patronage relationships with a limited group of people while simultaneously responding to the demands of the bulk of its clients, who have a broader notion of their citizenship rights. For a more conclusive test of the exchange models of machine support, we must turn to an analysis of party identification and party loyalty among the residents of the ward.

Seven Party Loyalty and Use of Services

The extent of use of party services and the characteristics of service users having been explored, it remains to find out whether the traditional models of machine support fit the data at hand. Both the material exchange model and the affectual exchange model explain support for the patronage party as resulting from networks of individual exchange relationships. The models assert that machine supporters do not base their voting decisions on their perceptions of how competing parties or candidates measure up to their values or long-term interests. Instead their decisions are based on short-term incentives received from party agents. The models differ on whether these incentives are primarily material or affectual, but agree that they are specific—capable of being granted to or withheld from individuals. In short, the exchange models assert that the service activities of the patronage party create a large number of individual obligations which are paid back in the form of votes on election day.

Is either of the exchange models empirically valid? In this chapter we test both of them by analyzing data from the survey of ward residents, data which reveal the sources of party identification and loyalty. In order to know what to look for in these data, we shall first derive from the exchange models a set of testable hypotheses.

Hypotheses

The material exchange model and the affectual exchange model of machine support are different in some respects and similar in others. Each model implies some unique hypotheses and both imply some identical hypotheses. Let us first examine the latter set of testable propositions.

Both of the exchange models assert that the party's service activities play a role in generating electoral support. If either model is correct, then, the data will support the hypothesis that users—persons who have been involved in service transactions with local party agents—are more likely to be loyal to the party than nonusers.

Both exchange models see the voter's sense of obligation as producing loyalty, although they differ on how this sense of obligation is generated. A second proposition therefore follows from either model: the stronger the user's sense of obligation, the more likely he or she is to be a loyal Democrat. That is, if party loyalty is cross-classified with each of three variables representing successively stronger levels of obligation to party agents, we can expect successively stronger association of party loyalty with the variables. In the group that requested services, loyalty to the party would be more likely among users who were satisfied with services they had received and more likely still among satisfied users who gave positive evaluations of the party agents serving them.

Both exchange models see the behavior of machine supporters as a rational response to immediate incentives, which can be understood by an analysis of perceived costs and benefits. As Banfield and Wilson state: "Control [of votes] becomes possible when people place little or no value on their votes, or, more precisely, when they place a lower value on their votes than they do on the things which the machine can offer them in exchange for them."[1] They recognize that the voter plays a part in determining the value of the things exchanged; the values the voter places on the incentives and on the vote determine whether he or she will be influenced. Voters of different social position and cultural background will place different values on favors and votes. The two exchange models disagree about how the voter will evaluate the favors offered; hypotheses based on these assumptions will be examined shortly. But the two models agree that the voter who attaches little importance to his or her vote is more amenable to exchanging it for the incentives offered by party agents. The survey data include a measure of the value placed by a respondent on his vote and on the election outcome: the political efficacy scale. The third hypothesis, then, is that satisfactory use is more strongly associated with loyalty among those with low political efficacy scores than among those with high scores.

The fourth hypothesis can also be expressed in economic terms. Just as economic resources can be either capitalized or maintained as liquid assets, a person's vote may be more or less flexible and thus available for use in exchange transactions. A person who participates in local politics and in voluntary organizations, is informed about issues, and feels competent to follow political events is likely to have stable political preferences linked to a coherent belief system. Such a person's vote will express these preferences, preferences which are not easily altered because they are founded on basic values. In contrast, nonparticipators have invested less thought and action in their preferences. They lose nothing by changing their vote and therefore they are more amenable to influence through either material or affectual exchange. The fourth hypothesis implied by both models is that satisfactory use will be more strongly associated with loyalty among those with low scores on the political participation index.

We turn now to hypotheses which are specific to the different models because they derive from assumptions about how the value of a favor is assessed by the recipient. Under the material exchange model, the nature of the service received will have a bearing on the degree of obligation it calls forth. Here the distinctions among requests for general goods, routine services, and special favors become relevant. Since general goods cannot be withheld from an individual, granting such goods is less likely to produce strong personal obligations. Routine services of the party are usually taken for granted—that is, they are perceived as part of what citizenship rights entitle a person to receive without any reciprocation. Our fifth hypothesis therefore is that, if the material exchange model is valid, loyalty is more strongly related to receipt of satisfactory services that can be regarded as special favors than to receipt of general goods or routine services.

The importance of a service to the voter depends not only on the nature of the service itself, but upon the voter's ability to secure that service without the party's aid. The bulk of party services consist of assistance in expediting matters through public bureaucracies; in most cases the person who possesses bureaucratic competence can do this without the party's help. But it is difficult for the person without such competence to deal directly with the agencies of government, and alternative sources of aid may be out of reach because of the same lack of competence. What the bureaucratically competent person views as an officeholder's duty, the bureaucratically incompetent person sees as an important personal favor. The sixth hypothesis, then, is that if the material exchange model is valid, satisfactory use will be more strongly associated with loyalty among those low in bureaucratic competence.

Under the affectual exchange model it is assumed that what generates a sense of obligation on the part of the voter is not the market value of the service received but its symbolic value—the degree to which it communicates the party agent's generosity, and his affection for the voter. Presumably, services delivered in face-to-face personal encounters in the precincts are more effective in carrying this message. Moreover, services performed at the ward level are more likely to be defined by the voter as benefits to which he is entitled by citizenship rights, rather than as evidence of an affectual bond. Precinct-level service contacts are more likely to become the basis of friendship, or at least of a patronage relationship which the voter may mistake for friendship. Therefore the seventh hypothesis is that, if the affectual exchange model is valid, satisfactory precinct-level service contacts are more strongly associated with loyalty than are ward-level service contacts.

The eighth and last hypothesis also deals with the client's evaluation of favors under the assumptions of the affectual exchange model. The symbolic value of a service contact depends partly on the cultural presuppositions which the client brings to the transaction. If certain voters think and act in the context of a private-regarding political ethos, then those voters are more likely to interpret receipt of a service from a party agent as signifying an important personal tie. Affectual exchange should operate most effectively with those voters. In chapter 6 it was shown that, of the measures available, the best indicator of political ethos is the religious affiliation of respondents. Hence, the final hypothesis: if the affectual exchange model is valid, satisfactory use will be more strongly associated with loyalty among Catholics than among non-Catholics.

These eight hypotheses are derived from the exchange models of machine support by inductive interpretation, rather than by strict deduction. If one or two hypotheses are not supported by the data, the models are not necessarily invalid. But if we find most of the hypotheses to be false, we must reject the models from which they are derived. If the data do support the hypotheses, we have not proved the models because other theories may exist which could account for the relationships observed.[2] The tests described in this chapter are therefore not "critical" tests in the strict sense of the term, but they do have the potential of disproving the exchange models.

Party Affiliation

Respondents' loyalty to the Democratic party was measured by questions about their party identification and their voting behavior. The interview schedule included the Michigan Survey Research Center party identification instrument (question 18) in which each respondent is asked two questions and then placed on a seven-point scale according to his responses: strong Republican, weak Republican, independent Republican, independent Independent, independent Democrat, weak Democrat, strong Democrat. Voting behavior was the subject of question 19c: "There are so many names on the ballot at election time, it's very difficult to know all about every single candidate. If you went to vote and didn't know much about the candidates for some of the offices, what would you do?" Responses to this question were coded as partisan ("I'd ask the precinct captain for advice," "I always vote a straight ticket," "I'd go for the party on those") or non-partisan ("I'd follow the recommendation of the newspapers," "I always fully inform myself before I vote," "I'd follow the IVI-IPO sample ballot,"[3] "I wouldn't vote for any of them"). The phrasing of the question permitted persons to be counted as loyal even if they were not straight-ticket voters. Democrats who might occasionally split their tickets—to vote for Nixon in 1972 for example—were still counted as loyal if they said they would vote for Democrats in races about which they knew little. The party identification and voting behavior data were combined to yield three categories of party affiliation: *loyal Democrats* were all those who considered themselves strong Democrats, plus those weak or independent Democrats who gave partisan responses to the voting behavior question; *nonloyal Democrats* were those weak or independent Democrats who gave nonpartisan responses; *non-Democrats* were those who considered themselves Republicans or independent Independents. Two dichotomies which represent somewhat different dimensions of party affiliation were generated from these three categories. By combining loyal Democrats and nonloyal Democrats into a single category, a dichotomous *party identification* variable was created (Democrat, non-Democrat). If non-Democrats were excluded, the remaining two categories could be treated as values of a *Democratic loyalty* dichotomy (loyal, nonloyal) applicable only to Democrats. Each of these dichotomies was used as a dependent variable in testing the eight hypotheses derived from the exchange models.

Party Affiliation and Its Correlates

The ward studied is heavily Democratic. Sixty-seven percent of the voter sample considered themselves to be strong, weak, or independent Democrats. Only 18.9 percent identified themselves as Republicans. Twenty-eight percent considered themselves strong Democrats. The latter result is congruent with election outcomes in the ward: organization candidates in the ward's Democratic primary elections usually tally around 6,000 votes, or 27.7 percent of the estimated 21,600 persons registered to vote. Loyal Democrats as defined above constitute 43.4 percent of the voter sample, nonloyal Democrats 23.6 percent, and non-Democrats 33.0 percent.

Since they are dichotomies, the relationship of party identification and Democratic loyalty to other dichotomized variables can be indicated by Kendall's *Q* statistic, a measure of association in two-by-two contingency tables.[4] *Q* indicates the strength and direction of a relationship, rather than its statistical significance. The statistic can vary from −1 to 1, and can be interpreted as "the probability of correctly guessing the order of a pair of cases on one variable once the ordering on the other variable is known."[5]

Table 13 displays the *Q*-statistics for the relationship of party identification and Democratic loyalty to selected variables, each of which was dichotomized for this table.[6] As before, the variables are grouped into indicators of political participation, social status, political ethos, and community attachment.

The political participation indicators seem to relate to party affiliation in contradictory ways. Political efficacy is equally strong among loyal Democrats, nonloyal Democrats, and non-Democrats. Bureaucratic competence is higher among Republicans than among Democrats, and higher among nonloyal Democrats than among loyal Democrats. The political participation index is unrelated to party identification, yet shows a strong negative correlation with Democratic loyalty. These relationships become comprehensible if the nature of the three indices is recalled. The participation index, which

Table 13 Correlates of Party Affiliation

Association of:	Party Identification	Democratic Loyalty
A. with political participation indicators:		
Political efficacy	−.003 (158)	.093 (107)
Bureaucratic competence	−.306 (159)	−.329 (108)
Political participation index	.042 (160)	−.415[b] (109)
B. with social status indicators:		
Occupational status	−.257 (155)	−.462[b] (104)
Educational attainment	−.243 (158)	−.465[b] (108)
C. with political ethos indicators:		
Ethnic status	−.011 (160)	.175 (109)
Religion	.357[a] (160)	.020 (109)
Corruption-acceptance	−.314 (156)	−.001 (107)
D. with community attachment indicators:		
Homeownership	−.299 (160)	−.286 (109)
Length of local residence	.408[b] (160)	.113 (109)
Stage of life cycle	.058 (160)	.080 (109)
Localism index	.185 (160)	−.170 (109)

NOTE: Data in tables 13 to 22 are for combined sample of voters and clients. In these tables entries are Kendall's Q for 2×2 cross-classification of indicated variables. Number of cases is in parentheses. Values of the variables are:

Variable	Category 1	Category 2
Party identification	Democrat	Non-Democrat
Party loyalty	Loyal Democrat	Nonloyal Democrat
Political efficacy	R. scores 2 or more on three-item index	R. scores less than 2
Bureaucratic competence	R. scores 1 or 2 on two-item index	R. scores 0
Educational attainment	One year of college or more	No college
Ethnic status	High status ethnic origin	Low status ethnic origin
Corruption-acceptance	R. scores 2 on two-item index	R. scores less than 2

Values for other variables are given in notes to appendix tables 24 and 25. Non-Democrats are excluded from cross-classifications involving the party loyalty dichotomy.

[a]Chi-square for this relationship significant at the level $p < .10$.
[b]Chi-square for this relationship significant at the level $p < .05$.

primarily comprises behavioral measures, is our best indicator of the respondent's ability to link political action to a stable set of preferences. We see that such ability is uncharacteristic of those Democrats most inclined to vote a straight ticket: it is the ticket-splitting Democrats who are politically most active and aware. The political efficacy index is not as strongly related to Democratic loyalty because it focuses more narrowly on beliefs about the importance of voting, beliefs strongly held even by those who take little other interest in politics. The political participation index is less strongly related to being Republican than is bureaucratic competence because the G.O.P. is so poorly organized at the local level in the ward studied. Republicans tend to be wealthier and better educated, which enhances both their levels of bureaucratic competence and their political participation, but the organized activism of the Democrats offsets the Republican advantage in political participation.

The difference between Republicans and Democrats on scales of wealth and social status is clear in this sample as it is in most studies of party identification in the United States. Even stronger, however, are the status differentials between loyal and nonloyal Democrats, which are the strongest effects in the entire table. Loyal Democrats are disproportionately low in socioeconomic status. In contrast, higher status Democrats identify with the party only weakly and do not use party labels alone as a basis for electoral choice. The status differential may be interpreted as a reflection of both local and national patterns. Chicago's amateur Democratic club movement is preeminently a middle-class movement, while the city's trade unions are strong backers of the Regular Democrats. Nationwide, a pattern has emerged in which better educated voters exhibit less partisanship than poorly educated voters. This pattern contrasts with the findings of early studies of voting behavior, which found strong partisanship to be closely linked with high levels of education, issue-involvement, and political participation.[7]

Among the ethos indicators, the only significant relationship is that between religion and party identification: Catholics are of course more likely to identify with the Democratic party. Neither religion nor the other indicators of political culture is a good predictor of loyalty among the Democrats. The relationship of party affiliation to community attachment indicators is mixed. Long-time residents of the area are very likely to identify themselves as Democrats; this reflects the transiency of the high-rise apartment area of the ward, where the bulk of the Independents and Republicans reside. In contrast, a disproportionate number of homeowners identify themselves as non-Democrats or as nonloyal Democrats; this reflects the linkage of homeownership to higher income. Overall, community attachment as measured by the five-item localism index does not strongly predict either party identification or Democratic loyalty.

In summary, the loyal Democrats in this ward are more likely than other voters to be low in social status, poorly educated, lacking in bureaucratic competence, and politically inactive and uninformed. They are not, however, characterized by low ethnic status, feelings of political powerlessness, or attachment to their community. Their characteristics contrast sharply with those of users of party services, who, as detailed in chapter 6, are high in community attachment and fully representative of all statuses.

Tests of the Exchange Models

Table 14 displays the results by which to test our first hypothesis, which states simply that users are more likely to be loyal than non-users. The *Q*-statistics show that party identification is positively associated with use (Democrats are more likely to be users than are non-Democrats) and Democratic loyalty is negatively associated with use (loyal Democrats are less likely to be users than are non-loyal Democrats). Whether the hypothesis is confirmed or contradicted depends upon which aspect of party affiliation we focus on. If identification with the Democrats is taken to be the source of machine strength, then the exchange models are supported by the data, but if Democratic loyalty is so taken, then

Table 14 Involvement in Service Transactions and Party Affiliation

Association of:	Party Identification	Democratic Loyalty
with . . .		
Use	.193 (160)	−.260 (109)
Satisfactory use	.290 (129)	−.203 (89)
Positive evaluation	.486[a] (107)	−.227 (75)

NOTE: Values of the variables are:

Variable	Category 1	Category 2
Use	User	Nonuser
Satisfactory use	Satisfied user	Nonuser
Positive evaluation	User giving positive evaluation of party agent	Nonuser

Values for other variables are given in note to table 13. Note that satisfied users and users giving positive evaluation are subsets of the user category.

[a]Chi-square for this relationship significant at the level $p < .10$.

the models are not supported. In tests of the other hypotheses we will repeatedly find this divergence of results.

Table 14 also displays the results by which the second hypothesis can be tested. Respondents who reported having requested a service from the alderman, the Democratic committeeman, or a precinct captain were classified as *users;* all others were considered *nonusers.* In the interviews, each user was asked several questions about the service transaction he or she reported. Two of these questions were: "Were you satisfied with what he did for you?" and "What did you think of him after that?" Those who answered the first affirmatively were classified as *satisfied users.* Responses to the second item were coded as positive evaluations ("he's great," "a fine man"), neutral evaluations ("he's O.K., I guess," "same as any politician"), and negative evaluations ("just seeking publicity," "he's no good"). Almost two-thirds of the users were satisfied with the services they received, but fewer than 40 percent gave positive evaluations of the party agents.[8] Presumably, the voter's sense of obligation will be higher in cases where he is satisfied and highest in cases where he thinks positively of the party agent after the service transaction. Table 14 shows that party identification is related to use, satisfaction, and positive evaluation in the way predicted by the exchange models—the percent Democratic increases as nonusers are compared to increasingly obligated groups. However, Democratic loyalty diverges from the hypothesized pattern. All three variables are negatively related to loyalty and the proportion loyal is about the same among Democrats who are users, satisfied users, and users who gave positive evaluations.

Part A of table 15 presents results by which to test the third hypothesis, according to which satisfactory use should be more strongly associated with party affiliation at lower levels of political efficacy. The *Q*-statistics directly contradict the hypothesis: party identification is more strongly associated with satisfactory use at a high level of political efficacy. At a low level of political efficacy, Democratic loyalty is negatively associated with satisfactory use.

Table 15 Satisfactory Use and Party Affiliation, by Level of Political Efficacy and Political Participation

Association of:	Party Identification	Democratic Loyalty
A. with satisfactory use where political efficacy is:		
low	.172 (73)	−.419 (53)
high	.500[a] (56)	.087 (36)
B. with satisfactory use where political participation index is:		
low	.255 (77)	.014 (52)
high	.326 (52)	−.353 (37)

NOTE: Values of the variables are given in notes to tables 13, 14, and 25.
[a]Chi-square for this relationship significant at the level $p < .10$.

In part B of table 15 we find results which invalidate the fourth hypothesis, that satisfactory use should more strongly affect the party affiliation of nonparticipators. The association of party identification with satisfactory use is somewhat lower among those with low political-participation scores than among those with high scores. The *Q*-statistics relating satisfactory use with Democratic loyalty indicate that the percentage of satisfied users who are loyal Democrats is higher among nonparticipators than among participators; however, the percentage of loyal Democrats is just as high among nonparticipators who use no services at all, a fact which scarcely supports the exchange models.

We now come to the hypotheses that relate most directly to the material exchange model. Table 16 shows data relating to the fifth hypothesis, that specific goods will have more influence on party affiliation than general goods, and that special favors will have the strongest influence. The hypothesis is partly supported by the party identification *Q*-statistics, which show that Democratic identification is positively associated with satisfactory specific goods and is independent of satisfactory general goods. However, the association of party identification with satisfactory special favors and with satisfactory routine services is quite similar. As in our tests of the first two hypotheses, Democratic loyalty

Table 16 Satisfactory Use and Party Affiliation, by Type of Service Requested

Association of:	Party Identification	Democratic Loyalty
with . . .		
Satisfactory general goods	−.039 (84)	−.042 (53)
Satisfactory specific goods	.374[a] (119)	−.240 (83)
Satisfactory routine services	.374 (95)	−.336 (64)
Satisfactory special favors	.316 (97)	−.094 (65)

NOTE: Values of the variables are:

Variable	Category 1	Category 2
Satisfactory general goods	Satisfied requester of general goods	Nonuser
Satisfactory specific goods	Satisfied requester of routine services or special favors	Nonuser
Satisfactory routine services	Satisfied requester of routine services	Nonuser
Satisfactory special favors	Satisfied requester of special favors	Nonuser

Values for other variables are given in note to table 13.

[a]Chi-square for this relationship significant at the level $p < .10$.

diverges from the expected pattern. Satisfied Democrats who request specific goods are even less likely to be loyal than satisfied Democrats who request general goods. Neither satisfactory routine services nor satisfactory special favors is positively associated with loyalty.

Table 17 tests the hypothesis that satisfactory use has a stronger affect on party affiliation where bureaucratic competence is low. The *Q*-statistics for party identification accord with the hypothesis; those for Democratic loyalty violate it.

Table 17 Satisfactory Use and Party Affiliation, by Level of Bureaucratic Competence

Association of:	Party Identification	Democratic Loyalty
with satisfactory use where bureaucratic competence is:		
low	.618 (36)	−.238 (29)
high	.275 (93)	−.143 (60)

NOTE: None of the relationships is significant at the level $p < .10$. Values of the variables are given in notes to tables 13 and 14 above.

The hypotheses we have examined so far are not mutually exclusive. Taken singly none of them has proved valid with regard to Democratic loyalty, but it is conceivable that operating jointly they might yield the pattern which the material exchange model predicts. The size of the sample does not permit us to impose simultaneous controls for all the variables which have been hypothesized as specifying the relationship of satisfactory use with Democratic loyalty, but one type of simultaneous control would seem especially promising for the material exchange model. Our third, fourth, and sixth hypotheses have suggested the effects that characteristics of the user have on the level of obligation he or she feels. In contrast, our fifth hypothesis deals with the significance of the type of service received. Is it not possible that patronage relationships develop only in those cases where the most significant type of service is given at a satisfactory level to a voter with the "right" characteristics—that is, a propensity for placing a high value on the service or a low value on his or her vote? Table 18 shows results by which we may test this possibility. We see that there is at least a mild tendency for voters who receive special favors and are low in political efficacy or low in political participation to identify themselves as Democrats; moreover, all the recipients of special favors who were low on the bureaucratic competence index were Democrats. However, we still find no positive relationships between use of services and Democratic loyalty. Even where the characteristics of the voter converge with the nature of the service granted, the material exchange model fails to account even partially for party loyalty among Democrats.

Table 18 Satisfactory Special Favors and Party Affiliation for Requesters with Selected Characteristics

Association of:	Party Identification	Democratic Loyalty
with satisfactory special favors, where:		
A. political efficacy is low	.077 (62)	−.250 (44)
B. political participation is low	.243 (65)	.059 (43)
C. bureaucratic competence is low	1.000 (30)	−.418 (24)

NOTE: None of the relationships is significant at the level $p < .10$. Values of the variables are given in notes to tables 13, 16, and 25.

Let us now examine the propositions which we derived from the affectual exchange model. The seventh hypothesis, that party affiliation will be more strongly related to satisfactory precinct use than to satisfactory ward use, may be tested with the data in table 19. The *Q*-statistics for party identification support the hypothesis but the statistics for Democratic loyalty do not. Loyalty is negatively related to satisfactory service transactions with both types of party agent. There is a higher proportion loyal among satisfied Democratic precinct

Table 19 Satisfactory Use and Party Affiliation by Type of Party Agent

Association of:	Party Identification	Democratic Loyalty
with . . .		
Satisfactory ward use	.192 (103)	−.328 (68)
Satisfactory precinct use	.421 (92)	−.118 (62)

NOTE: None of the relationships is significant at the level p < 10. Values of the variables are:

Variable	Category 1	Category 2
Satisfactory ward use	Satisfied requester of service from alderman or committeeman	Nonuser
Satisfactory precinct use	Satisfied requester of service from precinct captain or worker	Nonuser

Values for other variables are given in note to table 13. Users who received satisfactory services from both ward and precinct agents were classified as satisfied precinct users.

users than among satisfied Democratic ward users, but the proportion loyal is highest among Democratic nonusers.

In table 20 we find some slender support for the eighth hypothesis, that satisfactory use will have a stronger effect on the party affiliation of Catholics than non-Catholics. Among Catholics there is a strong positive relationship between use and party identification and a small positive relationship between use and Democratic loyalty. Because of the small sample size, the latter relationship could easily be due to sampling error, but even if it accurately reflects the association of variables in the ward population, the relationship is substantively insignificant: among the Catholic Democrats 60.9 percent of the satisfied users were loyal to the party, compared to 55.6 percent of the nonusers. Even if we interpret this slight differential in loyalty as being caused by the processes described in the affectual exchange model, we cannot make the case that any substantial amount of party loyalty is generated thereby.

Let us again consider the possibility that variables

Table 20 Satisfactory Use and Party Affiliation, by Religion of Respondent

Association of:	Party Identification	Democratic Loyalty
with satisfactory use where respondent's religion is:		
Roman Catholic	.523 (41)	.109 (32)
Other	.101 (88)	−.375 (57)

NOTE: None of the relationships is significant at the level $p < .10$. Values of the variables are given in notes to tables 13 and 14 above.

which show little effect when taken singly may specify the relationship of party loyalty and service use when taken jointly. Our seventh hypothesis, derived from the affectual exchange model, deals with the type of agent contacted; might this not operate jointly with characteristics of the voters to affect loyalty? As shown in table 21, the relationship of satisfactory precinct use with Democratic loyalty is negative among voters with low political efficacy scores, and near zero among political nonparticipators and Catholics. It is particularly noteworthy that even the small number of Democrats who are Roman Catholics and have received satisfactory services from precinct-level agents are not appreciably more loyal to their party than those Democrats who used no services at all. The affectual exchange model clearly does not account for variation in loyalty among Democrats in the ward.

Implications of the Data

Choosing a Dependent Variable

We have seen that party identification and Democratic loyalty are not related to involvement in service transactions in the same way. None of the eight hypotheses based on the exchange models of machine support is well supported by the data if Democratic loyalty is taken as the dependent variable. But if party identification is used, then some of the hypotheses are well supported. Although the effect of service activities on Democratic

Table 21 Satisfactory Precinct Use and Party Affiliation, for Requesters with Selected Characteristics

Association of:	Party Identification	Democratic Loyalty
with satisfactory precinct use, where:		
A. political efficacy is low	.496 (55)	−.455 (40)
B. political participation is low	.557 (60)	−.053 (41)
C. respondent's religion is Roman Catholic	.250 (26)	.057 (21)

NOTE: None of the relationships is significant at the level $p < .10$. Values of the variables are given in notes to tables 13, 19, and 25.

loyalty is clearly contrary to what the exchange models predict, we cannot from these data alone rule out the possibility that the party identification of voters is influenced by exchange relationships with party agents. We have deferred until now the necessary theoretical task of choosing between party identification and Democratic loyalty as dependent variables. If the latter is chosen, the exchange models are invalid. Does it make sense to choose the former?

I think party identification makes little sense as a dependent variable for tests of the exchange models because its causal linkage to party services is implausible. It is highly doubtful that the kinds of services which the Democratic ward club can provide today[9] would suffice to convert Republicans into Democrats or even facilitate such conversion. Practiced politicians recognize this; they devote little effort to attempts to win over people who identify with the opposition. Studies of American politics have consistently found party identification to be highly stable, persistent from one generation to another, and rooted in the social position of the individual and his immediate forebears. Massive party realignments occasionally occur, manifesting themselves in what political scientists call "critical elections."[10] As Bernard Berelson and his associates found in one of the early studies of voting, over the short term most changes in political position by voters are small shifts in a broad spectrum; conversions are infrequent and usually involve only a small shift in position.[11] In light of these facts, it would be a mistake to take the correlation of party identification with satisfactory use as evidence of influence through exchange.

An alternative interpretation of the correlation is more plausible: it arises through a process of selection governing the use of, and satisfaction with, party services. Where Democrats have control over patronage services, Democratic voters are more likely to know of the availability of Democratic party services than Republicans. They have more frequent contact with party agents because precinct work is concentrated on mobilizing them. Their requests sometimes get more favorable treatment by party agents than similar requests from Republicans. These circumstances increase the likelihood that Democrats will be satisfied users. An additional selection factor is perceptual: Democrats are more likely than Republicans to express satisfaction with services received and to evaluate party agents positively. Non-Democrats are naturally suspicious of the motivations and procedures of Democratic party agents. In fact, over half the dissatisfied users in the combined sample were non-Democrats. I believe that the positive correlation between party identification and satisfactory use results primarily from selection factors such as these, rather than from influence through exchange.

In any event, it is more important to Chicago's Regular Democrats that they effectively generate party loyalty among Democrats than that they convert Republicans into Democrats. With its heavily ethnic, Catholic, working class population, Chicago is natural Democratic territory. In practice, any faction that controls the Democratic vote controls all Chicago elections. To maintain this control, the Regular Democratic Organization need not concern itself with Republicans at all. The touchstone of machine control is regularity, unfaltering acceptance of decisions made by party leaders. The party must prevent Democratic voters from exercising selectivity, so that they vote for candidates designated by party leaders. Any theory of the sources of machine support, including the exchange models under examination here, must explain intra-party loyalty, not party identification.

Loyalty as Simplification

If Democratic loyalty were positively associated with use of party services, we would have to consider the effect of the same kind of selection process that links service use to party identification. But the association of use with loyalty is consistently negative. How is this association to be interpreted?

Clearly, the association cannot be a directly causal one. It is not plausible that use of services would somehow cause Democrats to become less loyal. It also makes little sense to propose the reverse causal relationship: that party loyalty itself reduces the propensity to use party services. Yet the data show clearly that independent Democrats use party services more frequently than loyal Democrats do. To account for this fact, we must consider whether factors which determine people's degree of loyalty may also have an affect on their usage of services. What makes people into party loyalists?

By aggregating diverse interests into an effective whole, political parties serve an important function for a democratic political system. They also serve the individual, whose duty it is as a citizen to choose between alternatives at the polls. When a voter identifies with the positions of one particular party, the party affiliation of the candidates can serve to guide his choice. The informed voter has other information on the basis of which he makes a choice. He may believe that his own interests are advanced when the unity of his party is maintained, in which case he will strongly favor candidates from his own party. Party loyalty, however, may not always override other considerations: the voter may exercise selectivity on the basis of what he knows about a candidate's record, campaign promises, ethnicity, sex, looks, or other individual characteristics. I do not wish to imply that ticket-splitting is the only rational response open to an informed voter in our two-party system, or that it is wrong to vote a straight ticket. The point is that selectivity only makes sense when the voter has information about individual candidates which he regards as reliable.[12] When the voter lacks such information, he must either abstain from making a choice or find a simpler basis for his choice. For some, this basis is ethnicity, as they judge it from the names of candidates on the ballot.[13] For many, the simpler basis is party loyalty.

If party loyalty serves the cognitive function of simplifying electoral choice, then the kind of people most likely to be loyal are those who lack reliable information on which to base selectivity. The information about local politics that appears most reliable is that which derives from personal experience and the experience of trusted acquaintances. For some local residents, however, Chicago is a "mass society" which provides them with no personal linkage to the powers which govern their lives. The mass media devote little attention to the politics of the neighborhoods, and published political commentaries represent a tangle of conflicting opinions which are of little guidance to those with no other information sources. Some residents are able to develop ties through which they can make their voices heard or at least inform themselves about political issues and personalities. Since de Tocqueville, it has been recognized that voluntary associations in a democracy provide a mediating and linking structure which permit the effective and intelligent participation of citizens in the political system.[14] Members of voluntary organizations—even organizations with explicitly nonpolitical goals—are likely to become acquainted with others who are better informed than they about local politics. They can discuss politics[15] and may even meet their local political leaders. They are therefore less in need of a simplifying principle such as party loyalty to guide their voting.

The survey results reflect the association of organizational membership with party loyalty. Respondents were asked if they belonged to any block groups, community organizations, political clubs, or service organizations. Almost none said they belonged to political clubs, but 4.7 percent of the voter sample claimed membership in block groups, the same percentage belong to community organizations, and 29.2 percent belong to service organizations (groups other than a union, church, block club or community organization). Party identification had little association with membership. In the combined sample of voters and clients, there were 30.0 percent non-Democrats among those who belonged to no organizations, compared to 34.3 percent non-Democrats among those claiming membership in at least one organization. Party loyalty, however, was strongly associated with membership: among Democrats in the combined sample, 67.7 percent of the nonmembers were loyal, compared to 43.5 percent of the members (*Q* for membership and party loyalty is −.444).

As mentioned in chapter 6, membership in either local or nonlocal organizations is correlated with use of party services (*Q* is .531). To some extent this correlation reflects differential recruitment: people who are knowledgeable and involved enough in their communities to hold organizational memberships are more likely to make requests to local politicians. However, there is also a truly causal element in the relationship, in that members learn through their organizations to articulate their demands for services.[16] Local voluntary groups are vehicles through which group demands are voiced, but they also foster concern with neighborhood problems and encourage the expression of individual needs directly to politicians.

Voluntary organization membership thus is an important prior variable which may account for the negative association between party loyalty and involvement in service transactions. Membership in voluntary organizations provides the individual with the information and the contacts he needs to exercise selectivity at the polls and to make known his desires for services from party agents. The tendency of independent Democrats to use party services more than loyal Democrats is a spurious result of their higher rate of membership in voluntary organizations. The effect of organizational

Table 22 Selected Types of Use and Democratic Loyalty, Controlling for Organizational Memberships

Association of:	Democratic Loyalty
A. with use	
among voluntary organization	
members	−.404 (46)
nonmembers	.048 (63)
B. with satisfactory use	
among voluntary organization	
members	−.429 (34)
nonmembers	.220 (55)
C. with satisfactory precinct use	
among voluntary organization	
members	−.200 (16)
nonmembers	−.045 (46)
D. with satisfactory special favors	
among voluntary organization	
members	−.286 (21)
nonmembers	.292 (44)

NOTE: None of the relationships is significant at the level $p < .10$. Values of the membership variable are:

Variable	Category 1	Category 2
Organizational membership	Member of one or more block, community, or service organizations other than a church or union	Member of no such organizations

Values of other variables given in notes to tables 13, 14, 16, and 19 above.

membership is apparent in table 22. Loyalty and use are independent among non-members of organizations. Satisfactory use is positively associated with loyalty among nonmembers. This is in contrast to the negative association we found when organizational memberships were not controlled. Loyalty is independent of satisfactory precinct use and positively associated with satisfactory special favors among nonmembers, in contrast to the weak negative associations obtained without the control. The apparent negative association of loyalty with use thus reflects the fact that Democratic members of voluntary associations are likely to be selective voters and likely to request services from the party.

Conclusion

According to the material and affectual exchange models of machine support, involvement in satisfactory service transactions fosters loyalty to the patronage party organization. Data from the survey of ward residents show that users of party services are *less* loyal than nonusers. When we control for the user's sense of obligation, the type of party agent, the type of service requested, or characteristics of the user which should in theory govern perceptions of favors and votes, we still do not find that service activities promote party loyalty. This negative result is obtained under the assumptions of both the material and affectual exchange models. Democrats are more likely to be involved in service transactions than Republicans, but this may be dismissed as the result of selection factors rather than influence through exchange. Although party loyalty and use of services are negatively associated in the total sample, they are independent among those ward residents who belong to no voluntary organizations. Moreover, Democratic loyalists have low social standing and low rates of political participation. These findings lend support to the theory that for those voters who lack personal linkages to the local political system, party loyalty functions as a simplifying guide for electoral choice.

One final set of statistics will sum up the inability of the exchange models to account for the loyalty of the Democratic voters in this ward. It has been noted that, of the ward's voters, 33.0 percent have used party services and 43.4 percent are loyal Democrats. Only 10.3 percent of the ward's voters, however, are *both* satisfied users and loyal Democrats. That is, of the substantial number of voters who think of themselves as strong Democrats or who would vote for Democratic candidates about whom they knew nothing, less than one-fourth report receiving a satisfactory service from any Democratic party agent. This is hardly the "controlled" electorate we read about in descriptions of the classic urban machines. Having found that the party's service activities fail to influence directly the party loyalty of the voters, we can turn to a consideration of the strategies by which the party actually exerts its influence.

Part 4 The Patronage Party in Machine Politics

Eight The Struggle for Support: Symbol and Substance in Ward Politics

The preceding parts of this book have described the considerable investment made by the ward club in service activities on behalf of ward residents, and demonstrated that the partisan loyalties of individuals who receive favors are not influenced in the way that the traditional models of machine support postulate. These findings raise two important questions: if favors do not generate votes, how does the patronage party sustain the support of the electorate? And why does the party invest such great effort in activities which do not have the consequences its members anticipate? The latter question will be taken up in the next chapter. In this chapter I will attempt to answer the more basic of the two questions: how does the machine succeed?

To answer this question I shall draw on qualitative data I gathered as a participant observer of ward politics over a period of three years. These data strongly suggest that the key to the success of the ward club is the participation of party agents in the public political life of the local community. Existing studies of machine politics have largely ignored the public behavior of patronage politicians, except to ascribe to them a tendency to avoid "issues." Because these studies treat the party's electoral support as a controlled vote, they naturally assume that patronage politicians need to devote little effort to the public activities by which other politicians win support. However, the politicians in the ward I studied commit tremendous time and effort to the meetings, rallies, ceremonies, conferences, and confrontations which are so much a part of local public life. They are adept at generating support at public gatherings and are usually glad to participate in them. The patronage politicians can successfully dominate decision-making and influence election outcomes in the ward because they deal successfully with a continuous stream of demands from local groups. They are able to respond to these groups in ways that win support away from the less successful politicians and parties that actively compete for voter loyalties.

I do not wish to claim that machine politics is indistinguishable from reform politics at the ward level. Rather, I begin with the same assumption that guided the analysis of the ward club's compliance structure: because the club is a patronage organization it pursues goals somewhat at variance with the public interest and operates in ways condemned by those who hold democratic ideals. Moreover, the structure of the citywide machine is unusually tight because it uses material incentives to secure compliance from its members. Therefore the ward-level patronage politician acts under powerful constraints which closely limit the public methods he can employ to generate local support. The politicians I observed sometimes used tactics of which the machine did not approve, but their breaches of the party's informal rules were fully as illustrative of the nature of machine politics as were the instances in which these norms were obeyed. Thus, despite the uniqueness of the setting, the events I observed provide a basis for theoretical generalization about how the machine continues to succeed.

I will first discuss the conflicting tactical alternatives among which ward politicians must choose as they compete for support. In practice, they employ a combination of tactics which I call the *compound supportive strategy.* The effectiveness of any strategy depends partly on the context in which it is employed; I will set forth the structural conditions that contributed to the success of the compound supportive strategy in the ward I studied.

I will then turn to an analytic description of some representative tactics included in this strategy, paying special attention to the ability of patronage politicians to use symbols as a substitute for substance in their public political actions.

Contrasting Tactics

Since our constitutional forms mandate regularly occurring competitive elections, politicians at the local level—like those at higher levels—require broad popular support if they are to stay in office. The actions of politicians are consciously calculated to generate electoral support. There are several kinds of incentives which affect the way people vote, and several kinds of people whose support the politician may seek; it is therefore useful to distinguish several kinds of tactics which politicians can employ in the struggle for public support.

One important dimension that differentiates among tactics is the degree to which they involve actions related to controversial political "issues." Some tactics involve actions that are *issue-oriented* while other tactics are *issue-free.*[1] But which of the myriad conflicts and disagreements that are affected by the politician's actions are issues, rather than private quarrels? The most apparent property of issues is that they are controversies which involve large numbers of people; they are the conflicts which—at least potentially—arouse masses of citizens into action. But as Banfield points out, the potential for such arousal exists "precisely because the community believes the public interest is at stake or can be persuaded that it is at stake."[2] Thus group interests—even the interests of a large or powerful group or those of several competing groups—can be at stake in matters that are not really issues. It follows, then, that issue-free tactics are not limited to allocations of specific material inducements, but can involve allocations of general goods.

It has often been stated that patronage parties tend to follow an issue-free strategy.[3] It is true that the leaders and active workers in political machines are not motivated as much by ideology or principal as by material inducements; indeed, this is a defining attribute of the machine. However, as the earlier parts of this book have made plain, it is a serious error to presume that the incentives offered to party agents are of like kind to those used to generate voter support. The assumption that patronage parties avoid reference to issues in their public appeals carries implications about the motivations of their supporters and the linkages among them. We have explored these implications in discussing the traditional models of machine support: these models imply, in essence, that machine supporters either lack political morality or subscribe to a private-regarding ethos. But certain fundamental notions of the public interest are in fact institutionalized at all levels in the voting public, and the actions and communications of patronage politicians frequently have direct and purposive relevance—both substantive and symbolic—to the issues that such notions define. The informed and critical observer sees many of the patronage politicians' actions as detrimental to the collective good and contradictory to their rhetoric, but most of the voters are either unaware of such actions or judge them more favorably. The machine's stance on issues may be inconsistent and deceitful, but the defense of its venality from repudiation by the voters requires that it constantly demonstrate its concern for the collective welfare. Unless we presume that the political values of machine supporters are somehow deviant, issue-oriented tactics are not only compatible with the machine politician's successful strategy but essential to it.

What, then, is distinctive about the tactics used by the patronage politician? It is that he limits his efforts at winning electoral support to actions and expressions that reflect support for the central power-holders who control both the city government and the citywide party. I will refer to these as *supportive* tactics. The organization closely defines what actions its members may take, and it can strongly sanction deviations from its definition of regularity by withholding the flow of inducements over which it exercises formal and informal control. No elected official can afford to have his constituents withhold their support, but the patronage politician aligned with a successful machine is also markedly dependent on the exercise of power from above.[4] There always are groups of voters around who are dissatisfied with the status quo, voters whose support a local politician could secure by actions or statements which appealed to their perceptions of the public's interests or their own. However, the actions which some of these groups call for would directly threaten the leaders of the patronage party—or threaten the interest groups and constituencies which these leaders are obliged to protect in order to maintain their position of power. The machine politician must scrupulously avoid such *oppositional* tactics.

The distinction between supportive and oppositional tactics can be combined with the distinction between issue-oriented and issue-free tactics to yield four types of support-generating tactics among which local politicians must choose. As we have noted, according to the traditional models of machine support the strategy of the patronage politician is limited to issue-free, supportive tactics. His arch-rival, the reform politician, specializes in issue-oriented, oppositional tactics. Professional politicians outside the patronage party (in Chicago, the small Regular Republican contingent) attempt to build support primarily with issue-free, oppositional tactics. It is my contention that the importance of the fourth type—issue-oriented, supportive tactics—in generating support for patronage politicians has not heretofore been given sufficient recognition. Banfield and Wilson have noted in several works[5] that some leaders of big-city machines, notably the late Mayor Daley of Chicago, have used such tactics—appointing "blue-ribbon" commissions and building conspicuous public works—in order to court the loyalties of the outer-city and suburban voters who are becoming increasingly significant in metropolitan politics. Banfield and Wilson presume that the machine wins support in the inner city through affectual exchange.

However, in the ward I studied—one which included a slum district—Democratic politicians pursued a compound supportive strategy which included frequent and efficacious use of both issue-oriented and issue-free tactics supportive of the city machine.

The compound strategy is a problematic one for the practicing politician. This is because the two dimensions of variation among possible tactics, although analytically distinct, are linked together in a fundamental way. By definition, the patronage party pursues the material interests of its members; if this characteristic is to distinguish the machine from other types of political party in any meaningful sense, it implies that the patronage party works against the public interest in important ways. It follows that actions which appeal to people's concerns with the public interest have a tendency to arouse them against the machine. Not all issue-oriented tactics are oppositional tactics, but the most controversial of them are. The category of issue-oriented actions supportive of the machine is a constricted one which patronage politicians must exploit with great care. Indeed, in the ward I studied the use of such tactics was, as will be seen below, a continuous point of controversy among the leaders of the ward club.

This brings us to a third distinction among vote-getting tactics—that between substantive and symbolic action. As Murray Edelman has eloquently argued, political leaders maintain their authority not only by allocating goods, services, and power, but by skillfully manipulating symbols that convey "what large masses of men need to believe about the state to reassure themselves."[6] Political action can be seen as a type of symbolic interaction, in which the politician mentally takes the roles of his constituents in order to assess the meanings his actions will communicate. The use of symbols by politicians goes beyond the function of upholding the legitimacy of state and regime; legitimate regimes use symbolic acts as inducements for contributions of support just as they use substantive allocations.

In theory, then, the politician can choose among eight

types of vote-getting tactics: a symbolic and a substantive version of each of the four types of tactics identified above. In each situation, his choice is governed primarily by his comparative assessment of the costs and benefits that each type of tactic will generate for him. The benefits of symbolic tactics compared to substantive ones (i.e., their efficacy in generating support) depend on the psychic needs of potential supporters, which vary in turn with the social structural context: "where public understanding is vague and information rare, interests in reassurance will be all the more potent and all the more susceptible to manipulation by political symbols."[7] The politician measures the costs of alternative tactics in terms of their potential negative impact on his support from above and below. As we have seen, any recurring use of tactics defined by the patronage party as oppositional will cost the politician the party's support. Because of the party's venal nature, substantive action on most issues is potentially oppositional; the politician is less likely to bear this cost if he takes symbolic action with regard to issues. As we shall see below, the conditions in inner city wards are such that these symbolic acts can be highly efficacious in generating support. The compound supportive strategy of the patronage politician thus comprises not only issue-free tactics but a significant amount of issue-oriented action, much of which is more symbolic than substantive.

Patronage politicians differ in the degree to which they employ symbols associated with newer styles of urban politics, but all make regular use of symbolic, issue-oriented, supportive tactics as a relatively costless means of generating support. As was described in the analysis of aldermanic service activities in chapter 4 above, symbol often substitutes for substance when issue-free action is undertaken. But such substitution is even more frequent in the sensitive and constricted realm of issue-oriented supportive tactics. This does not mean that the machine's central powers would be indifferent to symbolic issue-oriented actions which they saw as oppositional (for example, participating in a public protest against a decision by the mayor). On the contrary, citywide leaders constantly monitor both symbolic and substantive public actions of local politicians for what they reveal about the loyalty of the latter.

Strategies in Conflict

The party's compound strategy is partly determined by the nature of the patronage party and the values of the electorate. Within these constraints, however, important variations in strategy are possible, based on differences in the personalities of politicians and differences in their power vis-à-vis the party and the voters. The party's hierarchical, secretive, and tightly organized structure conceals from view the competitive jockeying for power which is an inherent part of its internal politics. The struggle for power becomes public during primary fights and contested elections for the office of committeeman.[8] The competitors in these struggles create their own strategies by combining the alternative vote-getting tactics I have defined. In the ward I studied there was pervasive but unpublicized conflict between practitioners of somewhat different compound strategies.

The alderman with whom I worked considered himself to be a Regular Democrat, but his relationship to other party leaders was one of constant tension and occasional intense conflict. Young and highly energetic, he had won his first aldermanic race handily with the support of the ward club. During the campaign, he had deemphasized his Regular Democratic ties by organizing support through an ad hoc "citizen's committee" with its own storefront office. Once elected, he moved into the party's ward office but continued to play down his partisan ties in public.

While maintaining a broadly supportive stance toward the Regular Democrats, the alderman persistently used support-generating tactics that went beyond the issue-free, supportive strategy mandated by the unwritten rules of the organization.[9] He occasionally absented himself from the council floor during key votes to avoid having to take an illiberal public stand. Discontented with a passive legislative role, he introduced substantive legislation in his own name rather than submitting his proposals privately to the party leadership for introduction by the mayor. He deliberately sought publicity in citywide media. He made political speeches in wards other than his own without first securing the approval of the commiteemen of those wards. He did not scrupulously avoid contact with Independent politicians. He publicly criticized some practices of the city agencies that serviced his ward. In his role as ombudsman for ward residents, he sometimes worked against the interests of influential party contributors. He refused to include his party affiliation on any of the numerous giveaway items he imprinted with his name, in the newsletter he distributed to residents, or in his campaign literature.

The tension the alderman's activities created for the more traditional leaders of the ward club is well illustrated in the following incident: At a cocktail party in the alderman's home, I approached Ken, the president of the ward club, and Billy, who acted as the committeeman's driver and companion. I heard the two discussing a new building under construction in the ward's high-rise area. Joining them, I mentioned that the alderman had just sent a letter to the Streets Department downtown which would delay the granting of driveway permits for the site. This was part of the alderman's response to local residents who were organizing resistance to the construction of high-rise buildings. Both men were dismayed by the news. "We'll just have to talk to him about that!" said Ken. "That's incredible!" said Billy. "Maybe we better let the committeeman know about this." Ken informed me, wide-eyed, that the principal investor in the new high-rise was a close associate of Mayor Daley himself. Ken and Billy were astonished, but quite ready to believe that the alderman would take such an action. I realized at this point that we were talking of two different buildings. The driveway stop order did not pertain to the mayor's associate's building. The confusion was cleared up, and their consternation was somewhat relieved.

This misunderstanding illustrates the importance which members of the party attach to avoiding oppositional tactics, and suggests how easily supportive, issue-oriented tactics can lead to oppositional ones. The alderman's use of the high-rise issue to generate support was acceptable to the club leaders as long as it did not directly threaten the party—but they were keeping a nervous watch over what he was doing.

For the ward committeeman and other leaders of the club, the alderman's issue-oriented activities were a burden, an embarrassment, and an affront. His frenetic efforts to gain voter support generated a great deal of work which overloaded the staff and strained the office resources. The alderman paid no rent or other business expenses to the ward club while he used the ward office as his own. The committeeman considered him a freeloader and repeatedly tried to limit his use of the phone. The committeeman and his staff viewed the alderman's intransigent misbehavior as, at best, opportunism. He was distrusted and disliked. Of course, the committeeman had the option of expelling the alderman from the office and withholding from him the support of the ward organization. But he apparently recognized that the alderman enhanced the public image of the ward club and that he had become a political power with whom continued alliance was profitable. Thus he was not "dumped"—only harangued, harassed, and treated as an outsider.[10]

The troublesome alderman also ran afoul of the leaders of the citywide party organization. He was not given good city council committee assignments. His proposed reform ordinances were buried in committee or stripped of all substantive content before passage. On several occasions he was publicly criticized by party leaders, one of whom once announced to the newspapers that he had "put on the black hat," that is, deserted the Regular ranks. Alderman Thomas Keane, then city council floor leader, privately reprimanded him for failing to support the mayor on all issues. The staff members of the more powerful city council committees resisted his attempts to find out the status of ordinances he had proposed. Through interpersonal cues—who would talk with him, where he was seated at luncheons, whom he had to wait to see, what inside knowledge was shared with him—the alderman was put on notice by party leaders that his status as a Regular was in jeopardy.

The alderman and committeeman each tried to modify the other's political strategy, without much success. For the first two years of his first term, the alderman worked full time, instead of devoting his energies to a more financially rewarding career as do most members of the city council. The committeeman and other Regulars did not approve of this choice, apparently fearing that the alderman's commitment of time and effort would make his issue-oriented tactics more effective and potentially threatening to the party's central powers. They tried to persuade him to take up other employment, and he was often greeted with the jibe, "Hey, alderman, when ya gonna get a job?" The committeeman repeatedly told the alderman to act more like a Regular or be labeled an outsider. At one point of crisis he threw forth the challenge: "Are you for us or against us?" The alderman's verbal affirmations of loyalty were not sufficient; they had to be accompanied by deeds that were in keeping with a wholly supportive political strategy.

For his part, the alderman tried to persuade the committeeman that the "old" politics was no longer effective, especially during George McGovern's campaign for the presidency. After McGovern won the Democratic presidential nomination, the ward club leaders deliberated on how they should act. Since McGovern's forces had unseated Daley's Illinois delegation at the national Democratic convention in Miami Beach, there existed some possibility that the mayor would construe vigorous support of McGovern as disloyalty, but he did not clearly state his expectations. The alderman pressed for decisive action; he proposed that a McGovern campaign headquarters be established in the ward office. He talked about how important McGovern's social programs would be to the residents of the ward. The committeeman maintained that people would remain loyal to the Democratic party because of its long liberal tradition, making it unnecessary to link the Regulars with McGovern. He listed the accomplishments of past Democratic presidents. The alderman characterized this as "ancient history," stressing the need to respond to the changed demands of the citizenry. The committeeman's executive aide sided with the alderman, but the committeeman turned them down. He did speak in praise of McGovern at the opening of his separate ward campaign headquarters, and he cooperated halfheartedly with McGovern's organization during the campaign. In this exchange and others I observed, it was clear that the alderman had some influence on the ward boss, leading him, if only by example, to make more extensive use of issue-oriented tactics.

The conflicting strategies of the two politicians caused each to try to reduce the power of the other. The committeeman and his lieutenants pressed the alderman to relinquish his city council seat and run for a seat in the state legislature, a post he regarded as far less desirable. On a more petty level, the committeeman would regularly remove the promotional items which the alderman placed in the windows of the ward office and his staff would "forget" to turn on the lights which illuminated the alderman's name on the ward office sign. There were times when the alderman would deliberately make the committeeman appear unintelligent or uninformed when the two spoke at the same gathering. The two men often praised each other in public and at ward club gatherings, but it was at best an uneasy coexistence.

The competitive struggle of these political allies reveals something of the social forces that determine the vote-getting strategies of patronage politicians. Observers of such struggles, including some of the participants with whom I worked, tend to understand them in terms of competing "styles" that are grounded in the social class and cultural backgrounds of politicians and their constituents. The struggle appears at times as the clash of fundamentally different value-systems. Yet the marriage of styles that occurred in this ward suggests that the politician's choice of tactics is determined more by the pressures from those above and below him than by his moral predilections. The patronage politician must have support from both the voters and the party leaders, and issue-free tactics alone are often insufficient to secure support from below. Each politician develops his own personal approach, and Regulars sometimes disagree on what strategy is appropriate. The ward-level patronage politician is under considerable stress. Those under the greatest stress are those who, like the alderman with whom I worked, are most dependent on their superiors in the party for power resources, and have among their constituents no single dominant group with which they enjoy close ethnic or communal ties.

During the time of my fieldwork there were several other ambitious freshmen in the city council who felt similar pressures. Their collective attempts to gain greater freedom for themselves in the council's operations attracted attention in the metropolitan press.[11] These were men with polish, "attractiveness," and some fluency in the language of the "new politics." They used these attributes and skillful manipulation of the press to create a popular image of concern with the public interest. They remained reliably discreet and loyal to the party's leaders at the same time that they pressed for enhancement of their power position within the party. The party hierarchy responded with resistance and anger, and ultimately only a few of the dissidents gained substantially from their small rebellion. But because of the power base they were able to generate through their issue-oriented yet supportive tactics, they were not expelled from the organization. I do not have sufficient evidence by which to judge whether issue-oriented supportive tactics have always been an important part of the strategy of rising patronage politicians. However, these tactics are clearly an important element of the compound strategy used by Chicago's new generation of Regular Democrats. Given the political conditions of the 1970s, the party and its Young Turks need each other. Effective appeal to salient issues brought outcast Regular Jane Byrne to the city's highest office in 1979, and brought the established party leaders to court her support.

Background Conditions

How is it possible for the Regulars to maintain the support of large numbers of voters without making more substantive responses to demands that the public interest be advanced? The success of their compound supportive strategy rests partly on the skill with which they use symbolic tactics, which will be examined more closely later in this chapter. The successful interaction of politicians with the public has a structural basis as well. The success of their strategy is made possible by the ecological setting of the city ward, the interests of other community leaders, and the interests of the electorate itself.

Ecological Setting

The sheer size of the city and the fact that the ward constitutes but a small fraction of its area help keep ward-level politics separate from substantive interests of the citywide electorate. The official agencies which provide services to the ward are responsible to a citywide clientele. The important interest groups to which downtown decision-makers respond are not geographically concentrated in any single ward. Those who have power at the ward level generally have little clout downtown. Thus the political struggles that take place in the ward have little real consequence for the larger question of who will benefit from the way the city is governed. If the ward were a separate self-governing unit there would be far more pressure on its leaders to offer substantive solutions for matters involving the public interest. This fact has long been recognized; it provides the rationale for the replacement of the ward system with at-large constituencies, as advocated by the municipal reform movement in the United States.

Differentiation and segregation of population are hallmarks of the urban setting. But the boundaries of political districts such as wards rarely coincide with those of "natural areas" populated by people and institutions with distinctive characteristics.[12] The result is that wards typically are socially heterogeneous and politically fragmented.[13] These cleavages are sharper than those in autonomous communities. There is far more discontinuity in the city ward, since it encompasses but a few spatially proximate fragments of a larger and more complex system of stratification and segregation. The sharp divergence of interests among groups in the ward places the ward politician in a difficult position with respect to issues and group interests. Questions of social reform and allocations of goods among competing local groups are likely to be highly controversial. The politician will lose the support of one or another divergent group no matter what substantive position he takes. When the constituency is heterogeneous, substantive tactics involve high costs in support from below.

The spatial structure of the metropolitan housing market fosters the inner-city politician's avoidance of substantive, issue-oriented tactics. As American cities have grown and deconcentrated, people of lower status have tended to concentrate in the central cities and the middle class in the suburbs.[14] Large areas of the central cities are now politically deprived, with disproportionately few of their residents included among the better-educated, higher-income, politically efficacious citizens of the metropolis.[15] The ward politician operates in a context where relatively few people possess coherent political belief-systems or the information by which to make decisions based on such beliefs.[16] Of course each community has its elite, but in inner-city wards ignorance, apathy, and narrow localism are pervasive. In such a context, symbolic actions are easily substituted for substantive actions because people lack the expertise and the information by which to distinguish the two, and because, as Edelman suggests, such distance from politics enhances people's need for symbolic reassurance.[17]

The diversity of the population of the ward I studied and the poverty of some of its neighborhoods were described in chapter 2 above. Because of the ward's lack of autonomy, its heterogeneity, and its political deprivation, there is a great deal of apathy in its political life. The meetings at which citizens voice their demands and politicians make their responses are rarely well attended; the "average people" of the community are notably absent. The same activists attend gathering after gathering. Relationships between members of the small but active cohort tend to become regularized as successive problems are dealt with. Real cleavages exist, but most activist leaders realize that to arouse the public over oppositional issues will not advance their cause. Politics at the community level is therefore boring much of the time; participants are aware of the existing power balance and know the outcome of the decisionmaking processes in advance. Most task-oriented gatherings consist of a halfhearted discussion that is little more than a time-consuming ritual. When ordinary citizens who are not among the active circle do speak at these meetings, their statements or questions usually reflect a hopelessly uninformed or narrowly self-interested point of view. These inputs present no substantive challenge to the leadership—indeed they help legitimate the decisionmaking process. Those activists who do attempt to arouse "the people" achieve at most a small following.[18] In this apathetic and diffuse setting, substantive issue-oriented tactics are not essential for the maintenance of power.

Interests of Other Leaders

The use of symbols by patronage politicians serves some interests of community leaders outside the party. Public decisions are justified in terms of "what's best for our community," "the needs of all our citizens," "the future of this area," "the right thing to do." In public, leaders usually discuss their differences in a vocabulary of respectful discourse; they may disagree but they take care to make each other look important.[19] When decisions are made and publicly justified by deference to venerable symbols, the entire leadership benefits, including those who accept a decision only after fighting for a different outcome.

The opposition leadership shares with the Regulars an interest in the continued management of potential destructive conflict. Extreme polarization is not the goal of any of the established leaders, although those not aligned with the machine do seek to make oppositional issues public. When radical leaders seem within reach of too much power, the liberal Independent and Regular

Democratic leaders quietly ally to neutralize the threat. Despite their traditional rivalry, both groups view the radical activists and their followers as "irresponsible," since they seem to lack regard for the stake established leaders and others have in continued order. Given the cleavages within the ward's population, they judge a political leadership that avoids substantive action on some issues to be preferable to one that addresses issues which cannot be peaceably reconciled.

Most of the local community leaders seek to "improve" the community, that is, reduce crime, reverse the process of housing deterioration, improve the local economic climate, and upgrade local service facilities. They disagree about how these goals should be achieved. Some would improve the area by excluding present residents whom they regard as disreputable. Others want all present residents to enjoy the benefits of progress. The Regulars show little commitment to the poor, but they do work for the general goal of local improvement. Even the community leaders who feel solidarity with the poorer residents sense this. The belief is widely held that city services would rapidly deteriorate if Independent politicians gained control of the ward. Community leaders sometimes refrain from raising oppositional issues because the party's program advances their general goal.[20]

Community leaders also appreciate the ability of the Regulars to defend the community from others within the party. The party allows ward-level politicians to lobby for their local areas and to resist moves by others in the party which adversely affect their constituents. After all, some oppositional issues cannot be ignored. For example, there was a storm of protest from groups in the ward when the local branch of the city college system planned to expand, a move which would have required the demolition of scores of apartment buildings. The committeeman intervened. In private meetings with other Regular leaders, including the head of the college system, he worked out a compromise entailing a more modest expansion and far less destruction of housing. The Independents and some radicals joined the Regulars in ratifying the compromise. It was the most the community could hope for and it was certainly more than the local leaders outside the ward club could have achieved without the committeeman's help.

Interests of the Electorate

The interests and conscious concerns of the local politician's constituency are generally congruent with a strategy that avoids oppositional issues. The fact is that local politicians are empowered to respond only to a few of the strongly felt needs of urban dwellers, and these do not include concerns that can easily be linked to the public interest. It makes no sense for a local group to express its demands as oppositional issues unless it can elicit the support of a larger bloc of voters. To do this, the group must publicize its specific goals in terms of general goals which are more widely shared. A local group's goal—a new stop sign, additional police protection, a zoning change—is not necessarily of benefit to those outside the immediate locale and may indeed be against their interests. Recognizing this fact, the citywide news media treat most local demands as unnewsworthy. The mass media are unwilling to provide the needed access to broader publics and those publics are unresponsive to localized concerns. Agitation arouses more opposition than support. Thus local groups tend to separate their demands from the broader questions of power, resource allocation, and the public interest, sparing local politicians from having to make substantive responses to issues.

The support ward residents give to the patronage party suggests that they are usually more concerned with what services the local community receives than with the means by which those services are provided. Banfield and Wilson maintain that a fundamental culturally-based value difference separates the "public-regarding" citizens who oppose machine politics as inefficient and unfair from the "private-regarding" citizens who support machine politics despite its ill effects on others.[21] Their view is that a community elects Regular Democrats because its residents lack a sense of moral responsibility for outsiders. My data suggest an alternative formulation which stresses voters' interests instead of their values. Those who participate in local elections and decision-making processes are those most attached to the local community. Strong local attachment—being a settled resident—causes strong concern with the quality of local services. Local notables support patronage politicians not because they care less than other people about official corruption but because they care more about local services. People who lack local attachment, transient residents and those with highly cosmopolitan orientations, fail to participate effectively in local politics. The correlation of community attachment with involvement in local politics[22] makes the patronage politician's compound supportive strategy more likely to succeed.

Continuity of political commitments over time also contributes to the success of this strategy. Certain economic and ethnic groups have historically been loyal to the Democratic party and today continue to define it as best representing their interests. Party loyalties tend to be stable in individuals and in groups. Gosnell pointed out that in Chicago elections of the 1930s, there was great continuity of Democratic strength based on the belief that the Hoover regime was responsible for the Depression.[23] The New Deal and subsequent reform programs of Democratic administrations have reinforced the notion that the Democratic party is "the party of the little man." In a ward populated by racial and ethnic minority group members and working-class people, the Democrats are at an advantage. Candidates with Democratic endorsement will win unless oppositional issues dominate voter choice. It is sufficient, then, for patronage politicians to foster political quiescence by dealing only symbolically with the issues that divide Democrats and Republicans.

The background conditions described in the preceding pages prevail in many city neighborhoods, and they underlie the common tendency of local community leaders to emphasize compromise over conflict and to work for the perpetuation of the status quo.[24] The presence of a highly organized patronage party is not required for community politicians to avoid substantive issue-oriented tactics. But a political machine does require an environment in which its distinctive strategy can work. The structure of interests in the ward thus facilitates the patronage party's hegemony, but does not suffice to explain it.

Tactics

Given the ecological conditions and the constellation of interests which the patronage party is able to serve, party politicians must still legitimate themselves and win the support of voters.[25] By nature the patronage party cannot pursue a coherent program of substantive issue-oriented activity that would elicit ideological commitment from the voters. Instead, party politicians manage public impressions of their character and their actions through a variety of tactics, the most important of which are either issue-free or primarily symbolic. They promote an image of themselves that accords with the evaluative standards of their constituents: they represent themselves as concerned with the local community and effective in acting on its behalf. The tactics they use are not limited to the intense activity of election campaigns. During campaigns, speeches are made, "coffees" held, rallies engineered, pamphlets distributed, and posters displayed, while precinct workers canvass the neighborhoods, trying to persuade people to vote for the party's candidates. But these efforts can accomplish little more than mobilizing partisan support which already exists. That support is skillfully nurtured, in the periods between elections, by the public actions of politicians.

There are three recurring contexts of interaction in which the politician must manage public impressions. The first of these is indirect symbolic interaction with the public through media of mass communication, including not only the professional news media but all means of disseminating information about the party. The second context is public ceremonies—gatherings understood by participants to have a symbolic or expressive purpose rather than a substantive or instrumental one. At such ceremonies, the politician is face-to-face with the public, but he is not called upon to take substantive action on issues. The third context is task-oriented gatherings. These constitute the most difficult arena in which to manage impressions, because the responses of others are direct and instantaneous, and substantive questions must be addressed. In describing the tactics by which politicians legitimate themselves and win support, I will consider each of these three contexts.

Mass Media

Citywide media—the major papers and broadcasting stations—rarely report news about individual neighborhoods. They occasionally mention ward-level leaders as part of their regular coverage of city council and Democratic party central committee meetings. For the ward politician, the local community press is a more important medium, for it is aimed at his constituency and can devote space to his news.

In the ward I studied the local press is sympathetic to the Regular Democrats but not controlled by them. The chain of community papers which serves the area is owned by a Jewish family with strong roots in the Democratic party and close ties to Jewish leaders in the party, such as those in this ward. The family's newspapers often print stories which show Regular Democrats in a favorable light; their editorials frequently praise Regular Democratic politicians. However, some columnists and investigative reporters for these papers are openly hostile to the Regulars. Their critical commentaries and embarrassing stories are regularly published, and editorials criticizing the Regulars do sometimes appear.

The relationship of the politicians and the local press is a symbiotic one, but one without intimacy. Politicians need to have favorable publicity. The press needs the information and news which the politicians can provide. As a matter of course, politicians try to have favorable stories printed and try to keep negative ones from appearing. When they are successful in these endeavors, it is because reporters benefit if good working relationships are maintained. Reporters and editors willingly take stories which they know to be contrived. For example, a story will appear in which a local politician announces some "new program." The reporter knows that the program is really part of a citywide plan which the local politician had no part in initiating. Since the local administration of the program is coordinated by the ward club, it is not incongruous for the ward politician to claim credit, and the reporter cooperates for the sake of good relations.

The local politician can do little to prevent negative items from being printed. But the party tightly controls information, and discretion is one of its strongest norms of membership. Most of the time, reporters have no access to sensitive information about the party; when they do, they cannot verify it.

The ward club also generates favorable publicity through other channels. The club cooperates with city agencies which have their own extensive publicity networks. For example, when the Chicago police department began to loan electric etching pencils to citizens for use in marking possessions as a protection against theft, the ward club arranged to act as lender of one of the etchers. The police department provided the club with the etcher and publicity posters inviting inquiries at the ward office. The ward office is the distribution site for literature and giveaways connected with many other civic programs: senior citizen tax exemption forms, reduced transit fare card applications, Spanish-language driver training manuals, even litter bags. The publicity efforts of other agencies thus benefit the ward club. In another instance, several thousand plastic whistles imprinted with the committeeman's name were distributed by precinct workers. This was publicized as a crime prevention effort, similar to the "Whistlestop" program introduced in Chicago by the Hyde Park–Kenwood Community Conference. A local civic group had already begun to sell superior metal whistles for one dollar apiece. Instead of supporting this program, the committeeman launched his own. But the small plastic whistles were not loud or durable enough to be effective and no systematic effort at community education accompanied their distribution. Although useless as a crime prevention measure, the whistles publicized the committeeman's name and bolstered the ward club's image as a concerned community organization.

A more traditional program is the annual distribution of groceries at Christmas. The club is usually able to secure enough donations from local businesses to fill one hundred grocery bags.[26] These are distributed to families the precinct captains select according to their own criteria. The press is invited to photograph the committeeman, the precinct captains, and a few of the lucky recipients posing with the grocery bags. Pictures of the giveaway are always posted in the windows of the ward office.

Each year the alderman mailed an eight-page tabloid-format newsletter to every voter in the ward. This was devoted entirely to his own accomplishments on behalf of the community. Despite protest from the committeeman, he gave no mention to the ward club or its activities. Occasionally, the committeeman and the alderman would collaborate in writing a letter to be distributed to people in some part of the ward. For example, when complaints were received about curb and gutter repairs in progress, a letter was hand-delivered to every house and business along the affected street, apologizing for the inconvenience, explaining the importance of this civic improvement, inviting further inquiries, and, of course, claiming credit. Such letters cannot be distributed frequently, because precinct workers resist the extra work of delivering them.

Regular Democratic politicians at all levels complain bitterly about the treatment they receive from the press. They feel that critical coverage is unfair, and they would be happier if they could more easily insert favorable public relations pieces in the newspapers and the broadcast media. At the same time, they distrust the press and those politicians who seem too anxious for publicity.[27] Generally ward-level politicians are expected to "stay out of the papers." Nevertheless, community residents who are exposed to the local press and to the mailings of local agencies do receive information about patronage politicians, the bulk of which conveys symbolic reassurance that they are helping people in need and exercising leadership on the community's behalf.

Public Ceremonies

The group life of urban subcommunities is punctuated by gatherings that mark ceremonial occasions—ground-breaking and dedication ceremonies for public works, parades, fairs, block parties, award ceremonies, and the like. By virtue of their office, Chicago's ward politicians are often invited to participate in such affairs. If the local chamber of commerce sponsors a parade, the alderman and the committeeman will ride in the procession. If there is a community fair where local agencies and institutions set up information booths and exhibits, the alderman will have a table of his own. At functions such as church socials where overt political activity would be considered inappropriate, the master of ceremonies does not fail to announce the presence of all public officials who attend. The politicians themselves usually preside or make major speeches at dedications and ground-breakings. For particularly important occasions, officials from downtown will attend—the head of the city's Model Cities program, a representative of the mayor, or even the mayor himself. The committeeman or the alderman will have the honor of introducing the distinguished guest, and each will have his own opportunity for extended comments. These big occasions are important for the symbolic life of the community, and at the same time, they allow politicians opportunity for symbolic action to show that they are true community representatives.

At ceremonies, as in all public settings, the politicians in the ward I studied express their leadership status through their dress and their deportment. The male politicians wear fashionable suits, distinctively tailored but not flashy; females wear clothes of similar style. They are well groomed, and men do not remove their ties or suit jackets in public. They sit, stand, and move with a cultivated ease, aware that many eyes are upon them. They address the public without faltering. They treat these ceremonies as important even though they may privately be bored or amused.

In their public speeches, the politicians devote most of what they say to the appropriate sentiments and to the allocation of credit. They express confidence in the future of the community. They rarely refer to issues or conflicts; if they talk about problems at all, they do so with optimism for their solution. They heap praise on notables from downtown who are present. They may also make modest reference to their own accomplishments. Other speakers applaud the ward politicians' efforts on the community's behalf. The image of the politician is enhanced in all these exchanges, not only when he himself is praised, but when he gives credit to others, for in so doing he assumes the role of community spokesman. And the fact that he participates in these rituals with other notables underscores his status as an important person.

On these occasions, the politician plays to several audiences simultaneously. First there are the onlookers who are, in the ward I studied, usually few in number, inattentive, unresponsive. Sometimes those who plan the ceremonies arrange for groups of schoolchildren to attend, as a means of filling out the sparse crowd of agency personnel and passersby. There are no intensely-felt crowd experiences at these events. There is no undercurrent of excitement. People simply go through the motions. They salute the flag, they bow their heads in prayer, but they cannot be coaxed into responding with enthusiasm.

The second audience is the one made available by the mass media. Television crews are present on the rare occasions when the mayor makes an appearance. Coverage of most events is limited to the captioned photographs which appear in the local press, usually without an accompanying story. Typically, the photographs are posed, showing the notables engaged in some activity symbolic of the whole event: turning up earth, cutting a ribbon, and so forth. They convey to a wider audience the image of the ward politician as a knowledgeable and influential community leader.

The third audience is composed of the other elite

participants in the event. Many community leaders are present. The integrative function of these ceremonies is evident in the diverse sectors of community life which are represented by participating notables. Business leaders, clergymen, police captains, fire marshals, youth group organizers, public and private social service agency heads, leaders of property owners' and neighborhood groups, and ethnic minority group representatives share the rostrum with elected politicians or observe closely from the crowd. Community leaders attend to see and be seen. They circulate through the crowd, seeking each other out to make contacts, exchange greetings, and catch up on gossip. There is a striking contrast between the attitude of the few idly curious onlookers and that of the local leaders in the crowd. The symbolic actions of politicians at public events are directed as much at this knowledgeable and comparatively powerful audience as they are at the general public.

Task-oriented Gatherings

The politician's image as a concerned and competent community leader is put to the test at local meetings where issues and group demands are raised. These meetings occur under varied sponsorship in varied settings, and they are frequent enough that a politician who wished to do so could spend almost all his evenings at gatherings of this kind. Often several take place simultaneously, and the politician must leave one meeting early in order to make an appearance at the next. Most such meetings are planned in advance by formally organized groups which invite the alderman, the committeeman, and other politicians to attend. Some are arranged by the politician himself. Some are planned without the knowledge of the politician, who is suddenly confronted when an angry group of citizens arrives at the ward office demanding action. Some occur when there is an emergency situation requiring immediate action, such as the eviction of a family with nowhere to go. Meetings take place at the ward office, in the offices of social service agencies, in churches, in schools, and in homes. Sometimes the politician is invited for the purpose of getting acquainted with the group, to exchange ideas, to sit on a panel, to give a talk, or merely to lend importance to the occasion. Usually, however, he is asked to discuss specific issues and problems with which the group is concerned and to state what action he will take in response to its concerns. Often, the group has determined in advance what it wants the politician to do, despite the fact that he may be unable or unwilling to comply. Local groups consider the elected official to be responsible to them and at these gatherings they challenge him to act on their behalf.

Sometimes the actions that groups demand can be carried out at little political cost. This is particularly true of requests for allocations of goods over which the politician enjoys full control and of which he has a plentiful supply. These requests can be fulfilled and the support of the group maintained by substantive issue-free action. However, most non-controversial demands of this kind are handled in the routine functioning of the ward office; the agenda for task-oriented public gatherings most often comprises those matters too controversial or too costly to be otherwise handled. These include requests for allocations of goods that could cost the politician the support of competing groups of voters, and matters that are susceptible to definition as oppositional issues—action on these could cost the politician the backing of his party. Thus, the patronage politician is frequently asked to commit himself to actions which he cannot afford to take. When faced with such demands, the Regular Democrats in the ward I studied used a variety of tactics which often enabled them to resist group demands and yet still secure the group's electoral support, or at least maintain its acceptance of them as legitimate community leaders.

Quite apart from the patronage politician's response to group demands, his legitimacy is upheld partly by symbols of deference which are as manifest in task-oriented gatherings as they are in the ceremonial occasions described above. The organizers of meetings usually arrange for the invited guests to sit in special seats.

Politicians who are not so seated move to the front when called upon to speak, in contrast to ordinary citizens who speak from the floor. Someone introduces the politician before he speaks, ensuring that all recognize his position. When meetings are held at the ward office, the office personnel and club leaders protect the politician by keeping people out of his private office, determining beforehand what is wanted, and controlling the group's impatience. Politicians sometimes keep groups waiting longer than necessary as a means of underlining the difference in their status.[28] The politician's dress is almost always more formal than that of his assistants or the other participants. However, ostentation and conspicuous display of wealth are avoided in these situations. In accord with American values of equality and achievement, the intent is to mark the politician as a person deserving of special respect, not undue privilege.

It is critical to the successful maintenance of the patronage politician's legitimacy that he prevent his audience from applying to him the stereotype of the machine politician that is part of Chicago's political culture. In the columns of the press and in the public statements of reformers, the political arena in Chicago's communities is depicted as being populated by villains and heroes: by corrupt, venal, secretive, intolerant machine politicians, and by honest, idealistic, open, liberal Independents. The wide acceptance of these stereotypes works to the disadvantage of men with public ties to the Regular Democratic Organization. Each of the Regulars uses his interpersonal skills in his own way to break through the stereotype and establish a measure of trust. Ideologically committed opponents of patronage politics are not easily shaken from their view, but the majority of local residents lack a structured system of beliefs about the machine. They judge politicians by what they can detect of their personal qualities, and they find most Regulars to be likeable people.

Party politicians also attempt to break down the public's preconceptions about those who compete with them for leadership. Trained community organizers are the moving force behind some of the grievance-bearing groups that confront the politician. Group members view the organizers as skilled leaders with high motives. At every opportunity and with varying degrees of truthfulness, the Regulars attempt to weaken the following of the organizers by questioning their legitimacy. The Regulars suggest that the organizers are secretly linked to groups with bad reputations. They impugn their motives, implying that they are trying to enhance their personal power by exploiting well-intentioned people. They maintain that the organizers use unfair tactics, implied threats, and demogoguery to achieve their ends. For their part, the organizers attempt to force the party politician into the role of unresponsive machine hack and to assume for themselves the role of champion of the people.

Thus political conflict in the community is a struggle not only among opposing interests but also among competing public definitions of the character of individual leaders. As I have discussed, many leaders outside the party give the Regulars substantive support in situations where their interests converge. They also give symbolic support to the Regulars' image as legitimate leaders.

This outside support for the legitimacy of the Regulars is seen in the informal cohesion-maintenance rituals which the politicians and other community leaders observe. After every meeting, even the most acrimonious, there is an obligatory period of informal interaction between participants, in which those who have disagreed the most during the meeting seek each other out, shake hands, and express affection or at least respect for one another. For a time, a few of the most radical community organizers in the ward would refuse to shake the hand of a Regular Democrat. This was so marked a deviation from the behavior expected by most participants that the Regulars would deliberately approach these men after meetings to have their friendly overtures rejected and thereby win the sympathy of onlookers.

One reason that the politician succeeds in maintaining legitimacy and securing support at meetings is that he allocates his time so as to partly insulate himself from groups he cannot easily satisfy. He knows from experience that certain groups will invite him to a meeting, confront him with demands he cannot accept, then angrily denounce his attempts at symbolic support. Other meetings are potential battlegrounds for groups in conflict, in which the politician might be forced to take the costly step of choosing sides. He turns down these invitations, claiming unavoidable conflicts, or sends an assistant who makes no promise of action. He stays away from some other meetings because they offer too little potential for electoral support to justify any time commitment.

The allocation of time is also a means of showing recognition of a group's demands.[29] Ward politicians are too busy to attend every meeting to which they are invited, and when they go to a meeting or send a representative it is recognized by others as a token of concern. When he is present, the politician can emphasize his interest by staying for an unusually long time. He may underscore the significance of his time-commitment by mentioning that other groups are waiting to see him or that he has postponed an important activity to come to the meeting. Even if he should reject the group's substantive request, the fact that he shows no haste to leave can have impressive symbolic effect. He proves himself accessible, concerned, and, if others at the meeting are attacking him, courageous. The politician's use of time is but one of the aspects of his behavior that carry messages about his character and his intentions with regard to group concerns. In some emotionally-charged gatherings, politicians are judged by such criteria as which individuals they converse with, where they choose to stand, and with whom they enter and leave. Of course, competent politicians are aware that people make such judgments and they regulate their demeanor accordingly.

In task-oriented gatherings, more than in other contexts of interaction, manifestations of legitimacy alone do not suffice. Patronage politicians must also manage public impressions of their substantive actions. Whether or not they have taken substantive action on behalf of a group, they take steps to convince the group that they have. They come to public meetings armed with copies of correspondence, proposed ordinances, press releases, and newspaper clippings to document their efforts. These are prominently displayed or distributed for all to see, valuable props in the "spiel" with which the politician solicits approval for his record.

Like other politicians, Regular Democrats offer their audiences generous amounts of symbol-laden talk. The politicians sound various themes, but irrespective of the degree to which their vote-getting strategy includes issue-oriented tactics, patronage politicians communicate support for the general goals of their audiences. Bob, one of our precinct captains, once told me what he thought about the lack of substance in such rhetoric after a meeting in which both the alderman and committeeman had spoken:

> It was quite a show. About fifty of those people from the B—— building [a tenant group seeking code enforcement] showed. They just about filled up all the chairs in here. Then [the alderman] comes out in front of all those people and says: "I'm glad you came here tonight"—and I knew it was going to be one of those nights . . . . What killed me was when [the alderman] said "I'll help you prosecute that building inspector; just get me his name and address and some proof that he's been paid off." Now Tom, how many building inspectors who accept a bribe stop to leave their name and address behind? I tell you, he gave those people nothing but bullshit.

Later, the alderman referred to the same meeting:

> Part of my job is to be loved, part of it is to do something for people. Usually the two are mutually exclusive. Now take this meeting last night. [The committeeman] got up in front of those fifty people and said how he has always been against slums and code violations and all this other stuff. He gave them only words, but they applauded him. These people loved him. I worked my ass off for those people, I helped them write letters and gave them advice on who to keep after downtown, and I still don't know what they think about me.

In fact, the alderman did take some substantive action on behalf of the tenant group, while the committeeman did nothing of substance, as might be expected from their somewhat divergent vote-getting strategies. But the above comments show that symbolic, issue-oriented tactics were an important component of each politician's response to group demands. To cynical insiders like Bob, the emptiness of the rhetoric was manifest; but it apparently was just the kind of talk which the group wanted to hear.

The patronage politician's attempts to satisfy group demands are complicated by the tendency of his constituents to exaggerate his power. Based on widely-shared myths about the cohesion and absolute power of the Regular Democrats, many people assume that any politician affiliated with the Regulars can produce results favorable to them by exercising decisive control through hidden channels of influence. When people fail to get what they want, this assumption may lead them to believe that the politician is actively withholding the desired outcome, despite his claims that he is powerless. In task-oriented gatherings, people often make impossible demands. Politicians respond to such demands by carefully spelling out the legal and practical limits on what they can get done. Sometimes the atmosphere approaches that of a civics class, as the elected official reviews his formal powers or describes the legislative process in terms that his audience can easily understand. His aim is to encourage the group to revise its expectations. At the same time, he has an opportunity to show off his expertise, underscore the ignorance of troublemakers in the group, and affirm his status as a powerful insider.

Another means of satisfying demands with which the patronage politician is unable or unwilling to comply is by outright pretense. Documentary evidence may be employed to make inaction seem like action, as in the following incident:

A Regular Democratic alderman in one Northside ward had a personal friend who had contributed generously to his campaign fund and wanted to open a liquor store in his ward on a street where several taverns were already located. A local block group asked the alderman to help prevent this man from obtaining a liquor license. (The alderman lacks the authority to deny a liquor license, but he can have its issuance delayed.) He responded by writing several letters to the city's liquor commissioner requesting that the license be denied. At the same time, he privately asked the liquor commissioner to ignore his letters and secretly told his friend how he could minimize the objections of the residents. After a short delay the liquor license was granted, over what seemed to be the strenuous objections of the alderman.

Even if the politician is in sympathy with the goals of a group, he may find that the symbolic importance of complying with their specific demands is more crucial than substantive action on the issue. The technique of modifying group demands by assuming the role of educator must not be carried too far lest the politician appear to be refusing to act. At times, therefore, the politician elects to carry out what he knows to be senseless or impossible requests. One example of this occurred when a group protesting conditions in the schools insisted that the alderman write a letter to a certain Board of Education official. The alderman knew that this official had no jurisdiction or influence whatsoever in the matter with which the group was concerned. He tried without success to explain this to the group. Ultimately, rather than refuse their request, he sent a letter to the official, who naturally replied that he had no jurisdiction.

The Regular Democratic politician's chances of success in managing public impressions of his character and actions are enhanced by the cooperation of party loyalists. Members of the ward club and persons with secret ties to the club are the most helpful in this regard. Underlying the complex interaction that takes place at community meetings is a hidden network of loyalties which produces close cooperation between allies. When the politician is attacked by opposition leaders, he never lacks friends to defend him. His fellow Regulars do so with a vehemence that would be unseemly for him to display himself. Those with covert ties to the party can also be counted on to provide support—albeit more cautiously. A surprising number of the members of the decision-making bodies in the community have ties of this kind. Party leaders make deliberate attempts to place loyal Regulars in positions of community leadership. These allies are important to the party not only because they publicly support it, but also because they constitute a network which gathers and controls information of political importance. Through well-placed informants the Regulars learn about the activities of their competitors, and they can depend on these loyalists to conceal any information which might be harmful to the Organization. There is thus an intimate linkage between the success of the party politician in securing outside support and the complex internal compliance structure of the ward club itself.

Conclusion

In describing the tactics which Regular Democratic ward politicians use to maintain their legitimacy and secure support, I have stressed the ways in which they use symbolic actions as a substitute for substantive responses to group demands. I do not mean to imply that these politicians have no genuine concern for their constituents or that they never actually act in the public interest. If a Regular Democrat perceives a clear local consensus on an issue and can take action which will not threaten his status as a Regular, he may well pursue the issue with real effect. But the patronage party poses real constraints on its members which force them to avoid substantive action on many issues. These constraints increase the importance of the symbolic tactics I have described.

Considered solely in substantive terms, patronage politicians support a party which acts against the public interest, and do not often accede to the demands of local groups. We have seen in previous chapters that their delivery of services to individual voters does not result in any enhancement of the partisan loyalty of the voters. This makes their continued success seem somewhat mysterious. However, when we observe the active involvement of patronage politicians in the public political life of the community, and consider the symbolic meanings of their strategic actions, it becomes clear that their political strategy includes both issue-oriented and issue-free tactics limited only by the demands of party loyalty. It is their skillful use of symbolic tactics which permits patronage politicians to pursue this compound supportive strategy.

As we have seen, the use of issue-oriented appeals is a point of controversy among machine politicians, but the use of symbolic tactics cuts across differences in political style. Some machine politicians are more skilled than others at manipulating the mass media and cultivating an image of "openness," but because they cannot act substantively on oppositional issues the new-style Regulars rely on symbolic tactics as much as the old-style bosses do.

The Regulars' tactics for securing legitimacy and support are effective in part because of the ecological characteristics of the inner-city ward. In addition, their strategy works for the benefit of key interests in the ward. But people support the patronage party not because they lack a sense of political morality or subscribe to deviant political values, but largely because they remain unaware of the party's venal nature. The pervasive secrecy of the ward club is one means by which this venality is defended; the party leaders' persuasive use of symbols in mass media, public ceremonies, and task-oriented gatherings is the positive component of the party's successful strategy. Members of the ward club act in concert to foster an image of localistic concern and responsive leadership, using a variety of tactics including some that involve outright deceit. If the ward club's service activities are related at all to the party's success, it is because the program of informal aid to constituents is effective as a symbol that politicians can evoke in their public appeals. It is to this and other vital uses of the party's service activities that we now turn.

Nine The Importance of Service Activities

In the foregoing chapters I have shown that the exchange models of machine support place mistaken emphasis on the patronage party's service activities. I have argued that the source of the party's support actually lies in its appeals to the basic value-commitments of local residents. If the commitment model of machine support is valid, however, an important question about the patronage party remains unanswered. Since favors are not themselves the source of electoral support, why do ward clubs such as the one I studied continue to invest so much in the performance of these services? As Robert Merton points out in his exposition of functional analysis, "when group behavior does not—and, indeed, often cannot—attain its ostensible purpose there is an inclination to attribute its occurrence to lack of intelligence, sheer ignorance, survivals, or so-called inertia."[1] Were we thus inclined, we could simply take the party's service activities to be an outmoded holdover of an earlier time in which, we might reason, machine support was grounded in material exchange. However, it seems implausible that party members would long continue the time-consuming and frustrating business of doing favors for voters if that activity served no useful purpose; were they to be so foolish, they would soon be outdone by competing political organizations that invested their time more efficiently. To explain the fact that service activities continue despite their failure to achieve their intended purpose, we must consider what other functions these activities serve for the ward club, its leaders, and its rank-and-file members.[2]

As one illustration of functional analysis, Merton briefly outlined some latent functions of urban political machines.[3] He sought to explain the persistence of the machine as an institution by identifying its consequences for political decision-making, for business interests, for the social mobility of its members, and for the welfare of those who receive its services. The present analysis applies a similar logic not to the party organization itself but to one institutionalized pattern of purposive activity involving leaders and members of the organization. Taking for granted the existence of the patronage party, we ask why its members perform service activities.[4] Part of the answer to this question lies in the consequences of service activities for groups outside the party. The consequences of service activities for the internal functioning of the ward club are also relevant. But we must supplement the inventory of consequences for groups and organizations with identification of consequences for individuals. We must explain why lower-level participants in the party are motivated to perform service activities and why upper-level participants offer rewards for that behavior.

External Functions

One fundamental cause for the party's involvement in service activities is the fact that groups outside the party receive benefits from these activities which they cannot obtain as efficiently elsewhere. There is a continual demand, in the economic sense, for service activities. That is, people are willing to offer incentives to the party to do favors for them. (As has been demonstrated in the foregoing chapters, however, votes are not among the things people give in return for favors.) What is it about the party's services that makes them so much in demand?

Merton asserts that the distinctive aspect of the aid offered by patronage party agents is its nonbureaucratic nature. "Humanizing and personalizing all manner of assistance to those in need" is a service performed by the precinct captain that large-scale, legally constrained welfare institutions cannot provide.[5] However, this description of party services does not fit the ward I studied. Recall the following findings: (1) About half the service requests the ward club handles come directly to the ward office rather than to precinct agents. (2) Of those who do contact a precinct-level agent for help, comparatively few regard him as a "friend." (3) Most users of services are of different ethnic background from the leaders of the ward club. (4) Users of party services have about as much bureaucratic competence as other voters. (5) The ability of ward politicians to circumvent bureaucratic rules in the allocation of services has steadily declined during the last half-century. The important and unique aspect of the party's services is not, then, that they are offered in a highly personalized, informal manner or in a context of primordial ties. Their crucial property is that they are made available on the basis of local residence. By living in the ward almost anyone can claim the party's assistance in securing help from large-scale agencies. The ward club is locally based, locally oriented, unique in that it offers services to ward residents only. It mediates effectively between large-scale agencies and individual clients not so much by creating diffuse and intimate service relationships as by handling services on a delimited territorial basis that more clearly defines the rights of the individual.

The party's service activities also provide a means by which the individual's sense of responsibility to his community can be expressed. As was suggested by the data analysis in chapter 6, users of party services are motivated not only by individual need but by concern with the collective welfare of the territorial groups with which they identify. Direct channels of access to large-scale service agencies are available, but a variety of separate agencies serve various needs and the individual gains little by dealing separately with each. By bringing all his requests to the attention of the same locally based authority, a person establishes his identity as a concerned resident. He may even come to be known as a neighborhood leader. The sense of responsibility felt by the city dweller with strong community attachment is validated and made useful to him or her by contact with the localized service apparatus of the party.

Another function of party services is to advance the interests of community leaders who may or may not belong to the party organization. Leaders of block clubs, homeowner's associations, ethnic associations, churches, and service organizations need to demonstrate to their followers that they can get things done. Party agents are anxious to provide services to such groups because they are significant potential loci of political support. In the larger, citywide political context, these small groups are far less important. Neighborhood leaders see the ward club as a more reliable ally in the pursuit of their own goals and those of their followers because it is more directly concerned with their support than citywide politicians are. Within the political structure of the community, then, are vested interests that benefit from the availability of locally based patronage.

Organizational Functions

The desire of groups to receive from the party benefits that cannot be obtained from other institutions contributes to the persistence of service functions. But benefits to outside groups are not alone sufficient to explain the extraordinary investment of the party in such activities. The needs of citizens generate demand for favors from politicians in all kinds of communities, and elected officials at all levels of government typically spend some of their resources processing citizen complaints.[6] Why does the patronage party go beyond the typical pattern of answering complaints as they are received and actively solicit requests for aid? Part of the answer lies in the consequences of service activities for the integration of the club as a social unit. These activities are important as a type of communication and a means of legitimation; they link the members of the club to each other, to ward residents, and to the citywide party organization.

Service activities build cohesion within the club by

providing a means by which members can interact with one another and add meaning to their relationships. The success of the ward club in winning elections rests in part on its ability to maintain a relatively high level of organization throughout the year. When election campaigns are under way, the party enlists the aid of temporary help, but unlike amateur political campaign organizations, the ward club maintains a full complement of precinct captains and assistants at all times. Of course a patronage job is the fundamental tie that binds a member to the club, and his principal obligations to the club are to work in campaigns and contribute money dues. But as was suggested in chapter 3, this exchange does not alone create a stable and effective organization. The service activities, vigorously pursued year-round, bring precinct agents into recurring contact with club leaders, with the office staff, and with each other. Adequate handling of service requests entails more than the implementation of commands; it requires two-way communication in which subordinates direct the attention of superiors to necessary tasks. The performance of service tasks brings club members into contact with each other in a context quite different from that in which campaign activity is carried out. Service activities facilitate social processes, growing out of interaction, that enhance the organization's effectiveness. Members come to know each other's personal qualities and learn how to adapt to them. They judge each other's competence and motivation, creating an informal system of status ranks. They regulate each other's behavior, socializing new participants into the normative order of the group. Given the patronage party's lack of ideological foundation and the lack of affect among its acquiescent members, it is difficult to think of an alternative type of activity that could serve these organizational needs as effectively.

Service activities link the ward club to the community by promoting contact between party agents and ward residents and by legitimating the party's efforts to maintain itself. The party agent's institutionalized role as broker of services leads some voters to seek him out and provides him with a rationale for seeking out others.

These contacts are crucial because they promote communication in two directions. Precinct workers who are not strangers to their voters possess greater credibility as opinion leaders and can more effectively influence them. Acquaintanceship also makes it easier for party agents to gather important information from the voters. The ward club's efforts to mobilize voters are contingent on information about how each intends to vote. Through contact with residents, precinct agents and ward leaders also find out the concerns and opinions of the voters, the activities of competing political groups, the effectiveness of their own appeals, and other useful intelligence.

We have already touched on the role of service activities in legitimating the party in our analysis of the symbolic tactics of ward politicians. The ward club depicts itself as "dedicated to public service," and the services provided by party agents constitute evidence in support of this claim. Through the mechanisms of defended venality, the efforts of ward club members to win votes for the party are made to appear as efforts on behalf of the community. Although individual voters are not influenced by receipt of favors, the collective investment of the club in service activities undoubtedly enhances its stature in the eyes of the locally attached and helps the organization to maintain the voter loyalties it requires.

The linkages formed in doing favors extend downtown to the city's central governmental and political powers. The contacts club members make with party members employed in citywide agencies are useful to the ward club for getting the information and the action it needs. These contacts also help the local club's citywide reputation. Ward clubs and their leaders are judged by the votes they deliver and by the opinion of Democrats downtown. The club can build its stature in the eyes of City Hall by vigorously pursuing service requests to downtown agencies.

We have identified some beneficial consequences which service activities have for the organization, but this still does not suffice to explain them. If club members and leaders are unaware of the benefits, or if they perceive benefits to others and not to themselves, they will not perform the activities. Fortunately for the ward club, the functions we have described are neither entirely hidden from its members nor irrelevant to their own interests.

Motivations of Club Members

To the extent that club members are aware that service activities bring them benefits—real or imaginary—they are motivated to perform them. The motivations of the lower level participants in the party are complex and varied, but the club members have some important interests and perceptions in common.

As we have seen, the manifest intent of service activities is to win votes, although club members conceal this purpose from outsiders. Since the party does receive strong support at the polls, it seems to club members that service activities are having their anticipated consequence. This perception creates an incentive for club members to do service activities. They conceive of the party as a traditionalistic, semifeudal structure in which vertical ties between participants at all levels consist primarily of loyalty given in exchange for favors. They see that the way to rise in this structure is to build a following of voters, and they think this is accomplished by doing favors. Although the central finding of this study is that the exchange models of party loyalty are invalid, the club members' mistaken faith in the logic of those models keeps them working at doing favors.

There are, however, other more real benefits that club members can anticipate from doing favors. We have seen that the performance of service activities tends to build intimacy and moral commitment within the organization. These system goals have counterparts in individual goals. The precinct captain or worker needs to demonstrate to club leaders that he is sufficiently active to continue to merit the patronage he receives from them. He brings service requests to the attention of club leaders so they will believe him to be an active worker who can control votes. Service requests provide the club member with an excuse to initiate conversation with club leaders and office staff, during which he can casually gather useful information. Experienced party agents assign service tasks to subordinates as a means of teaching and testing them. Most important, members legitimate to themselves and their peers their involvement in the ward club by carrying out services for the voters in their precincts. They show thereby that they care about their community and are competent to represent the party to outsiders. Performance of service tasks allows involvement in a network of material inducements to be coupled with commitment to higher values.

The party agent finds service requests useful in his assigned task of representing the party to local residents. Party leaders require him to estimate the vote totals in his territory prior to each election and to muster out the loyal voters on election day. Voters tend to resist overt attempts to influence their votes or to discover their preferences. They are aware that the precinct captain or worker is a partisan agent, and they are naturally more receptive to contact with him if he offers them a service. After establishing contact and building trust on this basis, the party agent can then broach more sensitive topics with the voter. He can also refer to his record of service in defending himself against those who would attempt to label him a self-interested hack.

Individual club members also perceive that enhancing the effectiveness of the club is in their own individual interest. Since club members are the direct beneficiaries of the club leader's patronage, they want their leaders to be powerful in the party. They understand that the power of ward club leaders is dependent upon how the party's top leaders estimate the local club's effectiveness. Club members know the value placed on service activities by the citywide leadership. The more service requests they process, the more effective the club will appear, and the more they will seem to club leaders to be dedicated to the club's success. In addition, to the extent that they feel a sense of responsibility for their locality, club members understand that demands for change are most effectively transmitted upward in the form of service requests.

Motivations of Party Leaders

It is in the interest of club members to perform service activities largely because authorities in the patronage party, at the ward club level and higher, offer rewards for their performance. Why are these rewards provided? I have no data on why members of the Democratic Central Committee attach such importance to service activities. At a conscious level, many party leaders perhaps give little consideration to the functions of these activities and support them because they carry the weight of long-standing tradition. If asked by an outsider to explain these activities, they would probably give altruistic reasons. If asked by an insider, they would undoubtedly explain these activities in terms of the material exchange model ("you do a fella a favor and he'll always remember it") or the affectual exchange model ("this is how our people develop *relationships* with their voters"). However, as I have already remarked, the weight of tradition and belief in mythical outcomes are not sufficient to account for the investment party leaders make in service activities. There are at least four ways in which these activities bring real benefits to party leaders, benefits which may serve as motivations for their support of the activities.

The first benefit to leaders is that the performance of service activities builds the strength of the clubs they lead; these organizational functions have been discussed above. Skilled party leaders are probably aware that by encouraging an active program of service, they build strength into their human vote-mobilizing machinery.

A second benefit is that the performance of service activities by the club is useful to the ward politician in his essential task of securing voter support. The party expects the ward politician to influence his constituents to support him, without arousing public concerns which might damage the special economic and political interests upon which the party depends. Doing favors for individual voters is an issue-free supportive tactic clearly acceptable to the party, but—as this book seeks to demonstrate—this tactic is not effective in generating voter loyalty. Nevertheless, service activities can constitute an issue-oriented tactic used by ward politicians as part of their compound supportive vote-getting strategy. By channeling a sufficient number of complaints to the right authorities, the politician can draw attention to the need for a change in administrative practice or public law without seeming to arouse opposition to his party. Demands for improved handling of individual citizen complaints sometimes bring responses which help the ward politician secure the support of issue-oriented groups. For example, when complaints about abandoned cars increased dramatically in the ward I studied, it was possible for the alderman to effect changes in the procedures by which the Department of Streets and Sanitation removed the cars. In a series of discussions with officials of the agency, a variety of proposals was discussed and a new procedure was implemented on an experimental basis. This procedure proved effective and was made permanent. The alderman and the streets department were able to share credit for the change, which reduced the number of abandoned cars on the streets of the ward. Given the subordination of the ward club to the party's central powers, service activities provide one means by which the ward politician can raise substantive issues without seeming disloyal to the citywide leadership.

The third benefit of service activities results not from their actual performance but from people's beliefs about them. It is in the interest of party leaders to maintain among their subordinates in the party the belief that favors generate votes. The compliance of party members and the cooperation of elected officials are predicated on the belief that the party controls election outcomes, control which is thought to stem from service activities. It thus becomes imperative for party leaders to stress the importance of service activities; to deemphasize them would be to admit the party's lack of control over the electorate and invite disloyalty.

The fourth way in which service activities benefit party leaders is similar in that it stems from the symbolic value of the activities. While publicizing service activities within the party serves to underscore the invincibility of the boss, publicizing them to the external audience conveys the legitimacy and effectiveness of his leadership. It is worthy of remark that urban political machines have never merely delivered services—they have always done their charitable deeds with the maximum publicity they can muster. Chicago's inimitable alderman Vito Marzullo recently appeared on a national television newscast, explaining to a reporter that he performs favors for people. The cameras rolled as a poor, black mother of six told Marzullo of her hardships and he instructed an underling to write her a fifty dollar check from party funds. It is important to realize as we watch such a performance that this charitable act helps the alderman more by its influence on the television audience than by its influence on the recipient of the check. Such use of the media is not limited to the electronic age, for an examination of the pages of the *Public Service Leader,* the citywide publicity sheet published by the Regular Democrats during the thirties and forties, reveals that service activities of ward and city Regulars were given major coverage. The skillful use of mass media by today's ward politicians was described in the preceding chapter. The public relations value of service activities undoubtedly serves as one motivation for the continued support these activities receive from party leaders.[7]

Sources of Importance

It is well to note in the above inventory of functions of service activities that there are a number of benefits people derive from doing service activities which stem not from the favors themselves but from the responses of others to their performance. That is, certain people place a high value on services or the activities that deliver them and this permits people to exchange other valued things for them. The motivations of club members are based almost entirely on the values which other groups place on service activities. Ward residents value the service which the party provides and they give to precinct workers time, attention, and information (but not control over votes) in return for their services and offers of service. Doing favors helps the club member build the prestige of the ward club and his own power within it because club leaders and citywide party leaders place a high value on service activities. Thus, the value assigned to service activities by voters and by party leaders is institutionalized in a reward structure which motivates participants to carry out these activities. These exchanges strengthen the relationships between people in the party, linking voters to club members, members to the club, and club leaders to city leaders. Their commitments to each other are strengthened.

It is unclear to what extent these organizational functions of service activities are manifest to party leaders. They value service activities partly because they believe in the exchange models of support for the party. But their purposeful and frequent references to service activities in their exhortations to club members and to the public suggest that party leaders are also cognizant of the symbolic value of service activities. They may value service activities partly for the wrong reasons, but the top Democrats do not err in treating these activities as an important source of the patronage party's effectiveness.

Ten Machine Politics: The New Chicago Model

In this concluding chapter, we will review the basic assumptions of this study and summarize the evidence for the commitment model of machine support. We will also address some fundamental questions which remain unanswered to this point: How can the present findings be reconciled with the views of earlier researchers? What are the implications of the new model for the future of the political machine? And how might the present findings affect our evaluation of Chicago politics?

The Commitment Model: A Review

As was discussed at the outset, there have been two competing models which seek to explain machine support in terms of exchange. They are alike in that they stress the importance of the party's service activities as a mechanism for generating support. According to the material exchange model, voters have material motives which make them responsive to the material incentives offered by party agents. According to the affectual exchange model, voters have affectual motives which make them responsive to solidary incentives such as approval and friendship. I have here proposed an alternative theory, the commitment model, which attributes moral motives to voters and stresses the party's efforts to appeal to their localism and other value-commitments. Rather than recapitulate here the details of each model, I will discuss the broader assumptions on which the latter model is based. The tests of the commitment model which have been described in the foregoing chapters are partial tests of these assumptions.

Assumptions

Morality. The commitment model assumes that the success of the machine is morally problematic. The patronage party carries out activities which are reprehensible according to widely accepted standards of conduct, and we assume that evaluative standards (whatever their specific content) play an important part in guiding all human action, including political action. This normative approach to politics does not assume the existence of any single natural system of values, but it specifically rejects as inadequate a "political economy" approach which would regard the existence of perceived interests as sufficient to explain the machine's success. Under the right circumstances, normative inducements can be used effectively in the exercise of power. Even where the operative inducements are primarily nonnormative, any system of power that does not rely on physical coercion must show those whom it would control that it uses its power in morally acceptable ways—in short, the system must legitimate itself.

Discontinuity. The commitment model assumes that the sources of internal support for a patronage party are analytically separable and qualitatively different from sources of external support.[1] Internally, the ward club offers patronage jobs as incentives. Material inducements are necessary—although not sufficient—to evoke compliance from club members. In contrast, the voters are not materially motivated and do not respond to party services with unselective loyalty. Politicians must win their support by appealing to their values. I have used the phrase *defended venality* to underscore the patterns of activity that allow the machine's fundamentally different external and internal systems of control to coexist. By hiding its illicit activities and by skillfully using substantive and symbolic vote-getting tactics, the party succeeds in securing support from a potentially hostile moral environment.

Community. In comparing alternative models of machine support, I have assumed that the political orientations of urban residents are partly determined by the nature of their relationships to others in their subcommunities. The material exchange model sees machine support as arising from the disruption of such relationships among slum-dwellers; the affectual exchange model attributes machine support to the primordial and primary attachments of the ethnic "village." The commitment model is congruent with a more realistic notion of inner-city subcommunities as socially constructed collectivities with specific functions, eliciting limited and variable concerns which are nonetheless widespread. These communities of limited liability are based partly on instrumental motivations, but they also evoke moral and affectual orientations among those who become committed to them.[2] These orientations involve notions of right and responsibilities with respect to the local area. The vote-getting strategy of the patronage party takes these sentiments into account.

The need to preserve anonymity has caused me to be reticent about the characteristics of the ward which I studied. I hope I have made it plain that the ward is a fragmented, arbitrarily defined territory with substantial ethnic and class heterogeneity in each of its neighborhoods. Some block groups and other locally based voluntary organizations exist, and neighborly interaction is frequent in some parts of the ward. At the same time, there is no shortage of poor, ignorant, ethnically distinct, or desperate people in the ward. Thus, parts of the ward constitute settings in which, theoretically at least, material or affectual exchange could be used in service of the machine. For the most part, however, the subcommunities which fall within the ward boundaries are built on the limited localistic affinities characteristic of modern urban areas.

Complexity. Since I have assumed that there is fundamental discontinuity between the system of relationships within the party and the system which exists outside of it, and since I have assumed that the evaluative component of human orientations can never be ignored, it has been possible—indeed, necessary—to conceive of people and their relationships to each other as being complex. I have described the ward club as having a complex compliance structure which relies on patronage, control of sensitive information, and symbols of legitimacy to secure the obedience required for the organization's success. Aldermanic service activities are laden with multiple meanings: they are described by party agents as being intended to serve the public, they are in reality intended to win votes for the party, and they function in fact to enhance the club's effectiveness and build for it a positive public image. Ward residents who request favors from the patronage party tend to be locally attached, but that attachment is multifaceted. Use of party services is encouraged by each distinct component of community attachment—access, needs, rights, and responsibilities. As we examine the characteristics of people who give machine politicians their votes, we find them to be a mixed lot. They include, on the one hand, relatively isolated and ignorant people who maintain a fierce partisanship and, on the other hand, more selective, active, and locally attached people whose support is skillfully courted in the public political actions of ward politicians. The strategy which the politicians use in securing support is a compound of several types of vote-getting tactics. Their compound supportive strategy is designed to respond to people's perceived self-interest and concern with the welfare of their communities, without expressing disloyalty to the party hierarchy. In the structure of multifaceted relationships that is ward politics, people interact strategically,[3] taking into account the orientations of other participants. The stable pattern of domination by the patronage party is built upon people's ability to defend its venality in the context of the ambivalence, uncertainty, conflict, and distrust that the machine's very existence generates.

Since it is hardly deniable that human experience is a complex affair, it would be specious argument to define the exchange models in simple terms and reject them on the basis of that simplicity. We can imagine that the mechanisms of defended venality could be extended to bridge the moral gap that would result if large numbers of votes were controlled through various forms of bribery or friendship. Indeed, in the ward I studied there were a few precinct captains who clearly exercised a degree of control that made the vote in their precincts "deliverable." Some offered small bribes to homeless men; some specialized in providing friendship to elderly folk; some enjoyed an ethnic following; some simply manipulated the incompetents in "halfway houses." Material and affectual exchange can be used to influence certain people's votes. But my results show that these mechanisms do not provide the principal means by which the patronage party generates support in the ward I studied or—by extension—in the city as a whole.[4]

The Case against the Exchange Models

The central datum which contradicts the exchange models of machine support is the pattern of party loyalty which my survey of voters revealed. Users of party services are not more loyal to the party than nonusers. Even among groups of Democratic voters whom we would predict to be the most influenced by exchange, involvement in satisfactory service transactions does not enhance party loyalty.

Moreover, the pattern of public political activity by ward politicians belies the efficacy of favors as a means of influence. If the machine's vote were really controlled it would not be necessary for politicians to involve themselves so actively in local public life. What has been characterized by previous researchers as an "issue-free" strategy is more accurately seen as one incorporating carefully chosen issue-oriented tactics. These tactics are effective in securing voter support not only because of what they give to interest groups but because of what they signify to the public about the moral worth of politicians.

We can note some additional evidence against the material exchange model. The historical record suggests that the kinds of service which the party can provide have steadily become less and less valuable as objects of exchange. Most of those offered today cannot plausibly be seen as effective material inducements even for voters who are economically deprived. The survey data analyzed above show that users of party services are not drawn primarily from among those we would expect to be most strongly motivated by material needs. Moreover, the patterns of party loyalty among voters do not support hypotheses derived from the material exchange model.

The affectual exchange model, on the other hand, proved to be incompatible with the quality of communal attachments observed within the ward. The heterogeneity of ward residents, their transiency and the lack of intimacy among ward club members have already been reported. Networks of primary and primordial ties seem relatively unimportant in the ward's political life. Residential proximity forms the basis for networks of intimacy among some residents, but party agents are not typically included in these networks. Precinct captains are often assigned to precincts in which they do not reside,[5] and their assignments change frequently. Few voters consider the precinct captain a friend; many interact with him guardedly, knowing that he seeks to influence them. In this ward, the party and its loyal supporters are not linked by ethnicity. Most club leaders are Jewish, but the Jewish areas of the ward tend to support the Independent ticket. This is not to say that ethnicity is unimportant either to club members or the electorate. Jewish candidates tend to do well in Jewish precincts, and Jewish club members have a better chance of advancement in the ward club than non-Jewish members. But in this ward, ethnicity is more important in structuring relationships within the party than in generating external support.

Further evidence against the affectual exchange model emerged from the survey results. We noted a significant effect of political culture, as reflected in being Catholic, on the tendency to request favors from the party. However, I was unable to discover any systematic difference between users and nonusers in attitudes about corruption or in ethnic prestige. More directly relevant is the finding that even those users of party services who ought to be most prone to affectual exchange (i.e., Catholic, precinct-level users) are no more loyal to the Democratic party than are nonusers.

The Case for the Commitment Model

In setting aside the exchange models of machine support, we must not lose sight of the fundamental importance of the party's vote-getting ability. Indeed, a party cannot be a machine unless it strongly influences election outcomes, a fact which probably accounts for the widespread acceptance of the notion that machines control votes through exchange. Like its predecessors, Chicago's patronage party is, internally, a tightly organized exchange system involving politicians of diverse origins who have self-interested motivations in common. Mechanisms of the market assure that power, patronage, and other benefits of office are distributed among these men according to their ability to win elections. Influence over voters is the basic resource power-holders trade with one another for things they desire. People gain power in the party by building influence with the voters. Elected officials grant party leaders discretionary power over patronage appointments in return for help in winning votes. Party leaders give jobs to precinct workers so they will work in elections on their behalf. Thus, the patronage system and the ward club's compliance structure are inextricably linked to the party's success at the polls. A machine that loses elections loses control of jobs and other resources without which it can no longer operate as a machine. If Chicago's Regular Democrats do not control votes by exchange, how are their candidates able to win elections?

The candidate who runs for office with Regular Democratic endorsement enjoys several important competitive advantages. First and foremost, a large and experienced force of precinct workers, which effectively mobilizes existing support, is put to work on his behalf. Second, he enjoys the use of the Democratic party label, with which many of Chicago's voters identify. Third, he is publicly designated as a Regular and benefits from the name-recognition and good will built up by the Regulars in their forty years of power. Fourth, he gains financial backing. The Regular Democratic Organization is generously supported by business and organized labor, not to speak of the obligatory dues from patronage jobholders. Fifth, he benefits from the party's reputation for invincibility; challengers are not readily supported by contributors or voters because they are not expected to win. Finally, he enjoys the active support of incumbent Regulars throughout the city, who are skillful at eliciting the commitment of their constituents.

These are substantial advantages which make the machine hard to beat. But they do not add up to a guarantee of victory due to a massive delivered vote.[6] The outcome of the 1979 mayoral primary, in which machine-backed incumbent Michael Bilandic was unseated, is the most sensational recent evidence that endorsement by the Regular Democrats does not always bring victory. But Bilandic's defeat is not without precedent. In 1976 Erwin France, a long-term party loyalist, won less than a third of the primary vote when he attempted to unseat the anti-Daley incumbent congressman, the late Ralph Metcalfe. In the 1972 Democratic primary, organization candidate Raymond Berg failed to unseat incumbent Cook County state's attorney Edward Hanrahan. And as far back as the primary of 1936, the voters foiled the machine's attempt to replace incumbent governor Henry Horner with Herman N. Bundeson, city health commissioner under Mayor Edward Kelly.[7] In these and other races, machine support alone could not outweigh the successful appeals of the victors to the value-commitments of the voters.

The values to which Chicago politicians appeal are many. The survey data used in this study unfortunately do not permit direct testing of relationships between indicators of people's value-positions and their votes for specific candidates. In general, the explicit and implicit appeals of machine politicians are similar to those used by candidates for local office everywhere in the United States, with the important limitation imposed by the Regulars' need for loyalty to the city's central powers. In understanding the success of these appeals, it is useful to distinguish the responses of unselective Democrats from those who vote selectively.

Straight-ticket Democratic voters are isolated from the subcommunities in which they live. They particularly lack ties to local voluntary organizations. Because they need to simplify the task of casting a long ballot, and since they lack personally mediated sources of political information on which they could base selectivity, they vote on the basis of party alone. What makes them choose the Democratic party over the others on the ballot? They are not tied to the Democrats by relationships of direct exchange. These most reliable voters apparently perceive the Democratic party as serving their class and ethnic interests, defending "the little man" from the injustices of the American system. This perception is grounded not in what the precinct captain does for them as individuals but in the history of the nation's major parties over the last several decades.

How do the Regulars secure support from selective voters? The evidence points to the importance of the party's appeals to the localistic affinities of these more active and informed people. Users of party services are locally attached—they have this characteristic in common more than any other. The party uses service activities to show that it is responsive to persons who feel the responsibilities of local citizenship. By their substantive and symbolic actions in local public life, the patronage politicians persuade the voters that they are concerned about the local community and that they are acting to advance its interests. Here the discontinuity between the internal and external structure of the party becomes crucial. The party's normative appeal to the voters is successful because members of the ward club control sensitive information and assist club leaders in their vote-getting tactics. The successful defense of the party's venality is critical for the party's influence among the more active, informed, and locally committed members of the electorate. It was perhaps among such voters that Jane Byrne most effectively cut into the power base of the Regulars.

One additional datum may be adduced in support of

the commitment model. In designing this study, I postulated that many Chicago voters were politically pragmatic—that is, both cynical about the motivations of politicians and accepting of the corruption they perceived. I included in the questionnaire some items designed to measure this complex of attitudes, expecting them to predict both use of party services and loyalty to the Democratic party. As discussed above, the corruption-acceptance scale which was drawn from these items failed to predict either use or loyalty. While the measures I used are far from perfect, these negative results suggest that the commitment model is correct in attributing to machine supporters a sense of political morality no different from that which most Americans hold. From the perspective of the commitment model, it is highly significant that the crisis of confidence which brought down the Bilandic administration was occasioned not only by a breakdown of city services in the midst of a disastrous snowfall, but by serious allegations of corrupt practices by the police chief and the mayor himself.

Reconciliation of the Commitment Model

How can we reconcile this new model of machine politics with the existing literature, which for the most part supports the exchange models? Our answer will depend upon whether we assume that: (1) there has been little variation in the structure of patronage parties; (2) patronage parties vary cross-sectionally (that is, from place to place); or (3) patronage parties vary over time.

The assumption that party structure does not vary would necessitate the rejection of previous findings and espousal of the idea that the patronage party is a uniquely deceptive structure. We would have to propose that previous researchers such as Lincoln Steffens, Frank Kent, and Harold Gosnell were wrong. They misunderstood the structure of the machine and misreported it. They were deceived by the conventional wisdom of the participants in the setting they studied and failed to unearth the true sources of machine support. We might attribute their failures to faulty methodology, since they did not check the accounts of party agents against the behavior of individual voters, or to conscious bias against classic political theory coupled with unconscious bias against the people they described. Even well-informed, well-intentioned researchers make errors of this kind.[8]

I am reluctant, however, to assert that a model which suits the present case study is equally applicable to an earlier time. To do so would ignore changes that have taken place in the structure of American cities. The urban scene has changed greatly since the days of "Boss" Tweed: the urban poor were poorer and less enlightened, news media were less effective, and local authorities commanded more significant resources. It is not implausible that in American cities of the industrial period, networks of exchange based on patronage were more important sources of electoral influence than they are in Chicago today.

If we assume cross-sectional variation, we can accept the commitment model without relinquishing the exchange models. We would then posit that the machine has a plural structure. We would conclude that the patronage party is a Protean system, taking different forms in different settings. Since I have used data on one community, I have perhaps found only one of the several extant types of relationships between voters and the party.

One account suggesting such a plural structure is William Kornblum's study of South Chicago.[9] According to Kornblum, the Regular Democrats in South Chicago include *professional, ethnic,* and *amateur* precinct captains. The professional captain is a patronage jobholder assigned to a precinct with no indigenous party-linked leaders; he generates support by doing favors. The ethnic captain commands a following based on primary ties established prior to his alliance with the patronage party. The amateur captain appeals to the class interests and moral sentiments of more middle-class voters.[10] Kornblum explains that different settings require different types of captains. If the professional captain, for example, can be effective only in transient, dependent areas, then votes are influenced through material exchange in some neighborhoods but not in others.

It is conceivable that a survey of an entire ward, especially a heterogeneous ward such as the one I studied, might fail to capture the plural nature of the party's vote-getting method. In the ward I studied, captains in different precincts do use different vote-getting strategies, ranging from passing out bottles of wine on election day to organizing issue-oriented citizens' groups. However, when I tested the relationship of loyalty and use of party services for a subsample of interview respondents drawn from the ward's central area, the results were no different from those reported in chapter 7 for the entire ward. Even in the ward's most reliably Democratic, poorest, most transient area, favors do not produce votes; there is no intraward pluralism here. Yet the possibility of interward pluralism remains. Perhaps Chicago's strongest patronage wards, such as the Eleventh or the Twenty-fifth, do produce votes through exchange. Even if this were so, the citywide strength of the Regular Democrats must depend largely on other sources of support.

If we assume longitudinal variation in the machine's sources of support, the present findings would indicate that Chicago's patronage party has an adapting structure. To me this seems the most realistic interpretation. The exchange models of machine support were applicable in the past, but changes in the structure of government, the structure of urban subcommunities, and the orientations of voters have forced changes in the vote-getting methods of the party. Federal service programs have multiplied and private welfare agencies have become more specialized. The party has lost its monopoly on many services which the urban poor need. With the professionalization and automation of government administration, the politician's ability to intervene on behalf of his supporters has diminished, despite the continued strength of patronage in the hiring practices of local agencies. The waves of European immigration have long passed, and the ethnic villages have all but disappeared. Incomes and educational levels have risen. As the party lost the ability to deliver important services, as the demand for its services diminished, and as the motivations of its constituents changed, it turned increasingly to alternative forms of influence.

Banfield and Wilson describe this process: "Some machines . . . are managing to adjust to the changing circumstances and to substitute, little by little as necessary, one kind of inducement for another so that they gradually become less machine-like. The Chicago machine is one which has survived by 'reforming' itself piecemeal." They refer to the highly visible public works and superficial reforms undertaken by Mayor Daley in the early years of his administration. Their view is that these steps were taken to increase the party's suburban and downstate strength: "If a boss were concerned only with the central city, the old style of machine politics would work well enough."[11] My results gainsay their confidence in the efficacy of exchange. The adaptation of the patronage party has extended to the grass roots level in the central city; even in slum neighborhoods commitment outweighs exchange as a source of party support.

We may speculate that the adaptation of the patronage party proceeded historically through a "natural history" of three stages, each corresponding to one of the models of machine support I have described.[12] The machine has its origin in the slum areas of the industrial city, where immigrant populations exist in their initial stages of transiency and social disorganization. Ward bosses exercise control by a combination of coercion and control of unskilled private and public jobs.[13] The illiterate new Americans, unused to democratic ways, are easily manipulated into voting as the unscrupulous bosses direct. However, the effectiveness of this low-level patronage system works gradually along with other factors to raise the immigrant community's level of living and its ability to sustain an organized style of life. The "ethnic village" emerges, protected and represented by formally constituted ethnic associations and an exquisite network of familial, religious, and neighborly ties. The appeal of the ward boss gradually shifts from brokering favors to representing the ethnic group in the decision-making process at City Hall.[14] He and his cohorts become well-respected family men in the neighborhoods of second settlement. The patronage party's grass roots support is reconstituted on a more affectual basis, with party workers becoming established as the principal opinion leaders linking their ethnic neighborhoods to the still somewhat mysterious world of politics.

The further transformation of the patronage party becomes necessary as the assimilation and residential dispersion of the ethnic voting bloc proceed. These changes can be viewed partly as consequences of the effectiveness of the party in protecting the interests of its supporters, but they are primarily the results of external circumstances which permit the group's social and spatial mobility. As the ethnically distinct character of the neighborhoods dissipates and the income and educational levels of the voters rise, it becomes increasingly important for local politicians to show concern for the public interest. As their constituents become more integrated into the dominant values of the American system, the venality of the patronage politicians must be more carefully protected from publicity. The growth of public welfare institutions not only provides direct competition for the service activities of the party, but brings with it a pervasive change in public demand and expectation.[15] The service activities of the party become institutionalized as legitimate functions of elected officials. An increasingly demanding public perceives these services as theirs by right. Politicians who provide the services receive no special gratitude, but those who fail to provide them are seen as unworthy of office. The patronage party therefore continues to carry out its service functions while acting to generate voter support through normative appeals.

This evolutionary scheme has the attraction of pulling together the competing models of machine support. It is compatible with the notion of cross-sectional variation in machine structure, insofar as the citywide patronage party can be conceived as a coalition of ward or precinct clubs which represent constituencies that are in various stages of integration into advanced industrialism. However, the scheme carries the danger of turning attention away from the essential complexity for which I have argued. It is tempting to think of machine supporters in times past as having been moral Neanderthals or peasants in factory clothes. These unjust characterizations result from assuming that machine supporters were aware of the party's venality. But we should not underestimate the capacity of organized groups such as the patronage party for systematic concealment, deceit, and manipulation of reassuring symbols. By the same token, we must not mistake the rise of the new-model machine for "reform," for the machine's recent transformations are but changes in its base of external support that allow its internal structure to remain centered on a system of spoils.

Implications

Observers of Chicago politics have been predicting for decades the imminent demise of the Regular Democratic Organization. With the coming of each election campaign, hopeful opponents of the machine point to signs of its weakness; when the returns are in the usually victorious Regulars proclaim their strength. When Jane Byrne won the 1979 mayoral nomination, the press proclaimed the "end of an era"—yet Chicago politics continued as usual after her victory. Both the predictions of the machine's demise and the proclamations of its invincibility are in error, for both are predicated on the exchange models of machine support. The exchange models predict the inexorable decline of machine strength, since the societal transformations we have just discussed act to undermine the basis for effective material or affectual exchange. Chicago's machine is seen as an imposing dinosaur, surviving by some quirk of political climate but headed for extinction as its natural habitat shrinks. For their part, the more naive champions of the machine see its continued dominance as evidence that it yet controls votes.

In fact, Chicago's patronage party is neither invincible nor doomed. As Byrne and others have demonstrated, to win an election against a Regular Democratic opponent, one need only appeal to the value-commitments of the electorate more effectively than the Regular does. This is difficult to accomplish because of the advantages the party offers its candidates, but Independents are not destined for inevitable defeat by a controlled bloc of votes. Nevertheless, the continued success of most of the party's candidates suggests that we should not expect Chicago's Regulars to disappear soon. The ideal motives which are the real basis for the party's electoral support should be stable despite social progress. If patronage politicians are skillful and flexible enough, they can retain their power indefinitely, and could even increase it. The party gains and loses power incrementally, and its internal structure is dependent on its external strength. If the ability of party leaders to control elected decision-makers is damaged, then the patronage system will falter and the party structure will have to change. The influence of the party has been weakened to some extent by failure to placate emergent minority groups, by problems of succession, and by scandal. But as long as large numbers of voters remain committed to it, a patronage party can attain access to the resources it needs to thrive in a modern metropolis.

The findings of any study of patronage politics are inevitably consequential for the evaluative concerns which underlie this area of inquiry. As David Matza has pointed out, the evaluation of the political machine by early social scientists tended to be overly negative.[16] Echoing the analysis of advocates of municipal reform, social scientists pointed to the machine's adverse consequences both for its supporters and for the political system as a whole. The pejorative view was congruent with the material exchange model of machine support: the alleged use of mass bribery by office seekers subverted the exercise of popular sovereignty and pillaged the public wealth. Merton's functional analysis of the machine took a more benign view; in Matza's words, "the political machine was no longer to be conceived as a cancer; rather it was a blessing in disguise."[17] Merton gave explicit recognition to the ways in which various groups benefited from the machine, and pointed out that the entire political system of the city was helped since the boss was able informally to centralize power which was hopelessly dispersed by constitutional rules. This appreciative view was congruent with the affectual exchange model. Emphasis on the machine's positive consequences has enjoyed a wide currency, to the point where the municipal reform movement is characterized in some current political science texts as being nothing more than the self-protective backlash of the native bourgeoisie against the threat of an immigrant proletariat. The successes of the City of Chicago are taken by many to mean that the hegemony of the machine has made it "The City That Works," and a recent sociological analysis of patronage politics concluded only half-jokingly with the sentiment: "God Bless Mayor Daley."[18] Matza, however, feels that the positive and negative views of the machine roughly balance each other out, for "the credibility of the functional view was always suspect among men endowed with good sense and reason . . . . Not a cancer, not a blessing in disguise, the political macine could be seen for what it unalterably *is:* a pretty good racket."[19]

In one sense, this characterization of the machine is indeed unalterable: the patronage party is like other rackets in that it brings benefits to some people at the same time that it harms others. But the term *racket* carries strong connotations of bribery, intimidation, and fraud. It seems to presuppose that the machine brings no more genuine benefits to the voters who support it than, say, a narcotics ring or a numbers wheel brings to its respective clienteles. The findings of this study require modification of this traditional critique of patronage politicians and their supporters. The latter are not less moral than other citizens. While they may concern themselves more with class, ethnic, or local concerns than with the public interest in the broadest sense, they vote on the basis of ideal motives as much as other mass publics do. Thus, their support is not won as cheaply as has been commonly supposed. Patronage politicians must take an active role in local public life and demonstrate communal concerns both substantively and symbolically. On the basis of the information available to them and in accord with their commitments to local subcommunities, machine supporters vote for the candidates they think are best.

What of the morality of the patronage politicians themselves? Setting aside the unanswerable question of what their ultimate goals in life really are, it is clear that many of their day-to-day political actions are selfishly motivated. They routinely use deceptive and manipulative techniques to further their ambitions. For the sake of party loyalty they avoid dealing substantively with some important issues upon whose resolution the city's future depends. They make decisions on the basis of what is best for the party rather than what is best for the entire polity. As part of a powerful and secretive party, they enjoy a freedom to act selfishly which politicians in other settings do not share.

Yet the principal standard by which patronage politicians ought to be judged is not their motivations or intentions, but the consequences of what they do. To what extent do they advance the interests of their constituents? We have seen that a variety of structural mechanisms permit the successful defense of a party organized around venality. The costs of the patronage system are borne by the public. But these costs are either so widely dispersed as to be imperceptible to most Chicagoans, or concentrated among groups whose support the party does not need to have. And the party *does* need the support of most Chicagoans to maintain its control of decision-making. Since the party does not control votes through mechanisms of exchange, the broad support it receives indicates the breadth of its favorable outputs. Some of the benefits are, as we have seen, illusory. The benefits are not distributed to everyone, nor are they allocated according to universalistic standards of equity. But in Chicago, enough citizens have been content with their slice of the pie to keep the patronage party in power for the last half century. As we gain a more accurate understanding of how the political machine secures electoral support, we thus arrive at a more favorable evaluation of it in relation to our democratic ideals.

Appendixes

Appendix A Interview Schedule and Number of Interview Responses

(Paraphrase the following introduction:) My name is ______ and I'm from the Center for Social Organization Studies at the University of Chicago. You probably received our letter about the survey we are making of community attitudes in Chicago. We are interviewing a cross section of the people in the city, and your name has turned up as one of those that I am to talk to. All interviews are strictly confidential. They are combined in a statistical report and no person is identified. Do you have a few minutes to give your opinions on the questions we have?

First we would like to get some of your ideas about the sort of services you're getting from local government:

1. How long have you lived in the City of Chicago?

Response Category	Voter Sample	Combined Sample
1–21 years	38	56
22 years or more	68	104
	106	160
And how long have you lived in your neighborhood?		
1–9 years	54	74
10 years or more	52	86

2. Compared with the rest of Chicago, do you think government services in your neighborhood are better, worse, or about the same as the rest of the city? (If

Respondent doesn't know:) Would you say it's about average?

better	30	44
about the same	47	74
worse	25	34
don't know	4	8

3a. Whom would you call or go see if there was a big pile of boards and trash in your alley? (If R. says "streets department," etc.:) You mean downtown?

correct: ward superintendent, ward yard	5	10
precinct captain, precinct worker	10	10
alderman, committeeman	29	58
Mayor's Office of Inquiry and Information, Mayor's Office of Senior Citizens, Department of Streets and Sanitation downtown	24	36
police, newspaper, phone company	5	9
neighbor, relative, building manager	13	13
don't know, no response	20	24

3b. Whom would you call or go see if there was a big hole in the street in front of where you live?

correct: Department of Streets and Sanitation	26	39
precinct captain, precinct worker	12	14
alderman, committeeman	22	44
MOII, MOSC, city hall	19	29
police, newspaper, phone company	2	4
neighbor, relative, building manager	5	5
don't know, no response	20	25

3c. And if there was an abandoned car on the block?

correct: Police Department	51	80
precinct captain, precinct worker	6	6
alderman, committeeman	15	28
MOII, MOSC, city hall	4	9
newspaper, phone company	1	2
neighbor, relative, building manager	1	2
don't know, no response	28	33

3*d*. If you weren't sure whom to call or go see, who would you ask?

correct: look up the number, find out myself by calling	14	29
precinct captain, precinct worker	8	8
alderman, committeeman	8	24
MOII, MOSC, congressman's office	18	26
police, newspaper, phone company, local agency, community group	25	29
neighbor, relative, building manager	19	27
don't know, no response	14	17

4. Sometimes big agencies like the phone company or the city government don't do what they're supposed to. Do you think it does you any good to complain to them when this happens?

yes, does good	56	93
no, does no good	43	59
don't know, no response	7	8

5. Sometimes people with "connections" get better service from government agencies. Over all, how has this affected you—that is, do you think this has helped you or hurt you more?

helped more	23	39
neither helped nor hurt	52	79
hurt more	26	35
don't know, no response	5	7

6. Here's a question about the police. If all Chicago Policemen were honest and did their jobs strictly by the rules, what kind of service do you think you personally would get from the police—better, worse, or about the same as now? (If R. says "same," or praises police:) So the things we read in the papers sometimes about corruption haven't affected you?

better	61	95
about the same	39	57
worse	2	2
don't know	4	6
police do a good job now	22	32
no spontaneous praise of police	84	128

7. In general, if you had a problem to take up with a government bureau, would you do it yourself, or do you think you would be better off if you got the help of some person or organization? (If R. says he would get help:) Who would that be? (If depends or don't know:) Do you think there are some problems you might have with a government bureau that it would be better to handle yourself?

would help self	46	71
would get help	58	87
don't know, no response	2	2

8. Do you think any of the people in the Democratic party would help you out with a problem if you asked them to?

yes	76	113
depends, don't know	20	30
no	9	15
no response	1	2

9a. Do you have a Democratic precinct captain in the precinct where you life?

yes	82	134
no, don't know	24	26

9b. (If *9a* is no or don't know:) Do you know someone in your neighborhood who works with the Democratic party?

not applicable	84	137
yes	0	1
no	22	22

9c. (If *9a* is yes:) Do you know him, or somebody who works with the party?

not applicable	23	24
yes	60	99
no	23	37

9d. (If yes on *9b* or *9c:*) How well would you say you know the captain (this person)? Just by sight? Would you say he's a good friend of yours?

not applicable	43	56
by sight	23	34
by sight and by name	7	11
acquainted	21	39
know well, but is not a friend	9	9
know well, is a friend	5	11

10.	What about the Republican precinct captain?		
	don't know him	90	135
	by sight	7	13
	acquainted	6	8
	know well	3	4
11*a*.	Do you happen to know the name of your alderman?		
	correct identification	37	85
	incorrect, don't know	69	75
11*b*.	What about your Democratic ward committeeman?		
	correct identification of incumbent or his predecessor	12	29
	incorrect, don't know	94	131
11*c*.	Your Republican committeeman?		
	correct identification	2	10
	incorrect, don't know	104	150
12*a*.	In the last six months, have you noticed any problems around where you live that the city should be taking care of?		
	yes	74	117
	no	32	43
12*b*.	(If yes:) Did you have occasion to do anything about this?		
	not applicable	32	44
	did something	25	51
	did nothing	49	65
12*c*.	(If did nothing:) Is somebody else taking care of it?		
	not applicable	58	95
	other individual taking care of it	11	12
	other group taking care of it	4	8
	no	12	20
	don't know	21	25
13*a*.	Have you ever had occasion to ask your alderman for assistance with anything?		
	yes	22	65
	no	84	95
13*b*.	(If yes on 13*a*:) What was the most important thing he ever tried to help you with?		
	not applicable	84	89
	general good	7	19
	routine service	7	26
	special favor	8	26

13*c*. (If yes on 13*a:*) Are you satisfied with what he did for you?

not applicable	85	96
yes	14	44
no	7	20

13*d*. (If yes on 13*a:*) Do you feel that he helped you as a special favor, or that he would have done the same for anyone?

not applicable	91	111
special favor	1	6
same for anyone	14	43

13*e*. (If yes on 13*a:*) What did you think of him after that?

not applicable	86	97
positive evaluation	10	24
neutral	5	23
negative evaluation	5	16

13*f*. (If yes on 13*c:*) Did he ever ask you for anything in return for this?

not applicable, no response	90	107
yes, asked for something	2	8
no, never asked anything	14	45

14*a*. Have you ever had occasion to ask your Democratic ward committeeman for assistance with anything?

yes	7	15
no	99	145

14*b*. (If yes on 14*a:*) What was the most important thing he ever tried to help you with?

not applicable	100	146
general good	0	2
routine service	3	6
special favor	3	6

14*c*. (If yes on 14*a:*) Are you satisfied with what he did for you?

not applicable	102	149
yes	3	9
no	1	2

14*d*. (If yes on 14*a*:) Do you feel that he helped you as a special favor, or that he would have done the same for anyone?

not applicable	103	151
special favor	0	2
same for anyone	3	7

14*e*. (If yes on 14*a:*) What did you think of him after that?

not applicable	103	151
positive evaluation	1	5
neutral	2	3
negative evalution	0	1

14*f*. (If yes on 14*c:*) Did he ever ask you for anything in return for this?

not applicable, no response	103	151
yes, asked for something	1	1
no, never asked anything	2	8

15. What about your Republican committeeman?

yes, have asked assistance	1	2
no, never asked assistance	105	158

16*a*. Have you ever had occasion to ask your Democratic precinct captain for assistance with anything?

yes	14	30
no	92	130

16*b*. (If yes on 16*a:*) What was the most important thing he ever tried to help you with?

not applicable	93	131
general good	0	3
routine service	6	12
special favor	7	14

16*c*. (If yes on 16*a:*) Are you satisfied with what he did for you?

not applicable	94	135
yes	10	21
no	2	4

16*d*. (If yes on 16*a:*) Do you feel that he helped you as a special favor, or that he would have done the same for anyone?

not applicable	96	140
special favor	2	2
same for anyone	8	18

16*e*. (If yes on 16*a:*) What did you think of him after that?

not applicable	95	137
positive evaluation	6	12
neutral	5	9
negative evaluation	0	2

16*f*. (If yes on 16*c:*) Did he ever ask you for anything in return for this?

not applicable, no response	95	139

yes, asked for something	3	5
no, never asked anything	8	16

17. What about your Republican precinct captain?

yes, have asked assistance	1	2
no, never asked assistance	105	158

Very good. Now we'd like to have your views about politics in Chicago.

18*a*. Generally speaking, do you consider yourself a Republican, a Democrat, or what?

18*b*. (If Democrat or Republican:) Do you think of yourself as a strong Democrat (Republican)?

18*c*. (If Independent or other:) Do you think of yourself as closer to the Republican or closer to the Democratic party?

strong Democrat	30	41
weak Democrat	31	50
independent Democrat	10	18
independent Independent	12	20
independent Republican	4	7
weak Republican	10	12
strong Republican	6	8
other, not ascertained	3	4

19*a*. When is the last time you voted in an election?

19*b*. (If voted in 1972 or later:) Where did you go to vote?

did not vote in 1972 or later	7	12
voted in 1972 presidential or other 1972 election	23	38
voted in March 1974 primary or Democratic convention delegate electors balloting of 1974	76	110

19*c*. (If voted in 1972 or later:) There are so many names on the ballot at election time, it's very difficult to know all about every single candidate. If you went to vote and didn't know much about the candidates for some of the offices, what would you do? (If no clear answer:) Would you "go for the party" on those?

(Note: Up to two answers coded for each respondent.)

vote for neither	40	63
ask precinct captain or someone at polling place	9	11
follow newspaper endorsements	22	32

follow IVI-IPO sample ballot	9	13
vote by ethnicity, pick at random	7	14
vote according to party	35	48
make up own mind, ask family member or friend	21	32

20. Have you ever helped campaign for a party or candidate during an election—like putting in time or contributing money?

yes	27	47
no	79	113

21*a*. Last March 19 there was an election where they voted on the RTA. Do you remember what the RTA proposal was?

correct	78	113
incorrect, don't know	28	47

21*b*. Do you recall if the RTA proposal passed or not?

correct—it passed	76	114
incorrect, don't know	30	46

22*a*. Do you belong to any block groups?

yes	5	22
no	101	138

22*b*. community organizations?

yes	5	16
no	101	144

22*c*. political clubs?

yes	1	2
no	105	158

22*d*. service organizations, like fraternal or veterans' groups or charity work?

yes	31	57
no	75	103

23*a*. Are there any city or neighborhood newspapers that you read regularly?

23*b*. How often do you read it (them)?

reads city paper daily	75	120
reads city paper sometimes	21	27
never reads city paper	10	13
reads neighborhood paper weekly or oftener	26	51

reads neighborhood paper sometimes	24	37
never reads neighborhood paper	56	74

Now I'd like to read some of the kinds of things people tell me when I interview them, and to ask you whether you agree or disagree with them. I'll read them one at a time and you tell me whether you *strongly agree, agree, disagree,* or *strongly disagree:*

24*a*. Sometimes politics seems so complicated that a person like me can't really understand what's going on.

strongly agree	31	39
agree	34	52
disagree	28	45
strongly disagree	12	23
no response	1	1

24*b*. We may hear a lot about dirty politics, but some politicians really have the best interest of all the people at heart.

strongly agree	20	34
agree	65	97
disagree	16	22
strongly disagree	2	3
no response	3	4

24*c*. People who criticize the Chicago city administration don't know what they're talking about.

strongly agree	8	14
agree	33	51
disagree	40	57
strongly disagree	18	30
no response	7	8

24*d*. The way people vote is the main thing that decides how things are run in this city. (If not sure:) Does it matter who gets elected?

strongly agree	9	15
agree	38	60
disagree	38	56
strongly disagree	17	24
no response	4	5

24*e*. In a big city like Chicago, a truly honest man can't be successful in politics.

strongly agree	8	11
agree	32	44

disagree	45	70
strongly disagree	15	28
no response	6	7

24*f*. So many other people vote in elections that it doesn't matter much whether I vote or not.

strongly agree	2	3
agree	14	16
disagree	37	57
strongly disagree	52	82
no response	1	2

That completes the regular part of the interview. As I was telling you, we don't reveal the name of any person we interview, but we do get a few facts about the people we talk to. I mean like occupation, age, and so on. We do this so we can compare the ideas of different people in different occupations, for example; or compare the ideas of younger people with those of older people, and so on.

25. Do you own your home, or are you renting?

owner, buying	12	35
renter	91	122
inmate of institution	3	3

26. May I ask your age?

18–30	25	32
31–55	28	53
56 and older	53	75

27. Are you or anyone living with you receiving any veterans' benefits? unemployment compensation? social security? public aid? or anything like that?

receives public aid	13	20
receives other benefits	10	11
receives nothing, or social security only	83	129

28. What is your occupation? (As clarification:) What kind of work do you do?

professional, top managerial	8	17
semiprofessional, assistant managers	25	40
clerical workers, small retail owners	28	40
skilled workers	7	14
semiskilled workers	22	29
unskilled workers	12	15
not ascertained	4	5

29. What was the highest grade of school you completed? (If attended college:) How many years of college did you attend?

none	1	1
some elementary	8	9
eighth grade	5	6
some high school	22	31
fourth year high school	20	39
some college	25	34
fourth year college	14	19
graduate study	9	19
not ascertained	2	2

30. What is your religious preference? (If Protestant:) What religious denomination is that?

Roman Catholic	30	51
Protestant	45	59
Jewish	21	34
other, no preference	10	16

31. What nationality were your ancestors on your father's side (As clarification:) What country were they from? (If "American":) Your people go way back here, then?

white American	15	21
West, North, Central European	56	82
East, South European	25	43
black American	3	3
Latin American	4	5
American Indian	1	2
Asian	2	4

32. (Respondent's sex.)

Male	56	84
Female	50	76

Appendix B
Sampling and Interview Procedure

The sample survey on which this study is partly based was perforce conducted at minimal cost. Several features of its design were the result of the need to keep the project at a scale that a single researcher could complete within a reasonable time. This constraint led to (1) limiting the number of interviews to around 150; (2) designing the questionnaire to permit some interviews to be completed by telephone; and (3) drawing a small separate sample of ward office clients, to ensure a sufficient number of users of party services in the combined sample of voters and clients. Since all the interviews were conducted within a single ward, it was possible to make repeated follow-up visits to potential respondents and thereby achieve a relatively high completion rate.

Sampling Procedure

The *voter sample* was drawn from the official printed list of registered voters for the ward (including supplemental listings) valid for the March 1974 election—some 28,000 names. The population for the *client sample* was generated by organizing and editing the alderman's files.

During the period I worked with the alderman, his staff expended unusual effort in keeping careful written records of all service requests and the action taken on each. Most of these records included the names, addresses, and phone numbers of the complainants, notes and comments of office personnel, and copies of relevant correspondence. The alderman turned over to me in 1974 all his records for the period from April 1971 through June 1973. Each service request record was filed under the name of the agency to which the request had been forwarded. I reorganized the records by date of initial complaint and consolidated split and duplicate records. It was clear that the best records were from 1972, but that careful record-keeping on abandoned car complaints did not begin until midyear. I took all service requests initiated in 1972, substituting abandoned car complaints from the first six months of 1973 for abandoned car complaints from the first six months of 1972. I now had records of 609 discrete service requests, fairly representative of the complaints initiated during a year. It was necessary to define the population on a full-year basis, because the kind of complaint the office receives (and the kind of complainant) varies with the season. Next I eliminated from the set all records which lacked the name or address of the complainant, all those in which the initiator of the request was listed on the ward club roster as a club member, and those initiated by nonresidents of the ward. I then consolidated the records of discrete complaints, so that no person's name was listed more than once. There remained 355 names from which the client sample was drawn.

In sampling from the list of registered voters, I first ordered the precinct lists by average income. Each precinct was assigned to an income category according to the 1969 median family income of the census tract which contained the precinct. The categories were ordered from highest to lowest, and within each category, precincts were randomly ordered.[1]

I hoped to complete 100 voter interviews, but I did not know what the completion rate would be. I began by drawing a systematic sample of 100 names from the voter population, using a randomly chosen start and a uniform sampling interval that distributed the sample through the entire list. After some interviews were completed, I estimated the completion rate and calculated the number of additional names I would need in order to achieve 100 completions. Fifty-five supplementary names were picked systematically from the 100 "halfway" names, names listed halfway between two consecutive previously sampled names.[2] I continued interviewing, reestimated the ultimate completions, and supplemented the sample again with 15 of the remaining halfway names. There were 170 names in the full sample of voter names, distributed over the entire list of registered voters.

I used a similar procedure in sampling from the client list. I first categorized the 355 complainants by the area of the ward in which they lived and ordered them within categories by date of request. I drew a systematic sample of 50 names using a randomly chosen start and a uniform sampling interval. In order to achieve 50 completions, I later supplemented these with all 50 halfway names and then picked 12 additional names using a randomly chosen start and a uniform sampling interval. One of these 112 names was that of a person in the voter sample who had already been interviewed. This individual's name was deleted from the client sample, leaving 111 in the full sample of client names.

Interview Procedure

I hoped to complete as many interviews as possible by telephone. I consulted the telephone directory for the phone numbers of persons in the voter sample and those in the client sample whose numbers were not on file. For numbers not in the directory, I called Directory Assistance. By these means, I obtained phone numbers for 62 percent of the voter sample, including 77 percent of the voters in the high-rise area, 58 percent in the working-class area, and 37 percent in the central area.

A letter describing the purpose of the interview was sent in advance to each prospective respondent. Those whose telephone numbers were known received a letter stating that an interviewer would telephone them. Those whose telephone numbers could not be determined were asked to send their numbers and a time they could be reached. A stamped, preprinted reply card was enclosed with these letters, but only a handful were returned. (See figs. 3–5.)

THE UNIVERSITY OF CHICAGO

CENTER FOR SOCIAL ORGANIZATION STUDIES

DEPARTMENT OF SOCIOLOGY
1126 EAST 59TH STREET
CHICAGO · ILLINOIS 60637

TELEPHONE (312) 753-2967

Executive Committee:
EDWARD O. LAUMANN, *Director*
CHARLES BIDWELL
MORRIS JANOWITZ

August 24, 1974

Mr. John S. Listed
1000 West Survey Street
Chicago, Illinois 60601

Dear Mr. Listed:

The Center for Social Organization Studies of the University of Chicago is conducting a public-opinion survey of Chicago residents. The purpose is to get an accurate picture of the characteristics of the people in Chicago neighborhoods and how they feel about some important problems.

Your name has turned up as one of several hundred names selected by chance in order to give us an accurate cross-section of the population. We would like to include you in our survey. All interviews are entirely confidential. They are combined in a statistical report in which your answers cannot be identified. The interview takes about fifteen minutes, and is usually conducted by telephone.

In order that this sample be truly representative of people in Chicago, we cannot make substitutions. An interviewer will telephone you sometime during the next month. I am sure that you will find it interesting and worthwhile to participate in our survey.

If you have any questions, our interviewers will be glad to answer them.

Sincerely yours,

Edward O. Laumann, Ph.D.
Director

Fig. 3. Specimen letter to respondent whose telephone number is known

THE UNIVERSITY OF CHICAGO
CENTER FOR SOCIAL ORGANIZATION STUDIES

DEPARTMENT OF SOCIOLOGY
1126 EAST 59TH STREET
CHICAGO · ILLINOIS 60637

TELEPHONE (312) 753-2967

Executive Committee:
EDWARD O. LAUMANN, *Director*
CHARLES BIDWELL
MORRIS JANOWITZ

August 24, 1974

Mr. James E. Femeral
100 N. Lasalle Street
Chicago, Illinois 60699

Dear Mr. Femeral:

The Center for Social Organization Studies of the University of Chicago is conducting a public-opinion survey of Chicago residents. The purpose is to get an accurate picture of the characteristics of the people in Chicago neighborhoods and how they feel about some important problems.

Your name has turned up as one of several hundred names selected by chance in order to give us an accurate cross-section of the population. We would like to include you in our survey. All interviews are entirely confidential. They are combined in a statistical report in which your answers cannot be identified. The interview takes about fifteen minutes, and is usually conducted by telephone.

In order that this sample be truly representative of people in Chicago, we cannot make substitutions. If you would like the interviewer to telephone you rather than visit you in person, please fill out and return the enclosed, stamped postcard. An interviewer will contact you sometime during the next month. I am sure that you will find it interesting and worthwhile to participate in our survey.

If you have any questions, our interviewers will be glad to answer them.

Sincerely yours,

Edward O. Laumann, Ph.D.
Director

Fig. 4. Specimen letter to respondent whose telephone number is not known

NAME: ____

ADDRESS: ____

I would like to participate in the Center's survey.
My phone number is ____________________. The best days and times for the interviewer to telephone me for a short interview would be:

____________________ between __________ AM/PM and __________ AM/PM
(days of the week)

____________________ between __________ AM/PM and __________ AM/PM.

I understand that you will keep my phone number and the interview entirely confidential.

Fig. 5. Specimen respondent reply card

Persons without telephones and those who could not be reached by phone I interviewed in person. If a person had moved, I attempted to determine the new address. A person was listed as "moved" only if the new address was outside the ward or could not be determined. Neither the number of call-backs nor the number of return visits was limited. At the conclusion of the interview period, there remained no cases listed as "not at home." Of the 160 interviews completed, 76 percent were conducted by telephone, including 72 percent of the voter interviews and 84 percent of the client interviews.

Table 23 displays the final disposition of all cases. In the full voter sample, 78.8 percent of the names were valid, and 79.1 percent of the valid names were interviewed. In the full client sample, 62.1 percent of the names were valid, and 78.2 percent of the valid names were interviewed. The completion rate for the combined sample was 78.8 percent of valid names. Unfortunately, no independent data are available on characteristics of voters or clients, against which the

Table 23 Completion Rates for Voter and Client Samples

	Number	Percent of Total Names	Percent of Valid Names
Voter Sample			
Completed interviews	106	62.4	79.1
Moved from ward	32	18.8	—
Deceased	4	2.4	—
Total invalid names	36	21.2	
Insufficient English	1	0.6	0.7
Incompetent; incapacitated	2	1.2	1.5
Out of town	1	0.6	0.7
Refused interview	24	14.1	17.9
Valid names not completed	28	16.5	20.9
Total valid names	134	78.8	100.0
Total initial names	170	100.0	—
Client Sample			
Completed interviews	54	48.6	78.2
Moved from ward; moved with no forwarding address	18	16.2	—
No such address; unknown at address	11	9.9	—
Deceased	5	4.5	—
Not ward resident	5	4.5	—
Member of ward club	1	0.9	—
Did not actually initiate request	2	1.8	—
Total invalid names	42	37.8	
Insufficient English	2	1.8	2.8
Incapacitated	1	0.9	1.4
Refused interview	12	10.8	17.4
Valid names not completed	15	13.5	21.7
Total valid names	69	62.1	100.0
Total initial names	111	100.0	—

representativeness of the groups interviewed might be measured.

I wrote the responses directly in the questionnaire during the interviews, attempting to record as much verbatim response as possible. The interviews ranged in length from 10 to 40 minutes; the average interview lasted 13 minutes. The distribution of responses to each item on the interview schedule is summarized in appendix A.

Appendix C
Services Which Client Sample Respondents Failed to Report

Eight respondents in the client sample told the interviewer they had never asked assistance from the alderman, the committeemen, or a precinct captain. The alderman's records from which the client sample was selected describe the following contacts with these respondents:

Case Number	Date	Recorded Service
152	no date	Precinct captain asked alderman to write a letter requesting the planting of additional trees at R.'s place of business.
210	6/72	R. requested removal of abandoned car.
211	10/72	Alderman sent R. a letter congratulating him on his recent registration as a new voter.
216	7/72	R. complained about debris left on lot after demolition of building across street from home.
218	4/72	R. visited ward office and discussed with alderman's assistant how to get city sanitation bureau to pick up materials collected in her apartment building for recycling.

220	5/72	Alderman wrote letter at R.'s request regarding problem with his voter registration.
236	10/72	R. requested repair of broken street light; alderman wrote letter to Bureau of Electricity and got written confirmation that repair was completed.
239	10/72	R.'s name was listed with four others on note protesting "unnecessary" curb and gutter repair which was causing damage to lawns.

Note that in case 211 no service was requested and in case 239 the respondent probably did not initiate the request. These two cases were eliminated from the client sample before analysis.

Appendix D Multivariate Analysis of Service Use

This appendix describes the method and presents the results of a multivariate analysis of characteristics of users of party services, which was summarized in chapter 6. A multivariate technique was used to examine the effects of different components of community attachment on service use, and to test four hypotheses about service use which are described in chapter 6. The results indicate the effect of each predictor with other predictors statistically controlled, allowing us to detect if any of the simple correlations discussed in the text are spurious.

The method used was the modified multiple regression approach to multidimensional contingency table analysis developed by Leo A. Goodman.[1] This log-linear method is especially designed for data sets such as the one discussed here where variables are nominal or ordinal and one variable is viewed as the dependent variable. The advantages of this technique are that it facilitates tests for higher-order interaction effects among variables and does not rest on the assumptions of homoscedasticity and unrestricted range. These assumptions are required for ordinary regression models, but they do not hold in data sets of this kind. The analysis is carried out by first organizing the data into a complete multidimensional contingency table. A series of hypothetical log-linear models is then fitted to the table. In this procedure, maximum-likelihood estimates of cell frequencies under different models are computed using an iterative method.[2] The estimated cell frequencies generated by the different models are then compared with the observed cell frequencies by computing a chi-square statistic.[3] The smaller the chi-square value, the better the fit, and the stronger the explanatory power of the independent variable or variables in the model. By computing the relative reduction in chi-square values from various models containing different combinations of independent variables as predictors of the dependent variable, one obtains measures of association roughly analogous to coefficients of determination, multiple determination and partial determination in conventional regression analysis. One can also obtain effect parameters for any model, which, like regression coefficients in multiple regression equations, indicate the direction and relative strength of the effect of each predictor variable (or interaction of predictors) on the dependent variable.

Components of Community Attachment

It was shown in table 12 in the text that indicators of community attachment were all strongly associated with service requests of all types. Does each component of community attachment actually have a separate effect on service use? I used the modified multiple regression technique to find the answer to this question.

The first step of the analysis was to dichotomize each variable and construct a series of three seven-way contingency tables. Each table included the six predictor variables which appear in table 12, cross-classified with a different type of service request. The dependent variable in the first table was *requests for general goods:* general goods requesters constituted the first category of this variable, nonusers constituted the other category, and all other respondents were excluded from the table. The other two tables were constructed similarly, with *requests for routine services* and *requests for special favors* as the dependent variables.

Fortunately, tests for interaction effects among the predictors in these tables showed that all interaction effects involving the dependent variable could be ignored without significant loss of explanatory power.[4] We may therefore consider only the direct effect of each predictor on the dependent variables. Table 24 shows, for each type of service request, the effect parameters for a log-linear model which includes all six predictors and excludes all interaction effects. It would be possible to exclude from these models some of the smaller effect parameters without appreciably reducing the explained variance, but despite their lack of parsimony the six-predictor models are best suited to exposition of the findings. The zero-order effect parameters are also displayed in table 24. These represent the degree of relationship between a predictor and a dependent variable observed without controlling for other predictors.[5] These coefficients provide no new information; they simply recapitulate the relationships shown in table 12 in a form more readily comparable with the multivariate beta coefficients.

The simple additive models involving the six components of community attachment account for most (63 to 74 percent) of the variance[6] in the types of service use. The independent variables have about the same relative predictive power in the multivariate equations as they do in zero-order relationships. The zero-order effects we saw in table 12 are partly a result of interrelationships among predictors which are controlled in the modified multiple regression analysis, but none of the simple correlations is wholly spurious. The importance of each component of community attachment is demonstrated in that indicators of access, need, responsibility and rights each have substantial independent effects on service use. The moral and sentimental aspects of community attachment are at least as important as the other aspects.

The variations in the relative strength of the effect parameters in the models for different types of service use are also revealing.[7] The strongest predictor of requests for general goods is membership in local organizations; homeownership is the strongest predictor of requests for routine services; length of local residence is strongest in the equation for requests for special favors.

Table 24 Effects of Components of Community Attachment on Three Types of Service Request: Modified Multiple Regression Results[a]

	Dependent Variables					
	Requests for General Goods		Requests for Routine Services		Requests for Special Favors	
Predictors	Zero-order Coefficient	Beta Coefficient	Zero-order Coefficient	Beta Coefficient	Zero-order Coefficient	Beta Coefficient
Citation of party as service resource	.190	.020	.578	.344	.488	.280
Homeownership	.606	.226	.832	.616	.590	.318
Membership in local organization	.968	.752	.418	.188	.556	.364
Length of local residence	.300	.170	.564	.388	.606	.582
Reading community press	.514	.428	.442	.260	.656	.506
Stage of life cycle	.662	.500	.634	.492	.654	.438
(Constant term)		−.166		.046		.108
(Coefficient of multiple determination)[b]		R^2 = .629		R^2 = .738		R^2 = .628
(Number of cases)[c]		122		139		142

[a]These results are from analyses of three similar seven-way, 128 cell contingency tables. Each includes a different variable and the six predictors.

The categories for these dichotomies are:

Variable	Category 1	Category 2
Requests for general goods	Requester of a general good	Nonuser
Requests for routine services	Requester of a routine service	Nonuser
Requests for special favors	Requester of a special favor	Nonuser
Citation of party as a service resource	R. named alderman, committee-man, or precinct worker as source of routine services (Q.5)	R. named other resources only
Homeownership	Homeowner	Renter, inmate of institution
Membership in local organization	Member of block club or community organization	Member of neither
Length of local residence	Resident of area 10 years or longer	Resident of area less than 10 years
Reading community press	Reader of community newspaper once a week or more	Reader less often
Stage of life cycle	R. aged 31–55	R. of other age

The quantity .25 was added to each cell of each table before analysis.

[b]Based on likelihood-ratio chi-square statistic.

[c]Number of cases in tables varies because each includes only one type of service requester. Number of cases shown for each table reflects artificial increase resulting from addition of .25 to each cell of full table.

This pattern supports the interpretation suggested in the discussion of table 12 in chapter 6 that these predictors are indicators of responsibility, needs and rights, respectively. For all three types of requests, however, there remain substantial independent effects of two other predictors: reading the community press and being in the middle years of the life cycle. If community attachment consisted entirely of the four components I have identified and if the first four predictors in these multivariate models were very good indicators of those components, then we would not encounter these substantial additional effects. The multivariate analysis has thus not fully succeeded in reducing community attachment to an exhaustive set of theoretically distinct, empirically independent dimensions. Accomplishing that task would require more extensive data on the attitudes of respondents and their relationships to others in the community. The available data indicate nevertheless that several distinct aspects of community attachment, including moral and emotional ties, have positive and substantial independent effects on use of party services.

Tests of the Four Hypotheses

Having established the nature of community attachment's effects on service use, we now test whether this strong effect operates independently of the other hypothesized causes of use: political participation, socioeconomic status, and ethos. As indicated in chapter 6, political participation was measured by a six-item index, socioeconomic status was measured by the white-collar/blue-collar dichotomy, religion was used as the sole indicator of ethos, and community attachment was measured by a five-item localism index. Modified multiple regression techniques were applied to seven five-way contingency tables, with the results shown in tables 25 and 26. As in the analyses above, each contingency table included a different dependent variable and the same set of predictors. As before, none of the higher-order interactions involving the dependent variables was significant, so that only the direct effects of the four predictors are considered. Models including all four predictors are shown for all dependent variables, even though the smaller effects could be eliminated without substantially reducing the explained variance. The four-predictor models are quite powerful, explaining from 65 to 85 percent of the variance in the odds for different types of service use.

When service use (including all types) is taken as the dependent variable, we find that high political participation scores and blue-collar occupational status have small effects (raising the predicted odds of service use by about 40 percent); being Catholic, our indicator of ethos, has a moderate effect (raising the odds by a factor of 2.5); and having a high localism score has a very strong effect (raising the odds more than sixfold). The multivariate results thus confirm what the zero-order associations suggested: the data give little support to the political participation and poverty hypotheses, moderate support to the ethos hypothesis, and very strong support to the community attachment hypothesis.

The predictive models for ward use and precinct use differ somewhat. Blue-collar occupational status is more strongly associated with precinct use than with ward use, and the political participation index has a substantial effect on ward use but not on precinct use. These differences are partly a spurious result of differences among people who request different types of service, since all requests for general goods are directed to ward-level party agents. To eliminate the confounding effect of type of service requested, a separate contingency table was analyzed which included (with nonusers) only ward users who had requested specific goods, i.e., routine services or special favors. When the model for specific ward use is compared with the model for precinct use, there is no appreciable difference in the effect of occupational status, because the somewhat higher-status requesters of general goods are excluded. But the difference in the effect of political participation remains substantial. This is further testimony to the effectiveness of the outreach efforts of precinct-level party agents. They are able to reach nonparticipators as effectively as they reach politically active residents. The

Table 25 Multivariate Models for Service Use by Type of Agent Contacted[a]

Predictors	Dependent Variables							
	Service Use		Ward Use		Specific Ward Use		Precinct Use	
	Zero-order Coef-ficient	Beta Coef-ficient	Zero-order Coef-ficient	Beta Coef-ficient	Zero-order Coef-ficient	Beta Coef-ficient	Zero-order Coef-ficient	Beta Coef-ficient
Political participation index	.238	.180	.406	.308	.300	.240	−.048	−.086
Occupational status	−.136	−.188	−.118	−.148	−.250	−.212	−.202	−.238
Respondent's religion	.466	.466	.436	.478	.496	.534	.540	.484
Localism index	.912	.912	.848	.818	.818	.820	.944	.942
(Constant term)		.514		.146		−.056		−.468
(Coefficient of multiple determination)[b]	$R^2 = .841$		$R^2 = .850$		$R^2 = .765$		$R^2 = .681$	
(Number of cases)[c]	171		141		128		115	

[a]These results are from analyses of four similar five-way, 32 cell contingency tables. Each includes a different dependent variable and the four predictors. The categories for these dichotomies are:

Variable	Category 1	Category 2
Service use	User	Nonuser
Ward use	Ward user	Nonuser
Specific ward use	Ward user who requested specific good	Nonuser
Precinct use	Precinct user	Nonuser
Political participation index	R. scores 4 or more on six-item index	R. scores less than 4
Occupational status	White collar	Blue collar
Religion	Catholic	Non-Catholic
Localism index	R. scores 2 or more on 5-item index	R. scores less than 2

The quantity .5 was added to each cell of each table before analysis.

[b]Based on likelihood-ratio chi-square statistic.

[c]Number of cases in tables varies because each includes only one type of user. A few cases are excluded from each table because of missing data on occupational status. Number of cases shown for each table reflects artificial increase resulting from addition of .5 to each cell of full table.

Table 26 Multivariate Models for Service Use by Type of Service Requested[a]

	Dependent Variables					
	Requests for General Goods		Requests for Routine Services		Requests for Special Favors	
Predictors	Zero-order Coefficient	Beta Coefficient	Zero-order Coefficient	Beta Coefficient	Zero-order Coefficient	Beta Coefficient
Political participation index	.686	.524	.232	.246	−.068	−.110
Occupational status	.192	−.050	−.308	−.342	−.394	−.232
Respondent's religion	.516	.446	.450	.376	.490	.494
Localism index	.794	.640	.960	.922	.769	.832
(Constant term)		−.860		−.320		−.142
(Coefficient of multiple determination)[b]		$R^2 = .727$		$R^2 = .793$		$R^2 = .655$
(Number of cases)[c]		103		119		112

[a] These results are from analyses of three similar five-way, 32 cell contingency tables. Each includes a different dependent variable and four predictors. The categories for these dichotomies are as given in notes to tables 24 and 25.

[b] Based on likelihood-ratio chi-square statistic.

[c] Number of cases in tables varies because each includes only one type of service requester. A few cases are excluded from each table because of missing data on occupational status. Number of cases shown for each table reflects artificial increase resulting from addition of .5 to each cell of full table.

association of political participation and specific ward use shows that citizen-initiated contacts are somewhat facilitated by the resources and characteristics possessed by politically active citizens.

Predictive models for requests for three different types of service are shown in table 26. Requests for routine services are strongly related to localism and moderately related to each of the other predictors as hypothesized. Requests for general goods are more strongly related to the political participation index, and are independent of occupational status when the other predictors are taken into account. Interestingly, the effect of religion on these more public-regarding requests is as strong as its effect on requests for specific goods. However, the strongest effect of religion is on requests for special favors, which are predicted to be two and a half times as likely among Catholics as among non-Catholics. This strong religious effect was also observed in table 11; it lends credibility to our use of religion as an indicator of political ethos, since requests for special favors encompass those requests which most clearly contradict universalistic standards of public service. The political participation index has no positive effect on this type of request; apparently special favors answer needs so pressing that politically inactive people (who make fewer requests for routine services) are not deterred from making requests for them.

To summarize, we may distinguish between the weak predictors of service use—political participation and occupational status—and the two strong predictors. The former are not associated with all types of service use, and although the variations in their predictive power are instructive, they contribute little to the variance explained by the multivariate models. In contrast, religion and localism have strong independent effects on every kind of service use, and in each model they far outweigh the weaker variables in predictive power. Localism is much the stronger of the two predictors. To illustrate, let us consider alternative models for predicting service use. A model including localism alone accounts for 66 percent of the variance in the odds of service use. The addition of religion to the predictive model raises the explained variance to 81 percent. But if we then add the two weak predictors we achieve very little additional increase in the model's predictive power; as shown in table 25, the four predictors jointly explain 84 percent of the variance.

Notes

Preface

1 On the patterned differential between the access to knowledge enjoyed by insiders and outsiders, see Robert K. Merton, "Insiders and Outsiders: A Chapter in the Sociology of Knowledge," *American Journal of Sociology* 78 (1972): 9–47.

Chapter One

1 According to the *Oxford English Dictionary,* use of the word in the United States to denote the controlling organization of a political party dates back at least to 1876.

2 A machine is thus a subtype of the more general category of *patronage party:* a party that is organized primarily around the material interests of its leaders and members. Max Weber recognized patronage parties as a distinct type, calling American political parties of his day "the classic example of parties in the modern state organized primarily around patronage." See *The Theory of Social and Economic Organization,* trans. A. M. Henderson and Talcott Parsons (New York: Free Press, 1947), p. 410; the original edition was published in 1922.

3 The elusive nature of the machine is a central theme in Ralph Whitehead's obituary for Richard J. Daley, "Daley the Broker," *Chicago* 26 (February 1977): 186.

4 To say that democratic values are institutionalized in a competitive democracy is not to assume that commitment to these values is uniformly distributed or that people act only in accordance with their values.

5 It is sometimes implied that this contradiction is an illusion—that the biased observer misunderstands the motives of the patronage party, or that the actions of the machine merely clash with the value-premises of the observer, rather

than with values widely held by the public. The former claim is that of the machine politician, who avows his dedication to the public weal. The latter claim is implicit in discussions of the machine that matter-of-factly describe it as a style of city politics which neatly fits into the value system of America's industrial era. For example: "Americans responded quickly to the prospect of engaging in politics in order to secure direct, personal economic gain. Because Americans seemed to believe in salvation through material success, public life became simply another arena where financial rewards could be secured, and the public treasury offered still another opportunity for the individual to better himself. In this context, machine politics grew and flourished" (Stephen M. David and Paul E. Peterson, eds., *Urban Politics and Public Policy,* 2d ed. [New York: Praeger, 1976], p. 12). Certainly there are clear parallels between the structure of a machine and the structure of a business, between the ideology of the boss and the ideology of the capitalist. See Edward C. Banfield and James Q. Wilson, *City Politics* (Cambridge: Harvard University Press, 1963), pp. 116–19. Nevertheless, it is incorrect to suppose that machines of the industrial era were able to win public support without diguising their profit orientation.

6 See, for example, Frank R. Kent, *The Great Game of Politics* (New York: Doubleday, Page, 1926); Sonya Forthal, *Cogwheels of Democracy* (New York: Pamphlet Distributing, 1948; originally published in 1928); David H. Kurtzman, *Methods of Controlling Votes in Philadelphia* (Philadelphia: University of Pennsylvania, 1935); Harold F. Gosnell, *Machine Politics: Chicago Model* (Chicago: University of Chicago Press, 1937); H. Dicken Cherry, "Effective Precinct Organization" (Master's thesis, University of Chicago, 1952); Lucille Simmons Edley, "Strategies and Techniques of Politics: A Study of Ten Selected Precinct Captains from Chicago's Third Ward" (Master's thesis, University of Chicago, 1955).

7 A good example of such an eclectic treatment is in Thomas R. Dye, *Politics in States and Communities,* 3d ed. (Englewood Cliffs, N.J.: Prentice-Hall, 1977), pp. 247–55.

8 Studies of formal organizations have distinguished the types of motivation and the corresponding types of incentive which organizations employ to control the behavior of their members. Weber makes the distinction between *material, affectual,* and *ideal* motives. Clark and Wilson describe *material, solidary,* and *purposive* incentives. Etzioni makes the distinction between *calculative involvement, social-moral involvement,* and *pure-moral involvement* of lower participants in complex organizations. These parallel typologies are relevant to the

problem of how parties produce voter support and are directly applicable to the two traditional models of machine support and the alternative model described in this section. In this book, I use the words *inducement* and *incentive* as synonyms. Weber, *Social and Economic Organization,* p. 325; Peter B. Clark and James Q. Wilson, "Incentive Systems: A Theory of Organizations," *Administrative Science Quarterly* 6 (1961): 129–66; Amitai Etzioni, *A Comparative Analysis of Complex Organizations: On Power, Involvement, and Their Correlates* (New York: Free Press, 1961), pp. 10–11.

9 Roland L. Warren, *The Community in America* (Chicago: Rand McNally, 1963), pp. 53–94.

10 A venerable tradition links a breakdown of local affiliations to the growth of the industrial city. The leading statement is Louis Wirth, "Urbanism as a Way of Life," *American Journal of Sociology* 44 (1938): 1–24.

11 The idea that vital local communities are necessary to responsible political participation has been expressed by many theorists, but perhaps by none so forcefully as Robert Nisbet in *The Quest for Community: A Study in the Ethics of Order and Freedom* (New York: Oxford University Press, 1953).

12 Harvey Warren Zorbaugh, *The Gold Coast and the Slum: A Sociological Study of Chicago's Near North Side* (Chicago: University of Chicago Press, 1929), p. 254.

13 The concept of *social disorganization* has fallen into some disrepute, for it has too frequently been misused to disguise value-judgments. It retains its usefulness, however, as a term describing the failure of rules in a social structure, failure due either to normlessness, conflict of rules, or the breakdown of sanctions. For an elaboration of this concept and a discussion of its history, see Earl Rubington and Martin S. Weinberg, eds., *The Study of Social Problems: Five Perspectives,* 2d ed. (New York: Oxford University Press, 1977), pp. 55–91.

14 Historian Bruce M. Stave's recent analysis of the machine draws primarily from this tradition: "The immigrant, in reciprocation for the politician's largess, returned the vote as his *quid pro quo,* the favor for the vote" (*The New Deal and the Last Hurrah: Pittsburgh Machine Politics* [Pittsburgh: University of Pittsburgh Press, 1970], p. 3). Compare the following from a recent urban sociology text: "Jobs, welfare payments, Christmas and Thanksgiving baskets, and other favors or city services could be exchanged by members of the political party (or arranged for through city jobholders whose employment depended on doing such favors) for votes, election work, and the like" (Alan S. Berger, *The City: Urban Communities and Their Problems* [Dubuque, Iowa: W. C. Brown, 1978], p. 306).

15 James Bryce, *The American Commonwealth* (New York: Macmillan, 1916), 2:668, cited by Samuel J. Eldersveld, *Political Parties: A Behavioral Analysis* (Chicago: Rand McNally, 1964), p. 17.

16 Gosnell, *Machine Politics;* Robert K. Merton, *Social Theory and Social Structure,* 3d ed. (New York: Free Press, 1968), pp. 124–36; Banfield and Wilson, *City Politics,* chap. 9.

17 This viewpoint is reinforced by the many careful studies which have documented the persistence of ethnic and primary group ties in poor urban neighborhoods; for example, Herbert Gans, *The Urban Villagers* (New York: Free Press, 1962).

18 Banfield and Wilson, *City Politics,* p. 117.

19 Jane Addams, *Democracy and Social Ethics* (New York: Macmillan, 1902), p. 254; quoted in Banfield and Wilson, *City Politics,* p. 118.

20 This is the term used by Clark and Wilson for incentives based on approval and affection. See note 8 above.

21 Banfield has also employed cultural traditions as key explanations of behavior in certain of his earlier and later works. See particularly *The Moral Basis of a Backward Society* (New York: Free Press, 1958); and *The Unheavenly City Revisited* (Boston: Little, Brown, 1974).

22 On the role of an Old World cultural tradition in the politics of Irish immigrants, see Nathan Glazer and Daniel Patrick Moynihan, *Beyond the Melting Pot* (Cambridge, Mass.: MIT Press, 1963), pp. 223–29.

23 Banfield and Wilson introduced this term in *City Politics,* pp. 40–44, 234–40.

24 My usage of the term *exchange* runs counter to Peter Blau's more inclusive concept of social exchange, which encompasses "any behavior oriented to socially mediated goals." By Blau's definition, exchange includes the ideally motivated conduct which Max Weber classified as *wertrational.* It is true that the voter who casts his ballot according to his commitment to internalized values does so with some ultimate social reward in mind and that the party modifies its platform to gain the support of groups committed to certain value positions. But these are exchanges only in an abstract or secondary sense. They are qualitatively distinct from direct, short-term, person-to-person trade-offs of favors or friendship for votes, to which the term exchange will refer in this book. See Peter M. Blau, *Exchange and Power in Social Life* (New York: John Wiley & Sons, 1967), p. 5; Weber, *Social and Economic Organization,* p. 115.

25 Banfield and Wilson, *City Politics,* p. 115. The concept is

similar to Samuelson's notion of *private consumption goods,* Dahl's *divisible benefits,* and Clark's *separable goods.* See Paul A. Samuelson, "A Pure Theory of Public Expenditure," *Review of Economics and Statistics* (1954): 387–89; Robert Dahl, *Who Governs* (New Haven: Yale University Press, 1961); Terry N. Clark, "The Structure of Community Influence," in Harlan Hahn, ed., *People and Politics in Urban Society* (Beverly Hills: Sage Publications, 1972); and Clark, "The Irish Ethic and the Spirit of Patronage," *Ethnicity* 2 (1975): 305–59.

26 This view of the community has been elaborated in Morris Janowitz, *The Community Press in an Urban Setting: The Social Elements of Urbanism* (Chicago: University of Chicago Press, 1952); Scott Greer, "The Social Structure and Political Process of Suburbia," *American Sociological Review* 25 (1960): 514–26; Gerald D. Suttles, *The Social Construction of Communities* (Chicago: University of Chicago Press, 1972); and Albert Hunter, *Symbolic Communities: The Persistence and Change of Chicago's Local Communities* (Chicago: University of Chicago Press, 1974).

27 Daniel Katz and Samuel J. Eldersveld, "The Impact of Local Party Activity upon the Electorate," *Public Opinion Quarterly* 25 (1961): 1–24; Peter H. Rossi and Phillips Cutright, "The Impact of Party Organization in an Industrial Setting," in *Community Political Systems,* ed. Morris Janowitz (Glencoe, Ill.: Free Press, 1961); Phillips Cutright, "Measuring the Impact of Local Party Activity on the General Election Vote," *Public Opinion Quarterly* 27 (1963): 373–86; Raymond Wolfinger, "The Influence of Precinct Work on Voting Behavior," *Public Opinion Quarterly* 27 (1963): 387–98.

Chapter Two

1 Fred I. Greenstein, "The Changing Pattern of Urban Party Politics," *Annals of the American Academy of Political and Social Science* 353 (1964): 1.

2 For discussion see Theodore Lowi, "Foreword to the Second Edition," *Machine Politics: Chicago Model,* by Harold F. Gosnell (Chicago: University of Chicago Press, 1958).

3 For evidence, see Norman H. Nie, Sidney Verba, and John R. Petrocik, *The Changing American Voter* (Cambridge: Harvard University Press, 1976), chap. 4; and Jack Dennis, "Trends in Public Support for the American Party System," *British Journal of Political Science* 5 (1975): 187–230.

4 Eldersveld, *Political Parties,* p. 17.

5 Relevant case studies include: Don Trudeau Allensworth, "Grass Roots Politics in Suburbia: A Study of Republican and

Democratic Precinct Chairmen in Montgomery County, Maryland" (Ph.D. dissertation, American University, 1964); Lyman Arthur Kellstedt, "Precinct Committeemen in the Philadelphia Metropolitan Area: An Analysis of Role" (Ph.D. dissertation, University of Illinois, 1965); and Ronald Peter Gluck, "Politics at the Grass Roots: The Inducements and Rewards of Party Participation" (Ph.D. dissertation, State University of New York at Buffalo, 1970).

6 It is difficult to estimate how great a role machines play today. Greenstein's caution remains true: "Our knowledge of the distribution of types of local party organization is scant. We have no census of local political parties, either for today or for the putative heyday of bosses and machines. And there is reason to believe that observers have exaggerated the ubiquity of tightly organized urban political parties in past generations, as well as underestimated somewhat their contemporary prevalence" ("The Changing Pattern," p. 1).

7 The careers of two notorious turn-of-the-century bosses are described in Herman Kogan and Lloyd Wendt, *The Lords of the Levee: The Story of Bathhouse John and Hinky Dink* (Indianapolis: Bobbs-Merrill, 1943). A brief interlude of reform is described—with astonishment—in Steffens, *Autobiography,* pp. 422–29. The changing fortunes of the Republican and Democratic machines during the 1920s and 1930s are ably recounted in Gosnell, *Machine Politics,* chap. 1.

8 The analogy to a one-party nation-state is used in Peter R. Knauss, *Chicago: A One Party State* (Champaign, Ill.: Stipes Publishing, 1972). Knauss represents Chicago's Regular Democratic supporters as a coalition of capitalist interests and bourgeoisified white working-class groups which acts to exploit the new migrants at the bottom of the urban class structure.

9 Daley's career has been recounted in several recent books by Chicago journalists: Mike Royko, *Boss: Richard J. Daley of Chicago* (New York: E. P. Dutton, 1971; also in paperback edition by New American Library, Signet Books, 1971); Len O'Connor, *Clout: Mayor Daley and His City* (Chicago: H. Regnery, 1975); and William Francis Gleason, *Daley of Chicago: The Man, the Myth, and the Limits of Conventional Politics* (New York: Simon & Schuster, 1970). See also Milton L. Rakove, *Don't Make No Waves, Don't Back No Losers: An Insider's Analysis of the Daley Machine* (Bloomington: Indiana University Press, 1975). Daley's invincibility in the last years of his life is seriously questioned in Len O'Conner, *Requiem: The Decline and Demise of Mayor Daley and His Era* (Chicago:

Contemporary Books, 1977).

10 Gosnell's chapter title, "You Can't Lick a Ward Boss" (*Machine Politics*) remains apt today.

11 For a vivid description of the virtual nonexistence of Republican committeemen and organizations in some Chicago wards, see Rakove, *Don't Make No Waves,* pp. 166–74.

12 For evidence on this estimate, see David W. McCoy, "Patronage in Suburbia" (Ph.D. dissertation, University of Chicago, 1963).

13 That the Regulars should expend sufficient effort to produce this large number of votes in uncontested primaries is understandable, since each ward's performance in the primary determines the amount of patronage allocated to its committeemen.

14 Ernest W. Burgess, "The Growth of the City: An Introduction to a Research Project," in *The City,* ed. Robert E. Park, Ernest W. Burgess, and R. D. McKenzie (Chicago: University of Chicago Press, 1925), pp. 47–62.

15 See Homer Hoyt, "Recent Distortions of the Classical Models of Urban Structure," *Land Economics* 50 (1964): 199–212.

16 The lack of coincidence of ward boundaries, official "community areas," and boundaries perceived by residents of Chicago is illustrated with maps in Suttles, *Social Construction,* pp. 68–72.

17 The election was held during the lull between the presidential election and Christmas. There was little publicity. The community press made no endorsements. The only issue was control of the council by Regulars, and the outcome was of minor concern to most voters. The turnout was extremely low, and the Regular slate received an overwhelming majority. The 7 percent figure is based on the 1200 votes received by one candidate who was new to the area and did no personal campaigning. The vote was unevenly distributed: 300 came from two precincts with extremely effective captains; 80 percent of this candidate's vote was cast in 50 percent of the precincts. Thus a few precinct captains are highly effective and some are apparently quite ineffective.

18 Under the Illinois constitution, three state representatives are elected to the lower house from each legislative district. In no district may more than two of the three be from the majority party in the district. Thus even heavily Democratic districts must elect one Republican state representative.

19 I use the term *amateur* here in the special sense introduced by James Q. Wilson, *The Amateur Democrat: Club Politics in Three Cities* (Chicago: University of Chicago Press, 1962). It de-

notes the reformer's ideological orientation, rather than his principal source of livelihood, which may or may not be politics.

20 On the many advantages of combined methods in sociological research, see Sam D. Sieber, "The Integration of Fieldwork and Survey Methods," *American Journal of Sociology* 78 (1973): 1335–59.

Chapter Three

1 For more on the concept of compliance, see Etzioni, *Complex Organizations,* chap. 1.

2 These two types of power are based on the "vertical" and "horizontal" patterns of community interaction, respectively, as described in Warren, *Community in America,* chaps. 8, 9.

3 The count of patronage jobholders is based on the club's own records.

4 The alderman with whom I worked suggested that the Regular ethic could be codified, and pointed out several of the rules I have set down here. However, in practice there is no name for these rules. They are institutionalized only as a diffuse set of expectations and a specific set of traditionally prohibited practices for each role in the organization. In this partial codification, rules 7–12 specify the principle of discretion; the others specify loyalty.

5 The more overt expressions of disapproval are infrequent, because of political expediency, fear of the party's imputed power, indifference, or common politeness.

6 This is an intentionally ambiguous threat. Since public employees cannot legally be fired for failure to perform political work, an explicit threat of "vising" could lead to legal trouble for the committeeman. This statement could be interpreted strictly as meaning merely that club members who do not work will lose their positions in the club—but members of course understand the threat as relating to their sponsored jobs.

7 Shakman v. Democratic Organization of Cook County, 435 F. 2d 267 (7th Cir. 1970). On remand, Judge A. L. Marovitz held that "patronage employees may be hired or fired based on political affiliation so long as coerced political activity or contributions are not conditions of retention of that employment." See 356 F. Supp. 1241 (N. D. Ill. 1972).

8 For more on the limits of patronage power, see David W. McCoy, "Patronage in Suburbia" (Ph.D. dissertation, University of Chicago, 1963).

9 Precinct returns cannot be verified until the Election Board's

official canvass several days after the election. If the overall outcome has been favorable, no one bothers to check the captains' reports.

10 Precinct workers sometimes turn in false change-of-address cards to make club leaders think they have performed a thorough canvass.

11 "The effective application of normative powers . . . requires that lower participants be highly committed. If lower participants are only mildly committed to the organization . . . the application of normative power is likely to be ineffective" (Etzioni, *Complex Organizations,* p. 13).

12 In Etzioni's terminology, remunerative power is congruent with calculative involvement of lower participants in complex organizations. Ibid., p. 13.

13 In a study of Cook County patronage, it was found that even hard-core patronage workers (those to whom political sponsorship is vitally important) will not support the committeeman if it is revealed that he has violated the most basic moral principles. McCoy, "Patronage in Suburbia," chap. 5.

14 Gosnell, *Machine Politics,* p. 68.

15 Wilson, *Amateur Democrat,* pp. 180–88.

16 Ibid., pp. 347–55.

17 For a personal account of this change in orientation, see Rakove, *Don't Make No Waves,* p. 116.

18 The use of these tactics is advocated in Saul D. Alinsky, *Reveille for Radicals* (New York: Random House, 1946), chap. 8. Some of the opposition leaders were conscious followers of Alinsky.

19 William Foote Whyte, *Street Corner Society: The Social Structure of an Italian Slum* (Chicago: University of Chicago Press, 1943), p. 234.

Chapter Four

1 At the time of my field research, an alderman's salary was $8,000, and an aldermanic assistant's $10,000. In April 1975 these salaries were set at $17,500 and $12,072, respectively. An additional $8,000 was allowed for office expenses.

2 Their relationship is discussed in more detail in chap. 8 below.

3 Peter M. Blau, "Interaction: Social Exchange," in *International Encyclopedia of the Social Sciences,* ed. David L. Sills (New York: Macmillan Company and Free Press, 1968), 7:455.

4 For example, the manager of a shelter-care facility for former mental patients gets high-priority treatment, since his cooper-

ation with the precinct captain secures many votes for the party at election time. City workers removed abandoned cars from the grounds of this facility at the alderman's request, although they normally may not take cars from private premises.

5 For example, the ward office was in turmoil one day because an abandoned car had not been removed after several requests by a relative of Mayor Daley. And the alderman personally wrote several letters and made many calls over a period of months in an attempt to get the sidewalk repaired in front of the home of a wealthy bank executive who had contributed to his campaign.

6 In one respect, the public service goal does have a substantive effect on service activities. The office staff and ward club leaders sometimes originate requests for service, not for anyone's specific benefit, but as part of the overall upkeep of the ward. These requests are not given high priority, except when staff members perceive them as tests of their efficiency; they do not take precedence over the more political services. There is certainly no attempt to increase the demand for favors artificially by depriving the ward of needed services. Indeed, my impression is that poor neighborhoods in Chicago get no worse government service than middle class neighborhoods. The uniformity of service levels across city areas is suggested by data for Houston's centralized complaint bureau. See Kenneth R. Mladenka, "Citizen Demand and Bureaucratic Response: Direct Dialing Democracy in a Major American City," *Urban Affairs Quarterly* 12 (1977): 273–90.

7 If we define *credit* as a person's belief that a specific individual or collective actor is the cause of some event or situation which that person evaluates positively, we can refer to attempts to influence a person's beliefs about service delivery as attempts to *manage credit. Blame* refers to beliefs about the causes of negatively evaluated things, and efforts to manage blame can be included in a more generalized notion of credit management.

8 This possibility has been noted before: "The ward leader cannot arrange to have welfare payments made to someone not entitled to them; he can, however, tell a needy person who *is* entitled to payments how to apply for them. In doing so, he may, of course, manage to leave the impression that if he had not made a telephone call and used his 'influence' as a 'friend' the payments would never have been made" (Banfield and Wilson, *City Politics,* pp. 121–22).

9 Nevertheless, 16 percent of recorded complaints from citizens lacked this information.

10 An example occurred during the 1975 mayoral and aldermanic election. The alderman's campaign literature claimed credit for bringing two new schools to the ward and for removing many abandoned cars. Mayor Daley's local campaign leaflets mentioned the same schools and the same number of cars.

Chapter Five

1 This argument is implied in much of the work on the machine I have cited above. It is most clearly expressed in Greenstein, "Changing Pattern," pp. 1–13.
2 The procedure by which this count was made is described in appendix B.
3 This is corroborated by the pattern of complaints received from aldermen by the Department of Buildings. In 1971 the department received 696 complaints from aldermen, of which 49, or 7 percent, came from the alderman with whom I worked. There are 50 wards, so the average ward would account for only 2 percent of the complaints. Letter from the Commissioner of Buildings, February 1972.
4 These figures are from official counts which MOII staff kindly made available to me. The MOII does not break down recorded complaints by ward or other local area. For more on this agency, see Alan J. Wyner, "Chicago: Complaining to City Hall," *Executive Ombudsmen in the United States,* ed. Alan J. Wyner (Berkeley: Institute of Government Studies, University of California, 1973).
5 Mladenka, "Citizen Demand," p. 280.
6 Brian D. Jones, Saadia R. Greenberg, Clifford Kaufman, and Joseph Drew, "Bureaucratic Response to Citizen-Initiated Contacts: Environmental Enforcement in Detroit," paper delivered at the Southwestern Political Science Association meetings, San Antonio, Texas, March 27–30, 1975, p. 5.
7 The sampling methodology and interviewing technique are more fully described in appendix B.
8 The degree of sampling and nonsampling error in the estimates of a population proportion (such as the percentage of users) depends on the size of the proportion. To illustrate the limits of the data, let us consider the finding that 33 percent of the voter sample report using party services. If we assume that there is no bias in the sample—i.e., no nonsampling error—then the 95 percent confidence interval for the percentage of users in the voter population ranges from 28.4 to 41.9 percent. But if we ignore the possibility of sampling error, how would a biased sample affect the results? If we

assume the worse, that *all* uninterviewed voters are nonusers, then the percentage of users in the full sample of valid names is only 26.1 percent. If we make the less pessimistic but still conservative assumption that the proportion of users among uninterviewed voters is only half the proportion of users among interviewed voters, then the percentage in the full sample of valid names is 29.8. It seems plausible, then, that the nonsampling error introduced by the refusals to be interviewed does not exceed the probable sampling error for a sample of this size.

9 Greenstein, "Changing Pattern," pp. 7–8.

10 The correct resource for trash cleanup was ward sanitation superintendent or ward sanitation yard; for street repair, the Department of Streets and Sanitation; for abandoned car removal, the police department. Correct responses to the fourth item (Whom would you ask?) were those indicating self-sufficiency: "I'd look it up myself," "I'd pick up the phone and start calling around downtown," "I've always known just whom to call." The police department was the correct service resource for abandoned car removal, but I counted the police department as a nongovernmental resource when respondents cited it as a source of help with other services. For a more detailed breakdown of responses, see appendix A.

11 Only two voters gave correct responses to all four items. Only 19 percent of the voters failed to mention some governmental or political source of aid on all four items (that is, mentioned only outside complaint agencies, personal contacts, or no resource at all). Many voters cited both local resources and downtown agencies; only 27.4 percent mentioned downtown agencies and no local resources.

12 A new committeeman took office only a few months before the survey was conducted. His predecessor had held the office for almost two decades, and voters who named him were given credit for a correct response.

13 At the time the survey was conducted a Democratic precinct captain and one or two workers were assigned to every precinct in the ward.

14 This estimate is obtained by deducting from the official total registration figure the percentage of names in the initial poll sheet sample which proved invalid—i.e., deceased or moved out of the ward. As shown in table 23, 21.2 percent of the sample of listed names were invalid.

15 Given the wording of questions 13–17 it seems highly unlikely that any appreciable proportion of respondents would falsely claim to have had contact with party agents; overreporting can safely be ignored. We can assess the extent of

underreporting by examining the reports of the client sample, all of whom were on record in the alderman's files as having had some contact with the ward office. Of the 56 clients interviewed, eight claimed never to have requested any service. The ratio of actual users to reporting users is 9/8 or 1.12. If we apply this ratio to the 35 users who reported use, we can project 38 actual users among voters interviewed, or 37 percent. The actual contacts with the ward office by the eight clients who reported no use are described in appendix C. One of the eight had not requested a service and another did not initiate the request for service on file. These two cases were excluded when the ratio above was calculated.

16 Since we do not know which of the voters are nonreporting users, the data analysis in the following chapters must be based on use as the respondents reported it. Unreported use among the voters will to some extent conceal the characteristics of users, which are analyzed in chap. 6. However, underreporting does not represent much theoretical difficulty for the tests of the political significance of service use because there is little reason to suppose that services which the voter has forgotten or is unwilling to report will influence his political orientations.

17 Of the 35 voters who reported use, 62 percent had contacted the alderman. Of the 26 voters who had asked the alderman or Democratic committeeman for service, only four had never contacted the alderman.

18 U.S. Congress, Senate Committee on Government Operations, Subcommittee on Intergovernmental Relations, *Confidence and Concern: Citizens View American Government,* 3 pts. (Washington, D.C.: U.S. Government Printing Office, 1973), pt. 1, pp. 173, 278. The universe sampled was all civilians 18 years of age and older, living in private households, with Alaska and Hawaii excluded. The question was: "Leaving aside paying taxes and filling out forms for licenses or Social Security, have you ever gone to your local government to get them to do something, or has that not happened to you?"

19 Sidney Verba and Norman H. Nie, *Participation in America: Political Democracy and Social Equality* (New York: Harper & Row, 1972), pp. 30, 345, 352, 354. The universe sampled was the total, noninstitutionalized population of the United States, 21 years or older. The question was: "We were talking earlier about problems that you and the people of this community have—have you ever personally gone to see, or spoken to, or written to some member of the local community about some need or problem?"

20 Eldersveld, *Political Parties,* pp. 450, 536.

21 This adjustment is based on information available in Eldersveld's report. He tells us that 14 percent of his respondents had never voted and that 72 Democratic precinct leaders were interviewed in the 87 precincts (ibid., pp. 26, 463). If we assume that self-reported nonvoters are the only unregistered voters in the sample, that 15 precincts lacked Democratic leaders, and that lack of a precinct leader was independent of percent registration, we can conservatively estimate that 432 respondents were voters in precincts that had Democratic leaders. This figure was used as a base for the adjusted percentages. The relevant items on Eldersveld's interview schedule were: "Are there leaders or delegates in this precinct who represent the Republican or the Democratic parties?" "Do you know this person (these people) personally?" "Have you, or anyone in your family, ever gone to a precinct leader for information, advice, or for help in getting something done?"

22 The earlier studies described below do provide quantitative data on service activities, but these show only the number of party agents who report that they sometimes provide services of various types, not the number of people who receive each type of service.

23 The reference here is to the potential value, as an object of exchange, of a given type of service. Voters who receive services which are of a "valuable" type do not necessarily reciprocate with political support. Whether users of party services tend to respond with political support is a separate empirical question which is taken up in chap. 7 below. In chaps. 6 and 7 we will deal with variable characteristics of voters which might determine the value they place on services of a given type.

24 An ombudsman's function, as it is usually conceived, is to expedite matters that are already pending before administrative agencies. *Priority referral* describes the frequent cases in which the politician makes an initial request for service—a privileged request on behalf of someone else. The *unusual* treatment he requests is most often—but not always—preferential or expeditious treatment. The underlying distinction between priority referral and intervention is that in the latter type of service the outcome desired by the client and produced through the politician's action is contrary to the interests of the public or the political community. Thus the distinction rests not on whether the outcome violates the letter of the law or the typical conduct of persons certified as professionals, but whether it violates the spirit of the law and professional ethics as institutional expressions of the public

interest. This is admittedly a vague standard, but the distinction is nonetheless important.

25 Forthal, *Cogwheels of Democracy;* Gosnell, *Machine Politics;* Cherry, "Effective Precinct Organization."

26 Gosnell, *Machine Politics,* table 8.

27 Often the examples are reported in sufficient detail to allow categorization with certainty. For example, the following is a clear description of a grant of material value: "The captain . . . paid the rent of a voter for the seven months of his unemployment" (Forthal, *Cogwheels of Democracy,* p. 57). Others are not as well described, but can be categorized with a good measure of confidence. For example, the "street and alley complaints" mentioned by Cherry probably included matters handled by priority referral and by intervention, since in 1951, as now, the ward sanitation superintendents were political appointees sponsored by their respective ward committeemen and granted wide administrative latitude by city hall.

28 Each respondent was asked the question, "Have you ever had occasion to ask your alderman (Democratic committeeman, Democratic precinct captain) for assistance with anything?" An affirmative response was followed by: "What was the most important thing he ever tried to help you with?" The reported requests are categorized in table 8 according to the type of treatment typically given such requests in the ward I studied. I had to make subjective judgments here, since (1) respondents do not know the exact actions taken by party agents in response to their requests, (2) actions on an individual request may involve more than one type of service, and (3) similar requests do not invariably get similar types of service.

29 The earlier data probably exaggerate the ability of the average captain to deliver services. Forthal, Gosnell, and Cherry interviewed the party agents, not the voters. They did not attempt to verify the captains' reports. Forthal's and Gosnell's samples probably overselected the more active and effective of Chicago's captains. Cherry selected the most effective by design. All used specific queries about a variety of services instead of asking for a spontaneous listing by the respondents, a procedure which encourages reporting of services rarely—or never—provided. Depending on self-reports by precinct captains invites exaggeration of their importance in the party, in the delivery of services, and in neighborhood life. On the other hand, respondents in my 1973 survey may have underreported unsolicited favors and personal involvement because of the wording of the questions.

30 Gosnell, *Machine Politics,* p. 90.
31 Harry N. Karlen, *The Governments of Chicago* (Chicago: Courier Publishing, 1958), p. 10.

Chapter Six

1 For a summary of this literature, see Herbert McClosky, "Political Participation," in David L. Sills, ed., *International Encyclopedia of the Social Sciences* (New York: MacMillan and Free Press, 1968) 12:252–65. Three of the best-known works on the subject are: Gabriel A. Almond and Sidney Verba, *The Civic Culture* (Princeton, N.J.: Princeton University, 1963); Lester W. Milbrath, *Political Participation* (Chicago: Rand McNally, 1965); and Verba and Nie, *Participation in America.*
2 Janowitz and Marvick distinguish two independent components of these attitudes, which they call *self-confidence* and *self-interest.* Eulau and Schneider reserve the term *political efficacy* for the self-confidence dimension, which is the same as what Almond and Verba call *civic competence.* In this book political efficacy is used to refer to a combination of self-confidence and self-interest. See Morris Janowitz and Dwaine Marvick, "Competitive Pressure and Democratic Consent: An Interpretation of the 1952 Presidential Election," *Public Opinion Quarterly* 20 (1956): 381–400; Heinz Eulau and Peter Schneider, "Dimensions of Political Involvement," *Public Opinion Quarterly* 20 (1956): 129–42; and Almond and Verba, *The Civic Culture.*
3 See, for example, Morris Janowitz, Deil Wright, and William Delaney, *Public Administration and the Public: Perspectives toward Government in a Metropolitan Community,* Michigan Governmental Series, no. 36 (Ann Arbor: Bureau of Government, Institute of Public Administration, University of Michigan, 1958); U.S. Congress, *Confidence and Concern,* pt. 1, p. 110; and Karl A. Friedmann, *Complaining: Comparative Aspects of Complaint Behavior and Attitudes toward Complaining in Canada and Britain,* Sage Professional Papers in Administrative and Policy Studies, vol. 2 (Beverly Hills and London: Sage Publications, 1974), p. 58. A notable exception to this finding is Verba and Nie, *Political Participation,* p. 200, which shows little association in a national sample between "particularized contacting and social status or organizational membership." Note, however, that Verba and Nie do find social status to be strongly predictive of contacts with public officials about problems of importance to the general community.
4 Areal data on citizen-initiated contacts in Detroit seem to

reflect the offsetting effects of need and social status. See Jones et al., "Bureaucratic Response."

5 As has already been noted, it is characteristic of social exchange that the expectation of reciprocation is not explicitly stated. Party agents do not generally announce that their services are offered on a *quid pro quo* basis. Nevertheless, they may communicate their expectations through more subtle cues. The idea that loyalty is expected of users may have a life of its own in the local political culture. It may be communicated to the potential user by his friends and neighbors, or it may just go without saying. As long as potential users of party services perceive that requesting service will put them under significant obligation, differential rates of service use according to social class ought to appear.

6 The strongest statement of the "private-regardingness" of European peasant culture and the linkage of this culture to attempts to secure favors from officials is Banfield, *Moral Basis.*

7 John D. Kasarda and Morris Janowitz label these contrasting theories of the basis of community attachment the "linear development model" and the "systemic model" respectively. See "Community Attachment in Mass Society," *American Sociological Review* 39 (1974): 328–39.

8 See Nisbet, *Quest for Community;* Hannah Arendt, *The Origins of Totalitarianism* (Cleveland: World Publishing, 1958); and William Kornhauser, *The Politics of Mass Society* (Glencoe: Free Press, 1959).

9 It was not uncommon for people who made requests for service to the ward office where I worked to attempt to legitimate their requests by making explicit claims to being "good" or "law-abiding" citizens, long-time residents, or regular taxpayers. Clients usually voiced these justifications when they thought staff people were withholding services over which they thought the party had control. As noted in chap. 2 above, some citizens in the same situation would make claims to being "good Democrats" or having connections in the party. Unfortunately, I have no data on either the relative frequency with which these differing legitimations were heard or on the characteristics of clients who voiced them.

10 See Reinhard Bendix, *Nation-Building and Citizenship* (New York: John Wiley & Sons, 1964).

11 This is the perspective of Morris Janowitz, *Social Control of the Welfare State* (New York: Elsevier Scientific Publishing, 1976).

12 Since the overall sample size was severely limited by budgetary constraints, I sought to maximize the reliability of com-

parisons by including a roughly equal number of users and nonusers in the combined sample. However, since the interview periods for the voter and client samples ran concurrently, I did not know in advance how many client interviews I would need to achieve this parity. It seemed reasonable to expect that about 25 percent of the voters would report use of party services. Accordingly, the number of clients interviewed was set at half the number of voters interviewed. But a full third of the voters had used party services, so users somewhat outnumber nonusers in the combined sample.

As noted in chap. 5 above and detailed in appendix C, some of the clients did not report that they had requested services from the party. In most cases this was simple misreporting by the respondents, but in two cases a reexamination of office records showed that their contact with the office had not involved a service request. These cases are excluded from the combined sample, which thus ends up comprising 89 users and 71 nonusers. The two nonusers in the client sample were included in the combined sample in my earlier report of this research; they were counted as users in some tables and as nonusers in other parts of the report. See Thomas M. Guterbock, "Favors and Votes: The Service Activities of a Local Patronage Party Organization" (Ph.D. dissertation, University of Chicago, 1976), chaps. 3–4.

13 In chap. 7, we will also consider the possibility that precinct-level service contacts have more influence on the party loyalty of users than ward-level contacts.

14 On the distinction between general and specific goods, see chap. 1, note 25.

15 In chap. 5 above we employed a six-category typology of services, based on the power resource used by a party agent to deliver his services. The present three-category typology, based on the expected influence of services on the orientations of voters, is used because it generates the larger cell counts needed for statistical analysis. The three categories of requests are mutually exclusive and exhaustive of all reported requests. However, some persons contacted more than one agent requesting a different type of service from each, so that the three categories—general goods requesters, routine services requesters and special favors requesters—overlap slightly.

16 Many of the variables listed in tables 9 through 12 have more than two values, so that some information is lost when the data are summarized in this form. However, prior examination of complete two-way tables revealed no important non-

linear relationships between types of service use and these predictors. Some of these two-way cross-classifications are reproduced in Guterbock, "Favors and Votes," chap. 3.

17 There were two elections held in the area during the period between the 1972 presidential election and the survey. These were the March 1974 primary election and RTA referendum, and a special balloting (under new rules of the Democratic party) for electors of delegates to the Democratic mini-convention of 1974. Respondents whose answers to question 19 indicated that they had last voted in one of these elections are counted in table 9 as having voted in minor elections.

18 In this analysis memberships in block and community organizations are treated separately from other memberships to avoid creating an artificial relationship between political participation and community attachment indicators. Church and union membership are not counted as voluntary organization memberships.

19 The Regional Transportation Authority is a public agency with taxing powers, created in order to unify and improve mass transit throughout the six-county Chicago region. Any respondent's description of the RTA proposal that mentioned mass transit and a regional scope (e.g., "for buses to run to the suburbs") was scored as correct. Some replies were elicited with neutral probes. The proposal passed by a narrow margin in a referendum on March 19, 1974. The highly controversial proposal was widely publicized at the time of the referendum and there were prominent stories in the news media about a legal challenge to the referendum at the time of the survey, some six months thereafter.

20 This definition is from Brenda Danet and Harriet Hartman, "Coping with Bureaucracy: The Israeli Case," *Social Forces* 51 (1972): 7.

21 Janowitz, Wright, and Delaney, *Public Administration and the Public,* p. 124. To increase the number of codable responses I used a standardized probe when a respondent failed to answer affirmatively or negatively: "Do you think there are problems you might have with a government bureau that it would be better to handle yourself?"

22 See for example Janowitz and Marvick, "Competitive Pressure," p. 386n.

23 It is noteworthy that most of the respondents who acknowledge calling on the alderman or committeeman for assistance say they would not ask for outside assistance if they had a problem with government. Apparently they conceive of ward-level party agents as part of the government and not as

external sources of aid. This lends oblique support to the idea that community residents view party services as being available to them by right rather than as patronage.

24 It is useful to recall that a substantial portion of the American citizenry are "voting specialists," who vote in most elections but fail to participate in other political activities. See Verba and Nie, *Participation in America,* pp. 79, 89, 97.

25 The neat pattern of correlations of types of service use with this index is of course partly a result of choices I exercised in constructing it. My aim was not to deemphasize the ambiguities in table 9, but to create a single index that would adequately represent the political participation hypothesis in multivariate tests.

26 Respondents' occupations were classified into six status levels based on Laumann's occupational categories. For the present discussion, the top three status levels are collapsed into the white-collar category, and the lower three levels constitute the blue-collar category. See Guterbock, "Favors and Votes," p. 82; and Edward O. Laumann, *Prestige and Association in an Urban Community* (Indianapolis: Bobbs-Merrill, 1966), pp. 157–58.

27 Question 27 on the interview schedule (see appendix A) distinguishes public aid from veteran's benefits, unemployment compensation, social security, and other transfer payments. I use the term *welfare recipients* to refer to persons who said they or a member of their household receive public aid.

28 The ethnic diversity of the ward's population is such that no single ethnicity is represented by a large number of respondents in a sample of this size. The first group comprised those who indicated that their "ancestors on (their) father's side" were American. Persons of British, Irish, Scotch, Scandinavian, French, Dutch, German, and Austrian ancestry were grouped into a second category, representing the ethnic groups of the "old migration." Persons of Italian, Greek, Croatian, Hungarian, Polish, Slavic, and Russian ancestry were grouped into a third category, representing the "new migration." The composition of these categories agrees with the mean social standing scores for white ethnic groups given by a national sample (N = 445) surveyed by the National Opinion Research Center in research conducted by Robert W. Hodge and Paul Siegel. The social standing scores are listed in Edward O. Laumann, *Bonds of Pluralism: The Form and Substance of Urban Social Networks* (New York: John Wiley & Sons, 1973), table 3.2. If these scores are trichotomized using cutpoints of 51 and 35, each of the resulting ordered

categories contains the ethnic groups that are included in one of my three ethnic categories.

29 A more detailed breakdown of the voter sample reveals high rates of use for the Irish and for persons of German-speaking descent, and very low rates for Russian Jews. However, contrary to what might be predicted from Clark, "Irish Ethic," Irish Catholics do not have higher than average rates of use (although Catholics as a group do). Small cell sizes make these results quite untrustworthy, in any case.

30 Clark, "Irish Ethic," pp. 321–24.

31 For example, Verba and Nie (*Participation in America,* pp. 98–101) report that Catholics tend to follow a parochial and partisan style of political participation, rather than a communal style. Much of the varied data reported by Clark, "Irish Ethic," can be taken to show the particularism of Catholics in general. Also relevant is the debate about political ethos as a factor in voting: see James Q. Wilson and Edward C. Banfield, "Public-Regardingness as a Value Premise in Voting Behavior," *American Political Science Review* 58 (1964): 876–87; and their "Political Ethos Revisited," *American Political Science Review* 65 (1971): 1048–62.

32 Seymour Martin Lipset, "Religion and Politics in American History," in *Religion and Social Conflict,* ed. Robert Lee and Martin E. Marty (New York: Oxford University Press, 1964), pp. 109–17.

33 In the last analysis the distinction used here between group factors and value-elements becomes clouded by the reciprocal causal links between the two types of factor. The "immigrant ethos" may have its origin in the weakness of democratic institutions in certain European countries at the time of the great immigrations to America, but this weakness is certainly related to the traditional strength of the Catholic church and its doctrines in those countries. Thus the general cultural characteristics of American ethnic groups may be functionally independent of theological factors at present, yet may still be rooted in religious value-elements in a historical sense.

34 Lipset, "Religion and Politics," p. 113.

35 The association between these two items was in the expected direction and moderately strong (Kendall's $Q = .548$). The questionnaire included six attitude items which were meant to show a "pragmatic" political orientation, but the scale was modified in subsequent analysis as described in Guterbock, "Favors and Votes," pp. 95–104. Tables and statistics for the two-item corruption-acceptance scale in that discussion are incorrect, because of an error in the algorithm for computing

the scores. This error is corrected in the results presented here, with no substantive change in the outcome.

36 Apparently many of the public-regarding respondents answered question 5 according to whether they had themselves successfully made personal contact with government officials, rather than according to their conception of their own benefits from a larger pattern of universalism in public administration. If people's attitudes about police conduct are independent of their attitudes about corruption in other sectors, then question 6 will not effectively measure political ethos.

37 Kasarda and Janowitz, in "Community Attachment in Mass Society," found a linear relationship between age and community attachment. They were able to dichotomize age using a cutpoint of fifty, without losing significant information. Dichotomization into old and young categories would be inappropriate for the present data, since people older than 55 are substantially underrepresented among users (see Guterbock, "Favors and Votes," table 14). The rootlessness of the elderly is particularly marked in the ward I studied because it is located in a part of Chicago with a percentage of elderly far above the city average. Some reside in health care institutions or in large public housing projects. Many others are displaced "empty-nesters" whose children no longer reside with them.

38 Awareness of local politicians as a service resource is excluded from the localism index because such awareness may be as much a result of actual use as its cause. Including this variable in the index might therefore have artificially raised the apparent explanatory power of localism in mutivariate tests.

39 I am indebted to Mark Granovetter for his careful presentation of the opposing view in his comments, in a private communication, on my earlier report of this research, "The Political Machine and the Local Community: New Data and Their Implications," presented at the American Sociological Association Annual Meeting, New York, August 1976. These comments from a "social networks" viewpoint were the impetus for the more detailed examination of the community attachment hypothesis provided here.

40 This term is from Kasarda and Janowitz, "Community Attachment in Mass Society."

Chapter Seven

1 Banfield and Wilson, *City Politics,* p. 116.

2 For a more complete presentation of this reasoning, see Ar-

thur L. Stinchcombe, *Constructing Social Theories* (New York: Harcourt, Brace & World, 1968), pp. 17–19.

3 IVI-IPO: Independent Voters of Illinois-Independent Precinct Organization, two political organizations which jointly publish and distribute endorsements of liberal reform candidates from both parties. For an assessment of IVI's effectiveness through 1960, see Wilson, *Amateur Democrat,* pp. 65–85.

4 See Hubert M. Blalock, *Social Statistics* (New York: McGraw-Hill, 1960), p. 231. *Q* is calculated by taking the difference between the two diagonal products of cell frequencies and dividing by the sum of the diagonal products. In the case of the two-by-two table, this statistic is identical to the gamma statistic supplied by the CROSSTABS procedure in the SPSS computer program. See Norman H. Nie et al., *SPSS: Statistical Package for the Social Sciences,* 2d edition (New York: McGraw-Hill, 1975), p. 228.

5 Ibid., p. 228. If the number of cases is increased and the cell proportions are held constant, the *Q*-statistic is unchanged. Measures of association of this kind have a built-in disadvantage: if the cell frequencies are small, a large *Q* may result even though no statistically significant relationship exists. However, since the present analysis requires comparison of cross-classifications with widely varying marginal frequencies, the *Q*-statistic is preferable to measures of association based on the chi-square statistic.

6 The construction of these measures from interview items is detailed in chap. 6 above.

7 See Angus Campbell and Warren E. Miller, "The Motivational Basis of Straight and Split Ticket Voting," *American Political Science Review* 51 (1957): 293–312. On the new pattern of independent voting, see Nie et al., *The Changing American Voter,* and Walter DeVries and Lance Tarrance, Jr., *The Ticket-Splitter: A New Force in American Politics* (Grand Rapids: Eerdmens, 1972).

8 Questions designed to measure more precisely a sense of obligation yielded too few affirmative answers to be statistically useful. Only ten persons in the combined sample thought they had received a special favor that the party agent would not have granted anyone who asked (questions 13*d,* 14*d,* and 16*d*). Only fourteen said the party agent had asked them for something in return (questions 13*f,* 14*f,* and 16*f*). For the wording of the questions, see appendix A.

9 These are described in chap. 4 above.

10 See Walter Dean Burnham, *Critical Elections and the Mainsprings of American Politics* (New York: Norton, 1970).

11 Bernard R. Berelson, Paul F. Lazarsfeld, and William N.

McPhee, *Voting* (Chicago: University of Chicago Press, 1954), p. 20.

12 Selectivity may be exercised without making sense. When asked how they would vote when they knew little about either candidate on the ballot, a few of the interviewed voters responded: "random, I guess," "just close my eyes and pick," or—as one put it—"eenie-meenie-miney-moe."

13 Some reported picking names of their own ethnicity, but two respondents said they took care to pick only "American" or "non-Jewish" names.

14 See Alexis de Tocqueville, *Democracy in America,* tr. Phillips Bradley, 2 vols. (New York: Alfred A. Knopf, Inc., 1945) 2:106–10.

15 Verba and Nie (*Participation in America,* pp. 178–80) show that a large proportion of members of "nonpolitical" organizations of various types report that political discussions do take place within their organizations.

16 Verba and Nie (ibid., pp. 200–205) demonstrate that organizational membership has the effect of enhancing political participation rates over and above the effect of SES.

Chapter Eight

1 Strategies built primarily around either issue-oriented or issue-free tactics correspond respectively to the *amateur* and *professional styles* of politics *as formally defined* by Wilson in *Amateur Democrat,* pp. 2–4: "An amateur is one who finds politics *intrinsically* interesting because it expresses a conception of the public interest . . . . The professional, on the other hand, . . . is preoccupied with the outcome of politics in terms of winning or losing." I choose not to use Wilson's terms because in subsequent usage he broadens their meanings to encompass other dimensions which are best kept separate here.

2 Edward C. Banfield, *Political Influence: A New Theory of Urban Politics* (New York: Free Press, 1961), p. 265.

3 For example, see Weber, *Social and Economic Organization,* p. 410; Wilson, *Amateur Democrat,* pp. 8, 16–21; Banfield and Wilson, *City Politics,* p. 116; Dye, *Politics in States and Communities,* pp. 247–51.

4 Compare Whyte, *Street Corner Society,* p. 211: "It is frequently difficult for the politician to reconcile his loyalty to his constituents with the conduct required of him by his political superiors. In explaining why he had not done more for Cornerville, Joseph Maloney spoke in this way to a club of corner boys: 'Sometimes you try to get a man a job through the

mayor, and then some issue comes up between you and the mayor. Should you fight him or should you keep quiet? You have to weigh that question carefully. If you fight, you might lose a man a life-job, and he'll always say, "If Joe didn't pick that fight, I would have my job today."' On the other hand, if the politician never fights, his superiors conclude that he is easily brought into line and need be given only the crumbs of political patronage."

5 Banfield, *Political Influence,* pp. 256–62; Wilson, *Amateur Democrat,* p. 19; Banfield and Wilson, *City Politics,* p. 116.

6 Murray Edelman, *The Symbolic Uses of Politics* (Urbana: University of Illinois Press, 1964), p. 2.

7 Ibid., p. 38.

8 William Kornblum, *Blue Collar Community* (Chicago: University of Chicago Press, 1974), chaps. 6–8, analyzes in rich detail the dynamics of one such intraparty contest.

9 See chap. 3 above.

10 A year and a half after I concluded my field research, the alderman was indeed expelled from the ward office. It would have been most revealing to see if he could have won election to a third term without the ward club's support, but before the election he relinquished his council seat to accept an appointive office.

11 The dissident group was dubbed the "coffee rebellion" by city hall reporters, because one of the aldermen, when asked what had transpired at one of the group's first caucuses, told reporters only: "We drank coffee."

12 The concept of "natural area" is explained in Harvey W. Zorbaugh, "The Natural Areas of the City," *Publications of the American Sociological Society* 20 (1926): 188–97. Suttles has effectively criticized the notion that such areas are natural in the sense which the classic theories of human ecology implied; see *Social Construction,* chap. 1. Nevertheless, the diversity of urban subareas is undisputed, and in the same book (p. 68) Suttles maps the noncoincidence of ward boundaries with those of Chicago's local communities.

13 Political fragmentation is to some degree deliberately fostered by the party leaders who control the City Council, which determines ward boundaries. Gerrymandering was so obvious in the ward boundaries established after the 1970 census that the Council was obliged by court order to redraw some of the boundaries to provide better representation to members of minority groups.

14 See Leo F. Schnore, *The Urban Scene* (New York: Free Press, 1965).

15 Janowitz has pointed out that this lack of leaders, which he

dubs "social absenteeism," can under certain circumstances weaken the patronage party organization itself. See *Community Press,* pp. 202–3.

16 On the lack of coherence of beliefs of nonelite adults, see Philip E. Converse, "The Nature of Belief Systems in Mass Publics," in *Ideology and Discontent,* ed. David E. Apter (London: Free Press of Glencoe, 1964).

17 Edelman, *Symbolic Uses of Politics,* p. 38.

18 For an account of the failure of a radical organizing effort in this kind of community, see Edwin S. Harwood, "Work and Community among Urban Newcomers: A Study of the Social and Economic Adaptation of Southern Migrants to Chicago" (Ph.D. dissertation, University of Chicago, 1967).

19 The form and functions of the "hortatory style" of political discourse receive extended attention in Edelman, *Symbolic Uses of Politics,* chaps. 6 and 7.

20 In such instances, the community leadership acts as a "growth-machine coalition," such as the ones described by Harvey Molotch, "The City as a Growth Machine," *American Journal of Sociology* 82 (1976): 309–32. However, the actions of local leaders with respect to competing strategies for community change can only partially be tied to the differing economic interests in land upon which Molotch's analysis hinges.

21 Banfield and Wilson, *City Politics,* p. 123.

22 For evidence on this relationship, see Scott Greer, "The Social Structure and Political Process of Suburbia: An Empirical Test," *Rural Sociology* 27 (1962): 438–59.

23 Gosnell, *Machine Politics,* chap. 5.

24 This tendency is noted by Janowitz, *Community Press,* p. 212.

25 The distinction between mechanisms of legitimation and the inducements by which contributions of support are secured is important for the analysis of organizations, political parties, and nation states. Weber makes the distinction in *Social and Economic Organization,* p. 325. Compare the contrast between legitimacy and effectiveness in Seymour Martin Lipset, *Political Man* (New York: Doubleday, 1960), pp. 64–71.

26 The success of the ward club in attracting donations of food and other consumer goods from local merchants is in large part attributable to the fact that several of its members were employed as licensing inspectors by various city departments. These patronage workers were in a position to be most persuasive in soliciting donations from local grocers, restauranteurs, and tavern keepers, who were quite willing to give donations in kind rather than the cash bribes which many city inspectors demand of them. On the pattern of petty bribery of city inspectors, see the series of articles about the Mirage

Tavern, *Chicago Sun-Times,* Jan. 8–Feb. 14, 1978.

27 For example, the alderman's tabloid newsletter elicited a pointed reaction from the Regular Democratic alderman in another ward. He mailed back a copy of the newssheet together with a note which said only: "Who the hell is this guy?"

28 The dramaturgical use of delay as a means of underscoring and enhancing status differences is analyzed in Barry Schwartz, "Waiting, Exchange, and Power: The Distribution of Time in Social Systems," *American Journal of Sociology* 79 (1974): 841–70.

29 The politician's allocation of time among different groups thus carries both instrumental and ceremonial significance, because the access which he grants has substantive value, while the action of waiting symbolizes deference to the group. On the mingling of objectively occasioned and ceremonial waiting, see Schwartz, "Waiting," pp. 864–67.

Chapter Nine

1 Merton, *Social Theory,* p. 118.

2 The functions of service activities I will describe are not all *latent* as defined by Merton (ibid., p. 105)—that is, they are not all both unintended and unrecognized. For example, the utility of service activities as public relations material is recognized and exploited by patronage politicians. Some of the consequences for individual club members are not widely recognized by other participants, yet are obtained intentionally. Moreover, the principal intended purpose for the club's service activities—that of creating relationships of indebtedness that will generate political support—can perhaps not properly be called manifest since it is systematically concealed from clients, who are key participants in service transactions. The hazy distinction between manifest and latent functions is less important in this analysis than the distinction between intended and unintended consequences, since a functional explanation of a given pattern of activity is logically incomplete unless one can identify in participants actual motives that lead to the actions to be explained.

3 Ibid., pp. 124–36.

4 Goode has suggested that such analysis is indistinguishable from exploration of causal relationships among social phenomena. I have not followed Goode's suggestion that the term *function* be excised from the sociological lexicon, but I share his conviction that this mode of analysis does not carry the conservative ideological overtones which critics of "functionalism" ascribe to it. See William J. Goode,

"Functionalism: The Empty Castle," pp. 64–94 in *Explorations in Social Theory* (New York: Oxford University Press, 1973). Identifying the functions of service activities serves to explain them but does not imply either that they are inevitable or that they benefit the larger social system. I am grateful to Joel Telles for his comments on these issues.

5 Merton, *Social Theory,* p. 128.

6 See Walter Gellhorn, *When Americans Complain: Governmental Grievance Procedures* (Cambridge: Harvard University Press, 1965).

7 The assertion that service activities have an effect on voter loyalties by virtue of their public relations value should not be taken as evidence for the affectual exchange model of machine support. In the latter pattern, the symbolic effects of service activities are contained within networks of face-to-face interaction and give rise to close personal ties involving emotional attachments. In speaking of public relations effects, I refer to symbolic effects easily carried through impersonal communication media, which give rise to commitment based on the value-orientations of those in the audience, often in the absence of personal acquaintanceship with party agents.

Chapter Ten

1 The use of different kinds of inducements at different levels of a structure of influence is illustrated in Banfield, *Political Influence,* pp. 315–16.

2 This view contrasts with that advanced by Molotch that community attachment is an expression of concern for collective economic benefits. See "Growth Machine," p. 311.

3 The notion of strategic interaction is elaborated in Erving Goffman, *Strategic Interaction* (Philadelphia: University of Pennsylvania Press, 1969).

4 For evidence on the applicability of the commitment model to city-wide returns from the 1972 election, see Thomas M. Guterbock, "Community Attachment and Machine Politics: Voting Patterns in Chicago's Wards," *Social Science Quarterly* 60 (1979): 185–202.

5 As of fall 1972 only 36.8 percent of the precinct captains and co-captains in the ward studied lived within their own precinct; 28.1 percent lived elsewhere in the ward; the same proportion lived outside the ward but within the city limits; and the remaining seven percent were suburban residents.

6 In his perceptive recent analysis of political machines in New York and Chicago, John M. Allswang also emphasizes that the notion of a "controlled" electorate is an unrealistic one, and

that a measure of rationality prevails among urban voters. See *Bosses, Machines, and Urban Voters: An American Symbiosis* (Port Washington, N.Y.: Kennikat Press, National University Publications, 1977).

7 Just after that election Harold Gosnell wrote: "The victory of Horner over Bundesen in the Democratic primary destroyed the myth of the invincibility [*sic*] which had grown up around the Kelly-Nash machine . . . . Horner was more in sympathy with the policies of the New Deal than were the Chicago bosses. Three hundred thousand voters in Chicago sensed this" (*Machine Politics,* p. 24). Gosnell was correct in sensing the selectivity of the electorate, but nevertheless the myth of invincibility remained intact for more than forty years thereafter.

8 A recent example of a study which parrots the conventional wisdom of practicing patronage politicians and fails to see the inadequacy of the exchange model in which they believe is Rakove, *Don't Make No Waves.*

9 Kornblum, *Blue Collar Community,* chap. 6.

10 Clearly, these are appeals to material, affectual, and ideal motives, respectively.

11 Banfield and Wilson, *City Politics,* p. 123.

12 I am grateful to Kenneth Wald for suggesting this. In a true natural history, a system is propelled into each new stage of its development by factors immanent in the preceding stage. Clearly, the "evolution" of the political machine is in large part a result of changes taking place in the larger system of which it is a part, as industrialism gives way to advanced industrialism.

13 See the description of the rise to power of "Hughey" McLaughlin in Oscar Handlin, *The Uprooted* (Boston: Little, Brown, 1951), pp. 209–10.

14 The present-day Chicago machine has its origins in the skilled ethnic politics of Anton Cermak, as recounted in Allswang, *Bosses,* chap. 4.

15 See Janowitz, *Social Control,* chap. 7; and Henry Cohen, "Governing Megacentropolis: The Constraints," *Public Administration Review* 30 (September /October 1970): 488–97.

16 David Matza, *Becoming Deviant* (Englewood Cliffs, N.J.: Prentice-Hall, 1969), p. 23. Allswang, *Bosses,* chap. 1, provides a useful review of both the pejorative and appreciative early studies.

17 Matza, *Becoming Deviant,* p. 60.

18 Clark, "Irish Ethic," p. 345.

19 Matza, *Becoming Deviant,* p. 60.

Appendix B

1 I ordered the precincts by income to make it possible to use the statistics for a stratified sample, which would have narrowed the confidence limits of estimates of population characteristics. However, the variance within implied strata was great enough that these statistics did not appreciably reduce the standard error of the estimates.

2 More precisely: To generate halfway names, divide the sampling interval by two, and add to the random start. Use this sum as a new start, and take a systematic sample using the original interval.

Appendix D

1 See Leo A. Goodman, "A Modified Multiple Regression Approach to the Analysis of Dichotomous Variables," *American Sociological Review* 37 (1972): 28–46. The Goodman and Fay computer program Everyman's Contingency Table Analysis (ECTA) was used for computation. A recently revised user's guide for the ECTA program is available from the Academic Computing Center, University of Virginia, Charlottesville, Virginia 22903.

2 The method is described by Leo A. Goodman, "A General Model for the Analysis of Surveys," *American Journal of Sociology* 77 (1972): 1035–86. See also James A. Davis, "Hierarchical Models for Significance Tests in Multivariate Contingency Tables: An Exegesis of Goodman's Recent Papers," in Herbert L. Costner, ed., *Sociological Methodology 1973–74* (San Francisco: Jossey-Bass, 1973).

3 Either the conventional goodness-of-fit chi-square statistic or the likelihood-ratio chi-square statistic may be employed. I have used the latter throughout.

4 None of the interactions was statistically significant according to the usual tests, but this was not the only criterion used. Because of the small size of the data base the usual levels of statistical significance are achieved only by very strong effects. Therefore, in selecting the most parsimonious yet powerful log-linear model out of the many possible models, I considered not only the size of the reduction in chi-square attributable to the inclusion of a given effect parameter in the model, but also the resulting increase in the coefficient of determination. Generally, if an effect resulted in an increase of .1 or more in the coefficient of multiple determination, I considered it significant even if the change in chi-square attributable to its inclusion fell somewhat short of significance at the five percent probability level. I used an eclectic strategy

for model selection, combining "forward" and "backward" stepwise selection with guidance by examination of effect parameters calculated under the "saturated" model, as recommended by Goodman in "Guided and Unguided Methods for the Selection of Models for a Set of *T* Multidimensional Contingency Tables," *Journal of the American Statistical Association* 68 (1973): 165–75. For the sake of brevity I do not report here the effect parameters for the most parsimonious models, which differ little from the effect parameters for the models in the text tables.

5 To my knowledge, such zero-order parameters have not been reported by other users of Goodman's techniques. Their use seems advisable for the same reasons that zero-order correlation coefficients are a helpful addition to a tabular display of regression coefficients from a series of multiple regression equations. The zero-order "beta" coefficients in modified multiple regression analysis may be computed by taking one-half the natural logarithm of the odds-ratio (or diagonal cross-product) in the two-by-two frequency table of the predictor variable and the dependent variable. (Users of the ECTA program can generate these coefficients by doubling the output "lamda" effect parameters for a fitted model that includes *only* the simple effects of the predictors on the dependent variable.) Note that the quantity .25 was added to each cell of the full seven-way table before the zero-order betas were computed. This is equivalent to adding the quantity 8.0 to each cell of the two-way table before taking the odds-ratio and computing the beta coefficient. The zero-order betas in table 24 are therefore smaller than they would be if computed from the raw data, but their size relative to each other and to the beta effects in the multivariate models is unchanged.

6 *Variance* has a special meaning in modified multiple regression analysis. As an example, take the seven-way table with requests for general goods as dependent variable. The variance in requests for general goods is the sum of the squared deviations of the 64 observed odds of requests for general goods (in the 64 possible combinations of predictor-variable values) from the overall odds of requests for general goods in the entire table. This variance is equivalent to the chi-square value for the fit to the data of the null hypothesis of conditional equiprobability (a model which includes [1] all possible interaction effects among predictors only and [2] the mean of the dependent variable). See Goodman, "Modified Multiple Regression," pp. 43–44.

7 The beta coefficients can be used to calculate the predicted

log-odds of each type of service request (i.e., the natural logarithm of the ratio of requesters to nonusers) for any combination of values on the six predictor values. For example, the predicted log-odds of being a requester of general goods, among people who are in category 1 of all six predictor variables, equals the sum of all six beta effects and the constant term (1.884). Hence the model predicts that the ratio of requesters to nonusers in this group is 6.6 to 1. The predicted log-odds for any combination of predictor values are calculated by adding to the constant term the beta effects for each variable that is at its first value, and subtracting the beta effect for each variable that is at its second value. In assessing the relative strength of the various effects, it is helpful to remember that when the beta coefficient is $\ln\sqrt{2}$ or .347, then the predicted odds (of the dependent variable being at its first value) are twice as high among cases in category one on the predictor variable as they are among cases in category two on that variable (holding constant the value of all other predictors and assuming no interaction effects involving the dependent variable change when the predictor variable changes value). A beta coefficient of $\ln\sqrt{3}$ or .549 triples the predicted odds.

Bibliography

Allswang, John M. *Bosses, Machines, and Urban Voters: An American Symbiosis.* Port Washington, N.Y.: Kennikat Press, National University Publications, 1977.

Almond, Gabriel A., and Verba, Sidney. *The Civic Culture.* Princeton, N.J.: Princeton University Press, 1963.

Arendt, Hannah. *The Origins of Totalitarianism.* Cleveland: World Publishing, 1958.

Banfield, Edward C. *The Moral Basis of a Backward Society.* New York: Free Press, 1958.

———. *Political Influence: A New Theory of Urban Politics.* New York: Free Press, 1961.

Banfield, Edward C., and Wilson, James Q. *City Politics.* Cambridge: Harvard University Press, 1963.

Bendix, Reinhard. *Nation-Building and Citizenship.* New York: John Wiley & Sons, 1964.

Berelson, Bernard R.; Lazarsfeld, Paul F.; and McPhee, William N. *Voting.* Chicago: University of Chicago Press, 1954.

Blau, Peter M. *Exchange and Power in Social Life.* New York: John Wiley & Sons, 1967.

Bryce, James. *The American Commonwealth.* 2 vols. New York: Macmillan, 1916.

Burgess, Ernest W. "The Growth of the City: An Introduction to a Research Project." In *The City.* Edited by Robert E. Park, Ernest W. Burgess, and

R. D. McKenzie. Chicago: University of Chicago Press, 1925.

Burnham, Walter Dean. *Critical Elections and the Mainsprings of American Politics.* New York: Norton, 1970.

Campbell, Angus, and Miller, Warren E. "The Motivational Basis of Straight and Split Ticket Voting." *American Political Science Review* 51 (1957): 293–312.

Cherry, H. Dicken. "Effective Precinct Organization." Master's thesis, University of Chicago, 1952.

Clark, Peter B., and Wilson, James Q. "Incentive Systems: A Theory of Organizations." *Administrative Science Quarterly* 6 (1961): 129–66.

Clark, Terry N. "The Irish Ethic and the Spirit of Patronage." *Ethnicity* 2 (1975): 305–59.

Converse, Philip E. "The Nature of Belief Systems in Mass Publics." In *Ideology and Discontent.* Edited by David E. Apter. London: Free Press of Glencoe, 1964.

Cutright, Phillips. "Measuring the Impact of Local Party Activity on the General Election Vote." *Public Opinion Quarterly* 27 (1963): 373–86.

Dahl, Robert. *Who Governs.* New Haven: Yale University Press, 1961.

Danet, Brenda, and Hartman, Harriet. "Coping with Bureaucracy: The Israeli Case." *Social Forces* 51 (1972): 7–22.

Dennis, Jack. "Trends in Public Support for the American Party System." *British Journal of Political Science* 5 (1975): 187–230.

DeVries, Walter, and Tarrance, Lance, Jr. *The Ticket Splitter: A New Force in American Politics.* Foreword by David S. Broder. Grand Rapids, Mich.: Eerdmens, 1972.

Dye, Thomas R. *Politics in States and Communities.* 3d ed. Englewood Cliffs, N.J.: Prentice-Hall, 1977.

Edelman, Murray. *The Symbolic Uses of Politics.* Urbana: University of Illinois Press, 1964.

Edley, Lucille Simmons. "Strategies and Techniques of Politics: A Study of Ten Selected Precinct Captains from Chicago's Third Ward." Master's thesis, University of Chicago, 1955.

Eldersveld, Samuel J. *Political Parties: A Behavioral Analysis.* Chicago: Rand McNally, 1964.

Etzioni, Amitai. *A Comparative Analysis of Complex Organization: On Power, Involvement, and Their Correlates.* New York: Free Press, 1961.

Forthal, Sonya. *Cogwheels of Democracy.* New York: Pamphlet Distributing, 1948.

Friedmann, Karl A. *Complaining: Comparative Aspects of Complaint Behavior and Attitudes toward Complaining in Canada and Britain.* Sage Professional Papers in Administrative Studies, vol. 2. Beverly Hills and London: Sage Publications, 1974.

Gans, Herbert. *The Urban Villagers.* New York: Free Press, 1962.

Gellhorn, Walter. *When Americans Complain: Governmental Grievance Procedures.* Cambridge: Harvard University Press, 1966.

Glazer, Nathan, and Moynihan, Daniel P. *Beyond the Melting Pot.* Cambridge, Mass.: MIT Press, 1963.

Gleason, William Francis. *Daley of Chicago: The Man, the Myth, and the Limits of Conventional Politics.* New York: Simon & Shuster, 1970.

Goffman, Erving. *Strategic Interaction.* Philadelphia: University of Pennsylvania Press, 1969.

Goode, William J. "Functionalism: The Empty Castle." In *Explorations in Social Theory.* New York: Oxford University Press, 1973.

Goodman, Leo A. "A Modified Multiple Regression Approach to the Analysis of Dichotomous Variables." *American Sociological Review* 37 (1972): 28–46.

———. "A General Model for the Analysis of Surveys." *American Journal of Sociology* 77 (1972): 1035–86.

Gosnell, Harold F. *Machine Politics: Chicago Model.* Chicago: University of Chicago Press, 1937.

Greenstein, Fred I. "The Changing Pattern of Urban Party Politics." *The Annals of the American Academy of Political and Social Science* 353 (1964): 1–13.

Greer, Scott. "The Social Structure and Political Process of Suburbia." *American Sociological Review* 25 (1960): 514–26.

———. "The Social Structure and Political Process of Suburbia: An Empirical Test." *Rural Sociology* 27

(1962): 438–59.

Guterbock, Thomas M. "Favors and Votes: The Service Activities of a Local Patronage Party Organization." Ph.D. dissertation, University of Chicago, 1976.

———. "The Political Machine and the Local Community: New Data and Their Implications." Paper presented at the American Sociological Association Annual Meeting, August 1976, New York.

———. "Community Attachment and Machine Politics: Voting Patterns in Chicago's Wards." *Social Science Quarterly* 60 (1979): 185–202.

Handlin, Oscar. *The Uprooted.* Boston: Little, Brown, 1951.

Harwood, Edwin S. "Work and Community among Urban Newcomers: A Study of the Social and Economic Adaptation of Southern Migrants to Chicago." Ph.D. dissertation, University of Chicago, 1967.

Hoyt, Homer. "Recent Distortions of the Classical Models of Urban Structure." *Land Economics* 50 (1964): 199–212.

Hunter, Albert. *Symbolic Communities: The Persistence and Change of Chicago's Local Communities.* Chicago: University of Chicago Press, 1974.

Janowitz, Morris. *The Community Press in an Urban Setting: The Social Elements of Urbanism.* Chicago: University of Chicago Press, 1952.

———. *Social Control of the Welfare State.* New York: Elsevier Scientific Publishing, 1976.

Janowitz, Morris, and Marvick, Dwaine. "Competitive Pressure and Democratic Consent: An Interpretation of the 1952 Presidential Election." *Public Opinion Quarterly* 20 (1956): 381–400.

Janowitz, Morris; Wright, Deil; and Delaney, William. *Public Administration and the Public: Perspectives toward Government in a Metropolitan Community.* Michigan Governmental Series, no. 36. Ann Arbor: Bureau of Government, Institute of Public Administration, University of Michigan, 1958.

Jones, Brian D.; Greenberg, Saadia R.; Kaufman, Clifford; and Drew, Joseph. "Bureaucratic Response to Citizen-Initiated Contacts: Environmental Enforcement in Detroit." Paper delivered at the Southwestern Political Science Association meeting, March 27–30, 1975, San Antonio, Texas.

Karlen, Harry N. *The Governments of Chicago.* Chicago: Courier Publishing, 1958.

Kasarda, John D., and Janowitz, Morris. "Community Attachment in Mass Society." *American Sociological Review* 39 (1974): 328–39.

Katz, Daniel, and Eldersveld, Samuel J. "The Impact of Local Party Activity upon the Electorate." *Public Opinion Quarterly* 25 (1961): 1–24.

Kent, Frank R. *The Great Game of Politics.* New York: Doubleday, Page, 1926.

Knauss, Peter R. *Chicago: A One Party State.* Champaign, Ill.: Stipes Publishing, 1972.

Kornblum, William. *Blue Collar Community.* Chicago: University of Chicago Press, 1974.

Kornhauser, William. *The Politics of Mass Society.* Glencoe: Free Press, 1959.

Kurtzman, David H. *Methods of Controlling Votes in Philadelphia.* Philadelphia: University of Pennsylvania, 1935.

Laumann, Edward O. *Bonds of Pluralism: The Form and Substance of Urban Social Networks.* New York: John Wiley & Sons, 1973.

Lipset, Seymour Martin. *Political Man.* New York: Doubleday, 1960.

———. "Religion and Politics in American History." In *Religion and Social Conflict.* Edited by Robert Lee and Martin E. Marty. New York: Oxford University Press, 1964.

McClosky, Herbert. "Political Participation." In *International Encyclopedia of the Social Sciences,* 12:252–65. Edited by David L. Sills. New York: MacMillan and Free Press, 1968.

McCoy, David W. "Patronage in Suburbia." Ph.D. dissertation, University of Chicago, 1963.

Matza, David. *Becoming Deviant.* Englewood Cliffs, N.J.: Prentice-Hall, 1969.

Merton, Robert K. "Insiders and Outsiders: A Chapter in the Sociology of Knowledge." *American Journal of Sociology* 78 (1972): 9–47.

———. *Social Theory and Social Structure.* 3d ed. New

York: Free Press, 1968. Originally published in 1949.

Milbrath, Lester W. *Political Participation.* Chicago: Rand McNally, 1965.

Mladenka, Kenneth R. "Citizen Demand and Bureaucratic Response: Direct Dialing Democracy in a Major American City." *Urban Affairs Quarterly* 12 (1977): 273–90.

Molotch, Harvey. "The City as a Growth Machine." *American Journal of Sociology* 82 (1976): 309–32.

Nie, Norman H.; Verba, Sidney; and Petrocik, John R. *The Changing American Voter.* Cambridge: Harvard University Press, 1976.

Nisbet, Robert. *The Quest for Community: A Study in the Ethics of Order and Freedom.* New York: Oxford University Press, 1953.

O'Conner, Len. *Clout: Mayor Daley and His City.* Chicago: H. Regnery, 1975.

———. *Requiem: The Decline and Demise of Mayor Daley and His Era.* Chicago: Contemporary Books, 1977.

Rakove, Milton L. *Don't Make No Waves, Don't Back No Losers: An Insider's Analysis of the Daley Machine.* Bloomington: Indiana University Press, 1975.

Rossi, Peter H., and Cutright, Phillips. "The Impact of Party Organization in an Industrial Setting." In *Community Political Systems.* Edited by Morris Janowitz. Glencoe, Ill.: Free Press, 1961.

Royko, Mike. *Boss: Richard J. Daley of Chicago.* New York: E. P. Dutton, 1971.

Schwartz, Barry. "Waiting, Exchange, and Power: The Distribution of Time in Social Systems." *American Journal of Sociology* 79 (1974): 841–70.

Sieber, Sam D. "The Integration of Field-work and Survey Methods." *American Journal of Sociology* 78 (1973): 1335–59.

Stave, Bruce M. *The New Deal and the Last Hurrah: Pittsburgh Machine Politics.* Pittsburgh: University of Pittsburgh Press, 1970.

Stinchcombe, Arthur L. *Constructing Social Theories.* New York: Harcourt, Brace & World, 1968.

Suttles, Gerald D. *The Social Construction of Com-*

munities. Chicago: University of Chicago Press, 1972.

Tocqueville, Alexis de. *Democracy in America.* Translated by Phillips Bradley. 2 vols. New York: Alfred A. Knopf, 1945.

U.S. Congress, Senate Committee on Government Operations, Subcommittee on Intergovernmental Relations. *Confidence and Concern: Citizens View American Government.* 3 pts. Washington, D.C.: U.S. Government Printing Office, 1973.

Verba, Sidney, and Nie, Norman H. *Participation in America: Political Democracy and Social Equality.* New York: Harper & Row, 1972.

Warren, Roland L. *The Community in America.* Chicago: Rand McNally, 1963.

Weber, Max. *The Theory of Social and Economic Organization.* Translated by A. M. Henderson and Talcott Parsons. New York: Free Press, 1947.

Wendt, Lloyd, and Kogan, Herman. *Lords of the Levee: The Story of Bathhouse John and Hinky Dink.* Indianapolis: Bobbs-Merrill, 1943.

Whitehead, Ralph. "Daley the Broker." *Chicago* 26 (February, 1977): 186.

Whyte, William Foote. *Street Corner Society: The Social Structure of an Italian Slum.* Chicago: University of Chicago Press, 1943.

Wilson, James Q. *The Amateur Democrat: Club Politics in Three Cities.* Chicago: University of Chicago Press, 1962.

Wilson, James Q., and Banfield, Edward C. "Political Ethos Revisited." *American Political Science Review* 65 (1971): 1048–62.

———. "Public-Regardingness as a Value Premise in Voting Behavior." *American Political Science Review* 58 (1964): 876–87.

Wirth, Louis. "Urbanism as a Way of Life." *American Journal of Sociology* 44 (1938): 1–24.

Wolfinger, Raymond. "The Influence of Precinct Work on Voting Behavior." *Public Opinion Quarterly* 27 (1963): 387–98.

Wyner, Alan J., ed. *Executive Ombudsmen in the United States.* Berkeley: Institute of Government Studies,

University of California, 1973.

Zorbaugh, Harvey Warren. *The Gold Coast and the Slum: A Sociological Study of Chicago's Near North Side.* Chicago: University of Chicago Press, 1929.

Index